"I believe the secret sauce for tomorrow's complex cultural challenges lies hidden in the emotional power of authentic, informed leadership. Davis explores how virtually any person can become a more authentic leader."

—JON KATZENBACH, FOUNDER OF
KATZENBACH CENTER AT PWC

"Davis leaps past leadership jargon and gives readers actionable tools! What do I love about *Brave Leadership*? It is not your typical business book. It's a roadmap for the business of life."

—VINCE POSCENTE, *NEW YORK TIMES* BEST-SELLING
AUTHOR OF *THE AGE OF SPEED*

"*Brave Leadership* clearly describes and convincingly prescribes a solution to a hidden crisis holding back far too many people: fear. The stories will keep you turning the page; the practical guidance will make you glad you did. A thoughtful, useful addition to the leadership literature."

—SCOTT ANTHONY, MANAGING PARTNER OF INNOSIGHT
AND AUTHOR OF *THE LITTLE BLACK BOOK OF INNOVATION*
AND *SEEING WHAT'S NEXT* (WITH CLAYTON CHRISTENSEN)

"Kimberly Davis's perspective on leadership is both powerful and unusual. In addition, her prose is a delight . . . clear, hard hitting, personal, and authentic."

—CHRIS TRIMBLE, INNOVATION EXPERT AND AUTHOR
OF SIX BOOKS INCLUDING THE BEST-SELLING *REVERSE
INNOVATION: CREATE FAR FROM HOME, WIN EVERYWHERE*

"In these times, to be an effective leader, *Brave Leadership* is imperative. Fortunately, we're guided expertly along this path by a fantastic mentor and teacher. This is a book for every potential and current leader to own, to study, and to review . . . often!"

—BOB BURG, COAUTHOR OF *THE GO-GIVER*
AND *THE GO-GIVER INFLUENCER*

"It's high time we redefined *brave*, particularly in the context of management and leadership. Kimberly Davis's *Brave Leadership* challenges outdated assumptions and offers fresh perspective for emerging leaders who want to be true not only to the people inspired to follow them but to themselves. Davis's book is an essential road map to the kind of self-discovery that helps develop strong, confident, authentic leaders."

—DONNA FENN, AUTHOR OF *UPSTARTS: HOW GEN Y ENTREPRENEURS ARE ROCKING THE WORLD OF BUSINESS*

"*Brave Leadership* is a book written about real leadership, the kind that is expressed through a shaky voice with sweaty palms and a tightened stomach—like everyday leadership, if we are honest about it. Kimberly Davis takes us on a journey through the emotional, psychological, and physiological sensations that hijack our best. Wrapped in the warm and compassionate hug of her own experience, she whispers her magic into our ears and then pushes us out on the stage with a gentle, 'You can do it.' A must read for those who aspire to lead."

—MIKE COOK, AUTHOR OF *THRIVING IN THE MIDDLE*

"If you are looking for a way to become your authentic self, then look no further than this authentic author who shares her own story to encourage and allow you to become the person you choose to be. Kimberly gives practical examples, useful exercises, and solid suggestions to allow all of us to connect with our real self and to project this self in a manner that allows us to maximize our potential. *Brave Leadership* is worth the read and the practice."

—JEFFREY C. BARNES OF PRINCIPAL JEFF BARNES CONSULTING, RETIRED FROM GE CROTONVILLE

BRAVE
LEADERSHIP

Unleash Your Most **Confident**, **Powerful**, and
Authentic Self to **Get the Results** You Need

KIMBERLY DAVIS

GREENLEAF
BOOK GROUP PRESS

Published by Greenleaf Book Group Press
Austin, Texas
www.gbgpress.com

Distributed by Greenleaf Book Group

For ordering information or special discounts for bulk purchases, please contact Greenleaf Book Group at PO Box 91869, Austin, TX 78709, 512.891.6100.

Design and composition by Greenleaf Book Group
Illustrations by Thomas McKinney
Author photograph by Tim Sutton
Cover credit: ©Thinkstock.com/iStock Collection/foto-ruhrgebiet.
Cover design by Greenleaf Book Group and Kim Lance

Cataloging-in-Publication data is available.

Print ISBN: 978-1-62634-433-4

eBook ISBN: 978-1-62634-434-1

Part of the Tree Neutral® program, which offsets the number of trees consumed in the production and printing of this book by taking proactive steps, such as planting trees in direct proportion to the number of trees used: www.treeneutral.com

TreeNeutral

Printed in the United States of America on acid-free paper

17 18 19 20 21 22   10 9 8 7 6 5 4 3 2

First Edition

To Mom, Dad, Todd, and Tim; thank you for being my greatest champions. And to my son, Jeremy; may you always own your "brave."

A hero is no braver than an ordinary man,
but he is brave five minutes longer.

—RALPH WALDO EMERSON

CONTENTS

PART IV: A BRAVE NEW WORLD

Introduction

There's a saying in the world of training, development, and education that "we teach what we need to learn." That is so true for me. I would love to tell you that after spending most of my adult life studying and obsessing about what it takes to be my real self powerfully in this world—what I call *brave*—I have solved the great mystery and I'm here to give it to you in a magic pill so that we can all be brave all the time. But, alas, that's not the case. What I've learned is that brave is not an all-or-nothing thing. It's not like you have it or you don't. Or once you get it, you've always got it.

Brave unfolds one situation at a time.

And brave hasn't always come easy for me. I think that's why I've been so obsessed with it. When I was a kid, it felt effortless. I spent my childhood on a ranch in northwest Montana, twirling about the pastures, singing to the cows at the top of my lungs. (I was weird, but I was fearless!) If I wanted to do something, I just did it. I didn't think much about repercussions. I sang the solos in choir, played the big roles in school plays, won state while competing on the speech team, and interned at our local news station. I put myself out there for anything I wanted without giving it a second thought. I felt completely free to be who I was and to express myself in the world. It felt easy to be me.

But when I went to college to study theater, things changed. I seemed to misplace my brave. It didn't feel safe to be vulnerable in class. It didn't feel safe to question and explore and try new things. It didn't feel safe to be me. What used to come with ease and grace became tight and unreliable. I stopped trusting myself.

I remember the visceral pain of auditioning: feeling small and alone as I stood on the empty stage waiting to be judged, like livestock at an auction. I would feel my throat tighten and then my jaws. My mind would swim as I fought to remember my audition piece. Nausea and an urge to pee would sweep over me like a tide. I couldn't breathe. It was so hot in there! The worse I felt, the more convinced I was that I couldn't perform. I'd push through, overcompensating for my body in revolt. With my hands shaking and my stomach in knots, I'd watch the director out of the corner of my eye as he scribbled my fate on the back of my headshot.

It was horrible! And I was horrified by myself! What was going on? What had happened to the passionate, powerful, fearless girl I had always been?

Yet when I managed to get cast in spite of myself, everything changed. When I would step on the stage and connect to the other actors in a scene, all my tension and fears and negative self-talk would melt away. On that stage, I could play full-out and stop censoring myself. I would experience this absolute freedom to simply *be*. The more I was able to let go and stop pushing and stop trying to impress and stop trying to prove myself to my director, to the audience, and to my classmates, the better my performance. I couldn't figure out what I was doing or why it worked, but when it did, it was magical.

It didn't escape me that my only safe place for self-expression was hidden behind a character in a play. The minute I would step off stage and drop the cloak of whatever role I was playing and be left exposed—just me—the old sensations would come rushing back. I would sit waiting for my director's feedback, my jaws tense and my stomach tight, holding my breath as I staked my self-worth on the words about to come out of his mouth.

During those years, I lost that sense of efficacy and joy that came from simply being and expressing myself in the world, and I think I've spent most of my adulthood trying to recapture that sense of freedom. I've been fighting to reclaim myself. What I've learned along the way, by working with thousands of leaders and emerging leaders from every different industry imaginable, with different backgrounds and experience levels, is that I'm not the only one who is fighting this fight.

We're all fighting to be ourselves powerfully in this world—to be brave.

As I got older, I became a bit obsessed with the question "What does it take to be brave enough to be myself powerfully?" I wanted to get my mojo back (what used to come so easily felt like an impossible feat) and I wanted to make something of my life and knew that I was the one stopping myself.

As a kid, I was bold and fearless: I totally put myself out there. Maybe it was because I didn't know any better. So the question is, how do we, as adults, when we know that the world can be a tough and scary place—when we know that there is risk for people not liking you, disagreeing with you, or judging you and that failure is commonplace—how do we step out into the world and be who we are for real, powerfully, anyway? How do we cut through the emotional, psychological, and physiological sensations that prevent us from doing our best? This is what I was committed to figuring out.

I developed a voracious hunger and curiosity to understand. For two decades, I've read everything I could get my hands on about authenticity, purpose, confidence, self-esteem, business, leadership, communication, influence, presence, and purpose. After leaving the theater and following a circuitous path, I found myself propelled into the world of training and development, and the participants in those sessions became my education. I'd secretly study the hundreds of Fortune 500 employees who'd show up in my classroom. And when I'd step into their shoes and try to see through their eyes, I got it.

I recognized the pain that comes from trying to be who you think you should be, instead of knowing and being who you are.

I could feel the tension that had built up from years of internalizing the immense amount of change, overload, stress, anxiety, and ambiguity. I could see it manifest in their bodies and in the way they communicated with each other.

Through the course of the day, I'd watch them protect and defend and deflect, until they felt safe enough to say what was real.

And in their efforts to prove themselves—to each other, to their bosses if they were in the room, and maybe, more than anything, to themselves—I could see my own reflection. As it turns out, the theater world and business world aren't so far apart after all.

As I made these observations, I noticed I was changing. When I'd get swept up in my sincere desire to listen between the lines and understand what they were thinking and feeling and truly connect with them, I started to have a lot more fun. I stopped being stressed about what they thought about me. Instead, I worked to draw them in, probing to dig deeper, challenging them, and holding up the mirror so they could see themselves as I saw them. The days flew by! And even though I was exhausted when it was over, in the moment, it felt effortless. I suspect this is what professor of psychology and management Mihaly Csikszentmihalyi calls *flow*.[1]

The crazy thing was that the more effortless it felt to me and the more I was able to be myself and focus on them, the more the participants would transform. I'd see light bulbs go off all over the place. The groups became energized and the rooms would fill with laughter as real change took place right before my eyes.

It was magical.

And I recognized that feeling. It was the same feeling I got when I was on stage and truly connecting with the other actors in a scene. And I wondered, if I could do this on stage and in the classroom, how could I do it in life? Eventually, it hit me. I had had the tools all along and I couldn't even see them.

It is these simple but powerful tools that I share with you today. While this content originated in the acting world, it is just as relevant outside the theater. These tools are a powerful mechanism to help us—myself included—get out of our own way so we can bring our true selves, more powerfully, to whatever situation we're facing. They help with leadership, influence, presence, and presenting. They help us understand the needs of our employees and our customers, and they help when the stakes are high. These tools make it possible to be mindful and purposeful in the face of vulnerability, stress, ambiguity, change, and all of life's challenges, for greater results.

They help us be brave.

While we think that we need to fit into some kind of mold or follow some kind of prescription to get results, the most amazing leaders on the planet are those who dare to be their *real* selves, constructively and powerfully. There are no formulas for true greatness. No credential, title, or alma mater can guarantee a fulfilling and successful life. It's something we must extract from our deepest self every day.

I'm hoping this book will be something different—more personal than your traditional business book—because authentic leadership is a personal journey. Giving you formulas and expounding academic jargon isn't going to get you any closer to the heart of this conversation. Together, we've got to risk getting real.

Hopefully, this book will give you a new perspective, a chance to explore, tools to help you be brave when you don't feel brave, and an opportunity to see yourself, the world, and the impact you can have with new eyes.

Consider this book to be something that none of us need and yet we all weirdly want—permission. Permission to be *you*—your most confident, authentic, and powerful self.

For real.

Brave.

PART I

WHAT IS BRAVE?

1

Who Are You as a Leader?

*Welcome. Whether our journey together lasts
for years or just one day, I can't tell you how
excited I am to take this first step with you.*

—FRASIER CRANE, *FRASIER*, SEASON 11

Who you are as a leader has an impact. Like it or not, your behavior and actions (whether conscious or unconscious) have an effect on the people around you. Their decisions and the way they feel and perform are in direct correlation to how you show up in the world. Who is affected by your ability to lead? Your customers? Your direct reports? Your boss? Your colleagues? Your shareholders? Your students? Your patients? Your team? Your family? Your community? These are the people who rely on you to be and bring your best. Their life is influenced by your performance. Picture these people in your mind. This is your audience.

———

Silence fills the air. My participants awkwardly shift in their chairs, glancing at one another, stifling uncomfortable giggles. Not knowing what to expect is nerve-racking. I take the stage and look at them. My stomach flutters. My fingers tingle. It's not anxiety; it's that I know what is in store for the day and I can barely contain my excitement. But I must. I must harness my most serious self. I am their casting director. This is serious business.

"As a leader, you are always on stage, as people are always paying attention," I say (seriously). "They're paying attention to what you do and to what you don't do—to what you say and, maybe even more so, to what you don't say. And every minute of every day, the people in your audience either cast you in their hearts and minds, or they don't."

The stakes are that high.

"My job is to cast you. I get to choose."

———

There are a lot of different ways that people define leadership. In my mind, it's pretty simple. A leader is someone people *want* to follow, not *have* to follow. They want to be a part of what you're doing, not have to be a part of what you're doing. They want to be there. They want to give you their best. They choose it. They choose you.

Leadership is a casting decision.

> 66
>
> *A leader is someone people want to follow, not have to follow.*

Do the people in your audience cast you in their hearts and minds as someone they want to follow?

If it is true, that as a leader you are always on stage, then that's a pretty vulnerable place to be, yes? You. In the spotlight. People watching. Deciding. Judging. To be and bring your most confident, powerful, and authentic self in the face of that kind of vulnerability is likely the hardest thing anyone can hope to do, especially in the workplace. It will require courage and a sense of responsibility beyond measure. It will require unwavering commitment and self-appraisal. It will require you to know and expose your most authentic self. It will require action in the face of the unknown and compassion in the face of frustration. It will require an awareness of the impact you're having and a surrender of control that may feel next to impossible. It will require you to step out of the quagmire of your fears and move forward when that's the last thing you want to do. It will require you to be brave.

Brave leadership is not for wimps.

But it's also not reserved for a privileged few. One of my intentions with this book is to demystify the whole leadership conversation. Many people seem to think that great leaders are somehow different than they are. I can't tell you how many inspiring, committed, influential people I've met who've said something akin to, "Yes, I'm the boss (or "Yes, I'm in charge of . . ." or "Yes, I run a team . . ."), but I don't really consider myself a leader!"

My goal is to help you see that you can be a great leader—a brave leader—if you choose to be. Whether you're the CEO of your company or a team leader at work, school, or in your family or community, you can lead bravely and have an impact.

I've had the great fortune to have long, meaningful conversations with thousands of leaders from all over the world, and I can tell you, they are no different than you. Most of them have not led charmed lives. Most of them have experienced intense periods of self-doubt. They've had heartaches and worries and fears like you. Some of them are quite well educated, with a string of impressive degrees on their resumes, and some of them have learned all they know in the trenches. Some of them are incredibly intellectual and some are more street smart. They're human beings like you and me. They are people who, sometimes by choice and sometimes reluctantly, have found themselves at the helm.

What I can tell you is that your unique path has set the foundation for who you are as a leader. It's how you leverage what you've learned from your past, how you act in the present, and how you shape your future that will determine your outcome. Goodness knows, my path has been anything but "traditional," but it has made me who I am, has given me a unique perspective and opportunities to lead in ways that I could never have imagined.

> **What is possible for you is often way beyond your vision for yourself.**

What is possible for you is often way beyond your vision for yourself.

I'm not going to kid you. This journey that is brave leadership is not going to be easy. It is going to force you to look at yourself perhaps more closely than ever before. Together we'll explore your barriers to brave—what might be unconsciously keeping you from being and bringing your best, real self powerfully to the workplace. We'll delve into mindset, look at your reactions and behaviors, and challenge how you experience yourself and the world around you.

As we move into Pushing Through to Brave, we'll identify specific actions you can take to overcome your barriers, uncover what drives you at your core, and put yourself on an active path to get the results you want.

Finally, I'll leave you with tools to create and sustain the brave new world you deserve.

What I know to be true is that whatever leadership role you may hold, now or in the future, you are a person first. Who you are as a leader and how you behave as a leader is influenced by who you are and how you behave in life. I learn as much about who I am as a leader from my interactions with my family and community as I do in the workplace. People are people, not titles. Don't be surprised when the stories I share venture outside corporate walls, as learning takes place all around us if we pay attention. In an effort to write a book about leadership and business, I don't want to rob you of life's classroom. Instead, I invite you to explore how your whole life influences the way you show up and lead.

This will demand a lot from you, and in exchange it will open up the possibility of full engagement, self-acceptance, ownership of your future, and incredible results. It will help you be braver. If, of course, you do the work.

Brave is an active path.

Many people, especially in the learning and development world, call the kind of work I do *transformation work*, but I don't see it that way. I think of the work I do as *excavation work* because I believe that everything you need to be a brave leader is already there. You simply need to get real about what you're doing that's working and what's not, learn how to make powerful and often minimal adjustments, and put them into action. I promise I'll be there every step of the journey.

I recently finished a coaching conversation with a senior leader who so vividly stands out in my mind. She reminds me of a young Maya Angelou because of the grace and poise and strength she brings to a space. Even in our short time together, I found her insightful and articulate. She is fearless in broaching difficult conversations. She has a big heart tempered by her engineer's logic. She is intelligent and wise. But she had no idea that these were her gifts. After our conversation, she said, "Thank you. I feel more confident. More sure of myself."

"I only said what's real," I replied. "This is who you've been all along. These are your superpowers!"

That is the work we are here to do together—to identify and leverage the unique qualities about you that make you special, while minimizing the ones that get in your way of being and bringing your most confident, powerful, and authentic self to the world. For me it's something worth fighting for. I'm glad you're here to join the fight.

Key Takeaways

→ Leadership is not about title, position, or power. A leader is someone people want to follow, not have to follow.

→ To be a brave leader, it's critical that you begin asking yourself, *Do the people I need to follow me* want *to follow me?*

2

A Whole New World

*The real voyage of discovery consists not in
seeking new landscapes, but in having new eyes.*

—MARCEL PROUST

H appy Anniversary!" I wrote in an email to my past-participant-turned-friend, Matt. He had reached out to me shortly after he attended one of my sessions, full of excitement, and in the months that followed, we had forged a friendship over shared blogs and common viewpoints. I treasure our conversations, however infrequent, and always feel energized after we chat. I finished typing, "I can't believe it's been a year . . ."

Within fifteen minutes of sending the email, my phone rang. *Wait a minute,* I thought, *upstate New York . . . Don't I know this number? It couldn't be . . .*

"Matt? Is that you?"

"I got your email, so I just thought I'd call." I could hear him smiling through the phone.

"It's great to hear your voice! What a surprise! I'm so glad you called! Can you believe it's been a year? Okay, so tell me what's changed?" I asked him. "Since we worked together, what's different?"

"Everything's different!" He laughed into the phone. "You know how when you're talking about something you really love, how easy it is to show excitement and how that excitement is kind of contagious? When you're passionate about something, it doesn't feel hard. It just flows. It doesn't feel like work. Well now, that's how it is all the time—even with the stuff I'm not so passionate about. I don't get nervous or stressed in the same way. It's like I can be me—and that's cool because I'm much better at everything when I can be the real me. I can be that easygoing, influential, passionate guy, even when I'm doing normal routine work stuff. Because now I know, it's really not about the project or the meeting or whatever it is I might be doing—I'm up to something much bigger. You know, purpose."

As I type this, I'm smiling, thinking about my inspirational friend, his words echoing in my head, perfectly describing what it's like to be your most "confident, powerful, and authentic self"—my definition of brave. "I'm much better at everything when I can be the real me . . . it's really not about the project, or the meeting, or whatever it is . . . I'm up to something much bigger. You know, purpose."

> **Brave is being your most confident, powerful, and authentic self.**

I've had the opportunity to work with hundreds of leaders and aspiring leaders from all over the place who are smart and talented and truly care about doing a good job. But many of them feel a bit lost and confused, sometimes frustrated, and oftentimes completely overwhelmed—and for good reason. The leadership game has changed tremendously over the past ten to fifteen years, but few people talk about it and even fewer model the way.

It's hard to find good role models at the precipice of a new era. The rules of the past no longer apply. What it means to be brave at work today requires more of us than ever before, which can feel incredibly scary and uncomfortable. No longer can we compartmentalize who we are at work and who we are outside of work, because "who we are"—for real—shines through. And if who we really are doesn't connect with the people we lead, we can't get anything done.

For real.

WE'RE NOT IN KANSAS ANYMORE

In the past, work was much more predictable. There were clear systems in place—job descriptions and reporting structures—that made a leader's job fairly routine. At one time, you could tell people what to do and they'd pretty much do it. And if they didn't . . . "heads are gonna roll!" You could put the fear of God in them and the problem would go away. It was a simple paycheck exchange. A manager's job was to make sure that people did what they were told to do by the time they were told to get it done. And until fairly recently, this command-and-control leadership would have given you the results you were after.

If you tried that today, you'd pay a price that you may not even see . . .

Once upon a time, you'd leave school, get a job, and could expect to spend your happily ever after working at the same company until you collected your gold watch and lived off your pension. You'd punch in and punch out, slowly moving up the ladder. You'd go to work every day, and in exchange for your time and your loyalty you could expect something called *security*. Talk to any millennial you meet about security at work and they'll laugh. In the job market they entered, there's no such thing. Security as it existed ten years ago no longer exists today. While the Bureau of Labor and Statistics won't estimate the number of career changes people make in a lifetime (as they've never been able to reach a "consensus . . . among economists, sociologists, career-guidance professionals, and other labor market observers about the appropriate criteria that should be used for defining careers and career changes"),[1] industry experts believe that the average worker changes jobs between ten and fifteen times in a lifetime. Popular job sites claim that "job searching . . . has become an integral part of everyday work life."[2]

It is a different world. If you haven't been through it personally, you likely have vicariously. We all know people who've experienced the pain and anguish that comes with massive layoffs. It's called *downsizing* (or *right-sizing*). The business world has become a big Pac-Man game of the "big guys" consuming the "little guys," entire industries being gobbled up by a handful of players. Redundancies are eliminated, and jobs are sent overseas. Every effort is being made to make products and services less expensive so companies can stay competitive in today's global market-place. New technologies are replacing human beings. No longer can any of us assume that we're going to be working for the same company for our entire adult life. And with that knowledge comes a sense of insecurity and a lack of loyalty. People feel vulnerable. They don't know what they can count on and what they can't. They don't know who is in their corner and who is not. Trust in the workplace is at an all-time low. And the vacuum of safety sparks an instinct for survival. It's every man and woman for themselves. One foot in and one foot out. Just in case . . .

Take this reality and combine it with the fact that global companies designed to meet global marketplace needs are erasing borders, marrying cultures and languages at such a rapid speed that differences are over-looked and underestimated.

Daily, there are new technologies to adopt and adapt. It's like parenting—the second you feel like you've figured it out, get your rhythm down, and finally feel like you know what you're doing, BAM! The game has changed, and nothing you once did works anymore. Ambiguity, complexity, and uncertainty form the backdrop for stress, anxiety, and feeling overwhelmed. Many people at work are not in their happy place.

Yet this does nothing to curb expectations. When do we want things done? YESTERDAY! If you move too slowly, it's game over.

The workday never ends. Emails zip back and forth past the dinner hour into bedtime. iPhones are perched on our nightstands, poised and ready to respond at a moment's notice.

I can't help but picture someone caught up in the eye of a tornado spinning recklessly out of control, their desk, laptop, phones, and sticky notes swirling around them in the debris, perilously close to knocking them out.

But while you're in the midst of spinning, be sure to think strategically, creatively, and bring your whole brain to work, because all repetitive, routine tasks that you could, at one time, simply "phone in" have been eliminated. And if you're feeling frustrated that so much is being asked of you, you can always tweet about it or IM someone or maybe write a blog and then share it on Facebook or influence others on LinkedIn or post a lovely review on glassdoor.com. Or take an Instagram selfie of yourself in your not-so-happy place at work and pin it.

You almost have to laugh at the absurdity of it all. We can all recognize the truth in the craziness—how so much has changed in such a short amount of time—and yet, when you look at what many leaders are doing, it's the same ole thing. They're applying old rules to the new workplace and not getting the results they need. There is another way.

Key Takeaways

→ The world of work has changed dramatically over the past fifteen years. Security is a thing of the past. The workplace is more complex, uncertain, and ambiguous than ever, the speed of business has increased exponentially, and information channels have multiplied. Jobs require cognitive thinking and critical decision-making skills.

→ Companies must be able to harness the passion, engagement, commitment, and loyalty of their workforce to succeed in today's competitive marketplace.

➜ Command-and-control leadership is no longer effective in today's work environment as it repels top talent and retains the least confident, creative, productive, and effective workers.

➜ If you want to be a brave leader, it's critical that you *recognize that the kind of leadership that worked in the past is no longer effective with today's workforce.*

3

Dealing with Real

. . . you are the window through
which you see the world.

—GEORGE BERNARD SHAW

One of the hardest things to do in life is to deal with what is real, rather than what should be or how we'd like it to be. Dealing with what's real, especially at work, is not for the faint of heart.

To deal with what's real, you've got to get past your own "stuff," whether you like it or not. You've got to adapt to change, because change is what's real. You've got to deal with emotions (gasp!), unfulfilled expectations, and irritations, because that's what's real.

You've got to be willing to see goodness and beauty in those you'd prefer to condemn, and truth and frailty in those you'd like to worship, because that's what's real.

You've got to accept being human and all that means: the humanity of your boss, your coworkers, your direct reports, your suppliers, your competitors, and your customers.

Your own humanity.

And sometimes humanity is going to be messy and uncomfortable and inconvenient and time-consuming and scary, and sometimes it will be an absolute thrill, but you can't have one without the other. That's what's real.

And you've got to find a way, as E. E. Cummings said, "To be nobody but yourself in a world which is doing its best, night and day, to make you everybody else." Because what's real is that your best self is your most confident, powerful, authentic, and (dare I say) constructive self, and that's not always easy to come by. It takes courage. In essence, you have to find a way to be brave. Brave leaders deal with what's real at work.

Remember, in the last chapter, when I talked about what's going on in our "whole new world?" How do you think people are feeling in the whirlwind that is work—for real? If there's no security in the workplace and you're constantly engulfed in change, might you feel a bit insecure? Vulnerable perhaps? Could it be difficult to trust?

Think about it for a second: What's real when people feel insecure and vulnerable? When they don't trust? How are they showing up at work? How are they showing up at your meetings? If half of the company has been laid off, are they going to risk bringing their most off-the-wall ideas to the conversation? Are they going to speak out when they see a problem or disagree with someone? What's real?

What's real when people feel stressed and anxious and overwhelmed? What will they be like at work? Are they going to be their most innovative, optimistic, and productive selves? What's real?

What's real when people feel afraid, when they're worried about messing up or losing their job or looking foolish? Are they going to risk more of themselves, or are they going to play it safe? Are they going to give you the best they've got, or are they going to give you just enough so they stay off the radar? What's real?

And in this new work environment, were a leader to use the old standby, the tried-and-true command-and-control method, what are your most talented and valued employees going to do? Are they going to stick around?

Think again. That's what's real.

And the not-so-talented ones? Are they going to stick around?

You bet! That's what's real.

What's real if your top talent takes a hike and all the people that remain focus on playing it safe and staying off the radar? Can you survive in today's competitive marketplace? What's real is that the old rules at work don't work.

There's a fabulous metaphor that Dan and Chip Heath use in their book *Switch: How to Change Things When Change Is Hard*. They talk about how our emotions are like a three-ton elephant and compare our logic to an elephant rider (you know, the little guy perched high on top who thinks he's in charge). When the elephant and the rider want to go in the same direction, all is cool, right? But what happens, the Heath brothers pose, when the elephant and the rider want to go in different directions? Which will win?

I ask this question all the time in my sessions, and everyone laughs at the silliness of the obvious answer, because of course we all know that a three-ton elephant is going to win any day over the rider, no matter how strong, experienced, or smart the guy might be. Similarly, emotions will overpower logic any day of the week. And yet . . .

Emotions don't belong at work! It's *unprofessional* to show emotions at work! We check our emotions at the door, right?

Well, I don't know about you, but I've never figured out a way to extract my emotions and leave them at home. It would be nice, on occasion, to be able to simply remove them, like an artificial limb or something, but I haven't figured out how to do it. They tend to travel with me whether I like them to or not (and sometimes it's terribly inconvenient that they're there). It's not a me thing; it's a human thing.

That's what's real.

We can pretend that the emotions shouldn't be there and maintain that they don't belong at work. And due to people's mastery in masking their emotions, we may not even have to look at them! We can pretend that all is copacetic in our work world. It's a lovely fantasy that we can entertain, but consider the price. In today's business environment, what's really going on with the human beings inside our organizations? Frustration, fear, anxiety, insecurity, stress, vulnerability. That's what's real. You tell me who's in charge, the elephant or the rider?

THE PHENOMENON OF BEING REAL AT WORK

"You were so real! You were exactly the way you sounded on the phone!" she exclaimed, seeming shocked by her discovery.

"Well . . . I guess that's good, right? I mean, I do teach authentic leadership, it would kind of be a problem if I wasn't authentic, don't you think?"

We both stood there a bit dazed—she in happy disbelief, and me? Well, surprised, I guess. What does that say about our business environment when people are shocked by meeting someone who is real?

From my experience, people are tired of playing the game. All the posturing—what vulnerability and shame expert Brené Brown calls *jockeying for attention*—false pleasantries, snarky comments, and decisions made by spreadsheets that don't consider the human toll, have left people leery. They don't know who or what to trust, so they don't trust anyone or anything. Not their boss, not their company, not their colleagues or suppliers, and least of all themselves. Like an actor getting into costume, they put on their protective mask, emotional armor, and cloak of perfection and head into the office each day with their hearts anesthetized, ready to survive.

The problem is everything that can make our companies great is hidden behind those masks and that armor and those cloaks. Creativity, engagement, passion, commitment, excitement, loyalty, joy, and trust are all activities of the *heart*. They come from caring and connection and are accessed through vulnerability.

Yikes. Vulnerability at work? What? Am I nuts?

Probably. But that's what's real.

If we want a culture filled with creative, engaged, passionate, committed, excited, joyful, and trusting people, we have to make it safe for them to take down the mask, take off the armor, and remove the cloak. If we want to have relationships that make our businesses work, then we have to stop treating them like transactions. Nobody gives their best for a simple exchange of value—not employees, not suppliers, not our clients, and not you.

People give and commit their best because they care. It's a *heart* thing.

Every human hungers to be seen and to connect. But we're all running around our work world disguised and protected. Most of our weirdness and ineffective behaviors are simply because our disguises don't fit. We don't make eye contact when we present, not because we're bad presenters, but because we don't feel safe. We brag or put other people down or steamroll over others, not because we're superior, but because we're trying so hard to prove to ourselves and to the world that we're okay. We shut down in meetings, not because we aren't smart or have something to contribute, but because we're overly critical of ourselves and afraid of saying the wrong thing. All of it stems from trying to protect ourselves, trying to prove ourselves, or trying to be something we're not. Our power—our best self and our ability to powerfully connect with others—lies behind the mask.

There seem to be a million books and articles out there about how to make your people more creative, how to engage employees and unleash their passion. We know intellectually what we want our cultures to look like and how we want them to feel, but it's simply an intellectual and costly exercise unless we're willing to do the hardest thing of all—*get real*.

Being real at work is not easy. It is reserved for the brave. I dream of the day when real won't come as such a surprise.

Key Takeaways

→ If leadership is about ensuring people *want* to follow, not *have* to follow, you must *connect to the positive emotions* of people you lead and influence.

→ Emotion overpowers logic. While someone may logically understand something, if they're not emotionally bought in, you will never get their best work.

→ If you want to be a brave leader, *you must be willing to connect to the hearts of those you wish to lead and influence.*

4

Redefining Leadership

It's choice—not chance—
that determines your destiny.

—JEAN NIDETCH, FOUNDER OF WEIGHT WATCHERS

Think about a specific person in your life whom you truly respect (not a hypothetical person, but a real, living-breathing person you know), someone you would consider to be a leader, who has influenced you in a positive way. Maybe this someone is a boss or a colleague. Perhaps your someone is a teacher, mentor, or coach. You trust this person. You know you can count on them. You believe in them. You believe that they care about you and want you to succeed. How do you feel when you're with this person? What will you do for this person that you wouldn't necessarily do for someone you didn't trust or respect, someone who may or may not care about you?

One of the things people expect, when you run a leadership company, is that you've defined leadership. In my mind it's pretty simple. As I've said, a leader is someone people *want* to follow, not have to follow.

To *want* is a choice. I *want* you on my team. I *want* to give her my best. I *want* to be here. I *want* it. I choose it.

Leadership isn't a title; it's a choice. Do the people you lead choose you or not?

When you think about it, in today's business environment, that's everything. When people want to follow—when they want to be a part of what you're doing—how differently do they show up?

Well . . . how differently do *you* show up?

Let's get real: how differently do you show up in meetings when you want to be there versus when you have to be there? Is your computer open and are you checking your phone a million times if you want to be there?

How much effort do you put into projects when you want to be involved? I know for myself, when I want to do something, I go all out. When I want it, I don't hold back. I learn everything I can, I tell everyone I know, and I'm excited. I'll be so into whatever it is I want to do that I'll totally lose track of time. I can't hold back my ideas, and I'm so full of energy that my passion is almost contagious.

To *want* is powerful. To want gives you access to creativity, ideas, excitement, loyalty, energy, passion, advocacy, commitment, focus, innovative thinking, joy, and fun. Want unlocks full engagement. To want corrals the emotion in the workplace and unleashes it as a force for good. It aligns the elephants and the riders.

Back in the paycheck-exchange era, it was a lot easier to motivate someone with a carrot or a stick because whether or not they wanted to give you their best didn't matter quite as much. You weren't asking for their best, you were asking for their good enough. You didn't need people to think creatively or strategically or bring their ideas to work. You didn't expect people to go the extra mile and answer emails until eleven thirty p.m. or jump on a global conference call in their jammies. You didn't need

> *To want corrals the emotion in the workplace and unleashes it as a force for good.*

people to make decisions that would benefit the business or lead their teams or manage their own time. But now you do. Now you need them to take on a boatload of responsibility, be exponentially more productive, and think independently. Their good enough doesn't cut it. You can't succeed without their best.

Author Dan Pink, in his book (and brilliant TED Talk and RSA Animated video) *Drive: The Surprising Truth About What Motivates Us*, has done some compelling work around the shift in what it takes to motivate others at work. Pink shows there's a better way than the carrot or the stick to get the results we seek. "We know that human beings are not merely smaller, slower, better smelling donkeys trudging after the day's carrot." (I'd like to think so.)

Yes. And still . . .

That old carrot-and-stick thing is a hard habit to break. I teach this stuff and I have a problem with it! My son will be home from school for one of the many, many, many holidays that only school children, banks, and postal workers enjoy, and I'll optimistically try to get some work done, hoping he'll play quietly on his own.

"Honey, Mommy has to jump on a conference call. If you're quiet and you don't interrupt me, we can go out for ice cream later!" I say, beaming. And then, serious Mommy takes over and says, "But if you bug me, you won't get to have your play date with Tyler later this afternoon."

Habits are hard to break, but if we want to motivate others in this new era of work, this is something we need to change. In Pink's research, he identifies three things we need to feel motivated to "drive" ourselves in this new world of work: We need to have a sense of autonomy (the ability to choose how we approach our work), mastery (be able to experience ourselves getting better, knowing more, and improving), and purpose (working for a cause larger than ourselves).

I likely don't have to tell you that this is a motivation model that has yet to catch on. Our organizations are engulfed in a backlog of carrots and sticks. Old habits die hard.

It's no wonder that today leaders feel frustrated and overwhelmed, because the rules have changed. It's no wonder if you feel paralyzed and don't know what to do, because there are few models to follow. Every leader is facing an epic shift in what works.

I will never forget the day Julia showed up in my session with her head cocked to the side and her eyes fixed on some mysterious spot on the floor. I couldn't tell if she was annoyed or simply indifferent, but it was quite obvious that she was not a happy person at that moment. She did not want to be there and made it clear. The question was, why?

She didn't participate much the morning of the session. She listened intently. She didn't make eye contact, but I could see her wheels spinning—questioning, debating, and scrutinizing the conversation in her head. What was she thinking? It was hard to know.

During lunch, as we all sat around the table, she looked conflicted. Something was up, and I couldn't tell what it was.

"Julia?" I asked gently. "Are you okay?"

For the first time that day, she looked me right in the eye and, like a release valve going off, said forcefully, "I don't want to be a leader if I have to be like the other leaders at my company!"

I can't tell you how many times I've heard this same sentiment or something similar—countless. And it makes sense. For years and years, organizations thrived at the hands of leaders who mastered the ability to command and control. But it's a new world, and it requires a new kind of leadership. What worked back then no longer provides the same results. Great talent is no longer willing to hang out with bullies in the boardroom in exchange for a paycheck. They know they have options or can create options. And they will. And they do.

Because here's what's real . . .

We're redefining leadership. The leaders and aspiring leaders in today's workplace are the new models. How can you bring your most confident, powerful, and authentic self to the workplace in order to get the results you need? The change starts with you.

Lucky you, brave leader.

Key Takeaways

→ Because there have been so many changes in the workforce over the past fifteen years, there are fewer role models in senior leadership.

→ Our traditional means of motivation at work—the carrot and stick—isn't effective in getting the best results out of people in today's workplace.

→ Unless you harness the "want" of the people you need to lead and influence, your ability to succeed is compromised.

→ If you want to be a brave leader, you must *recognize you have a responsibility to model a new kind of leadership for tomorrow's leaders.*

5

Unlocking the Want

*It isn't sufficient just to want—you've got to
ask yourself what you are going to do
to get the things you want.*

—FRANKLIN D. ROOSEVELT

So what unlocks the secret want? What can you do to ensure that everyone you lead wants to be led by you and will bring their best?

So many of us are looking for the formula. We love that stuff! It's comforting to believe that if we simply followed some expert's "ten steps," then people would do exactly what we'd want and we'd be successful beyond our wildest dreams. (Just give us an acronym to memorize!)

But brave leadership is all about dealing with what's real, right? Here's what's real: There is no formula. There is no prescription for success. To want is a personal choice. Every time, in every situation, what it's going to take to ensure someone wants to be led and wants to be a part of what you're up to is going to be a little different—because every time you're going to have a different human being in front of you. We don't like that. It's harder to scale. But that's what's real.

Back in the Industrial Age, when workers simply exchanged their time for a paycheck, it didn't much matter if they *wanted* to give their best or not. But thanks to extraordinary inventions like the Internet and cell phones and all of the other technological breakthroughs of the last two decades, we shifted into what's called the *Information Age*. Now our global workforce is made up of "knowledge workers"—people, like you, who are paid to bring their brains to work to make decisions, which requires a different kind of leadership. There's a lot of discussion among thought leaders about what will come after the Information Age. Some say it'll be the Age of Understanding. Some say it will be the Age of Sustainability, and some the Human Age. And some say it'll be the Conceptual Age, ruled by artistry, empathy, and emotion. But whatever they call it, everyone agrees that it will require more transparency, more human connection, and thus rely more on the *want* of others than ever before.[1]

To *want* is that gut instinct. It's desire. It's all elephant. To *want* is a decision made by the heart. Yes, the head may weigh in and try to logic its way through, but in the end, the heart will win. If you don't want it, it shows.

You can't fake *want*.

Want is at the center of commitment, loyalty, engagement, satisfaction, creativity, passion, and joy. Want transforms deadlines into achievements, obstacles into adventures, and colleagues into collaborators. Want unlocks the best that people have to give and fuels the results organizations need to deliver.

To unlock the want in the people you lead, you must be willing to connect to their hearts.

GETTING REAL ABOUT AUTHENTICITY

There's a lot of conversation out there about authenticity and the need for authenticity in the workplace—and a lot of confusion about what that means. Some people think that *being authentic* means that they can be whatever they want. "My boss is authentic—he's authentically a jerk!" Some people think that authenticity is all about not caring what others think. Sadly, being authentic does not give you a free pass to show up however you want. Authenticity, in the framework of leadership and influence, requires much more.

My favorite definition of authenticity comes from Harvard Business School Professor and authentic leadership guru, Bill George (also the former CEO of Medtronic, who wrote the book *Authentic Leadership*). His definition of authenticity is "genuine, worthy of trust, reliable, and believable."

Here's where it gets tricky. Who gets to decide? Who gets to decide if you're worthy of trust or if you're genuine? Not you. (Sure, you can decide that, but it's not going to help you lead or influence.)

In the framework of leadership and influence, the people around you get to decide—your direct reports, your team, the people you lead, your boss, your colleagues, and your suppliers. These people are your audience. They get to decide if you're authentic. You do not.

Are you genuine, worthy of trust, reliable, and believable? How do you know?

That's what makes this so complex! What your boss is going to need from you in order to find you worthy of trust or reliable is going to be quite different from what your client may need from you or your direct report might need from you or what your colleagues might need from you. And does that mean that you become a shape-shifter? "I'll be whatever you need me to be . . ." No! What it requires is that you pay attention to the fact that everyone around you has different needs. Whether or not someone *wants* is anchored in those individual needs.

To unlock the want requires us to always be asking ourselves, "What does he need from me in this meeting to find me worthy of trust?" For real. "What does she need from me to experience me as genuine?" For real. How does that inform how you prepare, how you dress, the language you use, and how you connect? To be the kind of leader that people *want* to follow instead of have to follow, it's critical to ask yourself, "What do they need from me to experience me as genuine, worthy of trust, reliance, and belief?"

Unlock the want, and you access the heart. Without that, all you'll get is a paycheck exchange. You decide: Which is better?

CULTIVATING WANT BEGINS WITH CULTIVATING YOU

We've read all the books, the influencer posts, and the cute, quippy quotes on Facebook that make us think and reflect. We've been ever so subtly trained on how to play the game and win. We know the right things to say. We know how to talk the talk and walk the walk. We've worked so hard to do what we're supposed to do that we lose sight of what's real. What's real is that the people aren't going to experience us as genuine, worthy of trust, reliance, and belief unless we sincerely show up as someone who is genuine, worthy of trust, reliable, and believable. We may say and do the right things, but if we're not real, people know.

I was talking to a friend of mine recently who is a recruiter, and she told me how often people will sit down with her and say, "I love what I do because of the people. I'm curious about people. I like to know what makes them tick." She hears it all the time.

"But you know, Kimberly," she said conspiratorially, "these same people who say that . . . we'll be talking for almost forty-five minutes and they won't have asked me a single question about myself. All they do is talk about themselves! If they're truly curious about people, wouldn't I count? If that's really who they are, why don't they show it?"

Great question. Why don't they show it? Could it be that they weren't truly curious about people and they fed her a line in hopes of landing the job? Sure. Could it be that they were nervous because the stakes felt high and they tried to impress my friend? Sure. Could it be that they were amazing and perfect for the job? Sure.

But it didn't matter if they were nervous. It didn't matter if they happened to be perfect for the job. They didn't unlock her want. She didn't experience them as genuine. She didn't know if they were someone who was worthy of her trust. Would my friend want to put her reputation on the line to recommend a candidate she didn't find believable? Likely not.

Being genuine, worthy of trust, reliable, and believable—in the framework of leadership and influence—lies in the eye of the beholder. We can say and do all the right things, but if we can't bring our best real self, in the moment, regardless how high the stakes might be, we cannot get the results we need.

So how do you cultivate your best real self so you can hope to unlock the want in the people you lead? First you have to understand what might be standing in your way.

Key Takeaways

→ To want is a gut instinct. It's desire. To want is a decision made by the heart.

→ In the end, the heart will win. If you don't want it, it shows.

→ In the context of *Brave Leadership,* we define *authenticity* as "genuine, worthy of trust, reliable, and believable"—in the eye of the beholder. Thus, the people you lead and wish to influence get to decide if you're authentic, not you.

→ The people in your life have unique needs, so what they need from you to experience you as authentic will be different.

→ To be a brave leader, it's critical to ask yourself, *Do the people I need to lead and influence experience me as genuine, worthy of trust, reliable, and believable?*

PART II

BARRIERS

TO BRAVE

Disappearing Genius

Yesterday is not ours to recover,
but tomorrow is ours to win or lose.
—LYNDON B. JOHNSON

Back in the 1960s, two educators named Dr. George Land and Dr. Beth Jarvis did some interesting research.[1] NASA had come to them requesting a test that they could give to potential hires to measure for creativity. Since no such test existed, Land and Jarvis successfully developed one. But when that project was completed, they got curious, wanting to learn more about where creativity came from, so they gave the same test that they developed for NASA to a group of 1,600 three- to five-year-olds. The results were "astonishing," as 98 percent of the children tested as having a genius level of creativity. Fast-forward five years and the good doctors, once again, gave the same test to the same group of kids who were then eight to ten years old. The second time, only 30 percent of the children tested at the genius level for creativity. Fast-forward again, another five years. The kids were now thirteen to fifteen years old. The final time the kids were tested, how many do you think tested at the genius level? Only 12 percent.

Land said, in his TEDx Talk, that since the tests were administered by teachers, they were all too depressed by the results to test this same group of kids further.

But it gets even better. Since the findings were so shocking, they decided to give the same test to more than a million grown-ups (over the age of twenty-four; the average age was thirty-one). What do you think they found? (Hint: It wasn't pretty.) Only 2 percent of my fellow grown-ups tested as creative geniuses.

Frightening, isn't it? (If you have kids, especially teenagers, I highly recommend you keep this interesting piece of research to yourself, or you'll never hear the end of it!)

While this study was clearly done with a focus on creativity, I believe the results point to a much bigger issue. For when you think about what creativity means—and as I tried to find a good working definition of creativity I found somewhere between fifty and sixty different definitions out there—the only common denominator I can see is that creativity is simply a form of unique human expression. So it seems that while we may all be born completely unique in this world, the longer we're here, the less comfortable we are with owning how unique we are. It's much more comfortable to let our uniqueness go. Except, of course, for the mysterious 2 percent of us.

If we want to be and bring our most confident, powerful, and authentic selves to our leadership, we've got to figure out what's getting in the way of our ability to express our unique selves in the world.

So let's take a look at what is happening during that gap between the first two tests. What could possibly be going on during that time in our lives that would explain a 68 percent drop in creative genius?

ACTIVITIES! SOCIAL GROUPS! SCHOOL! OH MY!

When my son, Jeremy, was about four years old, we enrolled him in soccer. It was a sight to behold, twelve little people running about the field kicking balls every which way, while the coach (one of the dads) did his best to keep them running in the same direction. Jeremy would inevitably find a stick or a dandelion or a dirt clod on the ground that he found much more interesting than the ball, and I'd hear myself yelling, "No! Jerem . . . Jer . . . Jayyy! Put the [stick/flower/dirt] down, honey!"

It was quite futile. He had no interest in soccer at all. On game days, all the parents would line the field with their blankets and camping chairs, collectively cheering the kids on, "Yes! Yes! Run! Nooooo! The other way! Your goal is over there . . . No! Nooo! Kick the ball in the other direction!"

You could spy many of us applying the ever-so-innocent bribe to get our kids to play. "Come on, sweetie, you can do this! You love soccer! Soccer is fun! If you play one more time, the game will be over and we can go get a Slurpee!" My precious son would look at me like I was a nutcase, shake his head, and stubbornly flop on the ground in defiance. "No! I don't care if I don't get a Slurpee! Soccer is not fun! I hate soccer!"

Then we tried basketball.

Going to practice was an exercise in frustration. He didn't want to go, and truth be told, neither did I. It wasn't fun. It sucked. Waiting for his turn to dribble or pass or shoot, or whatever the coach was trying to get them to do, was excruciating. I sat on the sidelines whispering, "Jeremy. Jeremy, stay focused. No. Stop poking your friend. Listen to your coach. Jerem . . . Jay . . . Listen!" What was supposed to be a fun childhood experience was filled with, "No! No! Don't! Don't! Stop!"

At four years of age, Jeremy had gone from having the freedom to run and explore and follow his instincts, with loving redirection from his parents, to having to fit into a system with rules and parameters around behavior. Forced to do what others were doing. Instead of his unique way of expressing himself sparking smiles and amusement, it more and more often resulted in frustration and exasperation.

This isn't a Jeremy thing; this is a kid thing. It's a rite of passage. We all learn to follow rules and master the expected ways of behavior to fit into the system that is society. No matter who we are, part of growing up is learning how to play the game.

Soccer, ballet, swim class, play group, pre-K, Little League, summer camp, first grade, Cub Scouts, church—each group with a different set of rules and different cast of characters, all delivering their lines. "Sit still." "Keep your hands to yourself." "It's not talking time, it's listening time." "Inside voice, please." "Walking feet." "Come here. Come here. One . . . two . . . three . . ." "No-no-don't-don't-stop."

Now imagine if these messages—the lines that the different characters in our lives delivered—were visible.

It might look something like this:

The lines almost become boundaries for self-expression. The messages aren't inherently good or bad. They're just messages. Our brain, being the supercomputer that it is, at lightning speed will factor in our intelligence, our personality, and all the messages that make up our history, comparing and contrasting them with all it knows to be true in an attempt to figure out what it means.

The more structured activities and social groups we're in, the more characters there are, and the more lines they deliver. And all the while, our brain is working. *What does that mean? What does this mean?*

WHAT YOU SAY	WHAT THEY HEAR
"You're such a good piano player!"	*That must mean I should keep doing that!*
"You talk too loud."	*That must mean I better be quiet.*
"He's the real athlete in the family!"	*I can't disappoint my parents!*
"Don't be so stubborn!"	*I should keep my opinions to myself.*
"She's the smart one."	*But not pretty . . .*
"Big boys don't cry."	*Suck it up!*
"So beautiful!"	*They like me!*

Some of the messages jibe with our experience and interpretation of the world, and some don't ("You love soccer" vs. "I hate soccer!"). Which messages do we override? Which do we keep and which do we toss?

And being the powerful creatures that we are, the thought bubbles in our head—informed by the feelings we feel, the messages we've received, and the observations we make—become a whole new set of lines. Our thoughts add to the cacophony of messages to be interpreted.

The trouble is our brain sometimes has difficulty determining what is truth. Some of the messages may be opinions, some might be contextual, some might have the intent to help, protect, or encourage; some might not. Some might be misinterpretations or reactions. But like data on a spreadsheet, it's hard to tease out the nuance and know exactly what lies beneath the message. What is really true?

All of it and none of it.

But our brain doesn't know that. It's just busy trying to make sense of it all. And where there's not enough data, it fills in the gaps, trying to connect the dots and making assumptions. Taking in all the verbal and nonverbal messages that are sent and how often they're reinforced, it chews and digests and filters the information to make meaning. What does this mean? What does that mean? Everything and nothing.

I remember having this conversation during one of my presentations, and a woman in the front row got quite grumpy with me. "Excuse me," she said, scowling, "but I find this all very negative. I had a great childhood, and I resent being told that it's left me somehow scarred." At first, I regretted acknowledging her raised hand. (I don't think I said anyone was scarred, did I?) But then I realized that she had an excellent point that I had neglected to clarify. Our lines are not simply the consequence of our *bad* experiences. They're not good or bad; they just *are*. Our good experiences result in as many lines as our bad experiences. And they can create an equally big obstacle.

Reading psychologist Dr. Carol Dweck's book, *Mindset: The New Psychology of Success*, was a watershed moment for me. While I had already formulated my thinking about how the lines in our lives defined how we showed up and interacted with the world, I had yet to uncover the reason why good experiences could be as problematic as our so-called bad experiences. Dr. Dweck's research made it all make sense. It also put me to work—on myself.

Like the grumpy lady in my audience, I too was fortunate to have a good childhood, and yet I knew I had my lines. What gives? My parents and teachers were supportive and effusive in their praise. I was told I was talented and smart. I was told I was pretty. I was told I was a good singer. I was told many lovely things that make me blush to share them with you. I was lucky. But my luck also forged a mindset I had to overcome.

Dr. Dweck's work examined how the messages we receive from an early age can form what she calls a *growth mindset* or a *fixed mindset*.[2]

People who have a growth mindset believe that they can develop themselves to be better and better. They believe that talent and brains are only one part of the equation and that their success is an outgrowth of their efforts rather than their birthright. A growth mindset instills a love of learning, resilience, and a commitment to tackle big obstacles. I've had to work hard to cultivate my growth mindset, as it hasn't always come easily for me.

People who have a fixed mindset, however, believe that you either have it or you don't. You're either smart or you're not. You're either talented or you're not. You're either pretty or you're not. It's black and white. A fixed mindset is always looking for proof. *See! I got first place in the science fair. I am smart! They asked me to sing the solo. I am talented!* Every situation is a chance to confirm their intelligence or talent or validate their greatest fear that perhaps they aren't all that after all. With a fixed mindset you don't see that you can grow and develop; you simply are or you aren't, which is why praise, however well intentioned, can backfire.

You are so beautiful!

You are so smart!

You are so talented!

I used to love to hear those things as a kid! Manna from heaven! More of that! But then . . . When I didn't get cast as the lead in the play . . . *Wait. Maybe I'm not as talented as I thought. Maybe I don't have what it takes.* Or when the boys in high school didn't seem to notice I existed. *I'm not pretty. She was just being nice.* Or when I got a D on my math test. *I suck at math.*

Talented, beautiful, smart, wonderful, kind, and generous are words—lines—describing everything I wanted to be. But when consumed by my fixed mindset of the day, they became limitations.

If I'm not talented, I don't want to try. It hurts too much to fail.

If I'm not pretty and she says I am, then her words can't be trusted.

If I suck at math, why put in any effort?

Rather than seeing that talent, looks, and achievements can be cultivated—that a single incident doesn't define you—people with a fixed mindset *decide* about themselves and others, limiting what is possible. Meanwhile, the people with a growth mindset are off working to improve and grow and develop themselves to be better every day.

I remember one friend who was constantly told how brilliant she was as a child. She was convinced that she was so far superior to everyone else that everyone she worked with, who didn't acknowledge her superiority, was an idiot. I'm sure it was wonderful to hear her dad tell her how smart she was as a kid, over and over again. But her fixed mindset has left her relationships in ruins. Who wants to hang out with someone who treats them like they're "less than"?

It's fortunate for all of us that we're not stuck with either a growth or fixed mindset for life. Our mindset is something we can work on (and Dr. Dweck's book is a great place to start). Additionally, you might find that you have a growth mindset in certain areas of your life and a fixed mindset in others. Look at the areas of your life where you've decided about yourself—about who you are, what you're capable of doing, and what is possible for you—to find where your fixed mindset might be limiting you.

Our lines aren't good or bad; they just are.

THE TRUTH ABOUT WHO YOU ARE

I remember when I was about five years old, I desperately wanted to be a ballerina. I had a jewelry box with a ballerina inside that would pop up and twirl to the tune of "Twinkle, Twinkle, Little Star" as soon as I opened the lid. I had a blue tutu and ballet shoes that I proudly wore trick or treating. I thought ballerinas were the most beautiful creatures on earth, so of course I wanted to be one. I begged my mom for ballet lessons. She resisted, but I didn't give up. I begged and begged. When she finally caved, it was the happiest day of my young life. I remember walking up the steps of the Hockaday Center for the Arts, the hub of all things cultural in our little town, excited and scared. The teacher stood in the studio, tall and lean and statuesque, with her hair pulled back tightly. She wore bright red lipstick and a stern expression that told me that ballet was serious and important stuff. I was about to become a world-famous ballerina, and I could hardly wait.

When my mom picked me up after class, I was in shock. "It was hard," I whispered, hanging my head in defeat. "It wasn't what I thought it was going to be. I don't like it."

"It was just your first lesson," my mom said in a reassuring voice. "Give it time."

The next lesson was worse. I remember my scowling teacher tapping out the rhythm with a yardstick on the dance bar. In her presence, it seemed everything about me was wrong. My hair was wrong. The position of my feet was wrong. "Are you even listening to what I'm telling you?" she repeated sharply, assessing my wrongness.

Ballet, I discovered, was not as I had imagined.

"Please, please, don't make me go back. I don't like it!" I cried. My mother looked at me with her soft blue eyes and gave me a big hug. "I know. I know it's not easy. I'm sorry you're having such a hard time. It'll get better."

But it didn't. The next week, I left ballet in hysterics.

"I'm not going back! You can't make me! She's soooooo mean!" I said, sobbing uncontrollably.

"Okay," my mom said, pulling me into her arms. "Shhhhh . . . It's going to be okay," she soothed, rubbing my back as I wept. "I won't make you go back."

"I thought it would be different," I hiccupped. "Ballet was supposed to be fun."

"Oh, honey," my mom said gently, and then stroked my hair as she held me. "I'm so sorry." And with sadness and a hint of embarrassment she said, "I think you got my genes. You're not athletic, just like me."

YOU'RE NOT ATHLETIC.

I'm not athletic! That's why I hated ballet as much as I did! I'm not athletic! I was like my mom, and my mom is wonderful, so that was a good thing. I'm not athletic. Okay. Got it.

It was a message that jibed with my experience of myself and the world (and goodness knows I didn't want to feel the pain of ballet class again), so I did everything I could to reinforce it: When it came to physical education, I hung back, timid and worried about others finding out that . . . *I'm not athletic*. And on the playground, I was extra careful and didn't join in some of the games because . . . *I'm not athletic*. And when I was required to take dance class in college to satisfy the requirements for my theater degree, I hid in the back so nobody could see me and discover that . . . *I'm not athletic*.

"I'm not athletic" became my truth, and I lived according to that truth. I recruited everyone around me to support me in that truth. If I didn't want to participate, it was cool. ("She's not athletic.") Or they'd make me feel better if I didn't get the part I wanted in a play, because of course it must be so hard to be me in that situation (you know . . . *not athletic*).

"I'm not athletic" became a convenient excuse for anything outside my physical comfort zone.

Not until I was thirty-seven years old, when I heard someone talk about their life-changing experience doing the Komen 3-Day Breast Cancer Walk and got inspired enough to register, did I challenge that belief. What you learn, when you've committed to walk sixty miles over the course of three days, is that you've got to train. And train hard. And what you learn when you're training is that one day it feels hard, and when you keep doing it, it doesn't feel so hard. So you walk a little farther, and a little farther. Until pretty soon you're walking ten miles at a time, and then fifteen. And then, during the event, when you're walking alongside 2,500 other women, many who recently finished chemo and some who are still going through it (not one of them complaining, as they walked, about blisters or the heat or the never-ending hills dotting Seattle's route) is that your paltry excuses don't add up to much. And when, on day two, you're thirty-eight miles in and you still have two more to go before reaching camp, you discover reserves you never knew you had. And as I crossed the finish line after walking sixty miles, that first time I did the three-day walk, I realized something that changed my life: *I might just be athletic after all.*

Or not.

But it was no longer my truth.

Now, when my sweet mom said those words when I was five, her intent was nothing but beautiful. She was trying to soothe her distressed child and gave me an explanation for my experience that got me off the hook and made complete sense to me.

If I were to step into my mother's shoes at that time and think about what she knew to be true, these are some things that would have informed her reaction in that moment:

- She knew that I had been born with dislocated hips, had spent a considerable amount of time in a full-body spica cast as an infant, and ballet was probably physically impossible.

- She knew that, for whatever reason, when she was a kid she didn't participate in or enjoy activities that required athleticism, and I was her daughter, so I was highly likely to be a lot like her.

- She knew that watching her daughter in such distress over a silly ballet class was the last thing she wanted, and she didn't want me to endure that kind of pain any more than I needed to.

She was simply loving me. That's it. My little mind did what little minds do, latching on to whatever it could to make sense of the frustration and humiliation I felt in ballet class. In an effort to not feel that way again, I spent the next thirty years constructing a barrier to wall out those feelings.

The lines that define our lives are often of our own construct. Like lines in the sand, they can be crossed at any time, but since we can't see them, we don't know what's stopping us. We just feel something when we bump into them. Something unpleasant that makes us recoil or react. The feelings become like those electronic pet fences that keep dogs safely in the yard. They teach us what's permissible and what's not permissible. How far we can and want to push the boundaries. Who we should be and who we should not be. Who we are and who we are not. Don't like the way that feels? Back up. Don't do it again. Move into a more comfortable place. Like the way it feels? Push on! Do it more! We adapt. We exchange the freedom of self-expression to feel safe and be accepted, not consciously but necessarily. It's not a good thing or a bad thing—it's just a real thing.

So what is happening during the time our creativity takes a 68 percent nosedive? Perhaps this:

We unconsciously shrink ourselves back to live within the lines, exchanging the desire to express who we are uniquely for comfort. Staying within our comfort zone is a natural human strategy to satisfy our pesky human needs. But comfort zones can be lethal to leaders.

IT'S OKAY TO HAVE NEEDS

I remember when my son was an infant, we'd sit in the rocking chair and read to him, even before he could understand language. He was teething, so he'd chew on the thick, colorful board books, drooling happily as we'd bring the story to life. One of my favorite books was Todd Parr's *It's Okay to Be Different*. ("It's okay to be short. It's okay to be tall. It's okay to wear two different socks. It's okay to have freckles . . .") I always thought grown-ups could benefit from this book. We seem to need a reminder that it's okay to have needs, because we all do.

It's okay to need air.

It's okay to need sleep.

It's okay to need to feel safe.

It's okay to need to belong.

It's okay.

That's part of the deal when you're human. We all have needs.

As early as 1945, psychologist Abraham Maslow created a research log he called his *Good Human Being Notebook*. He wanted to understand why some people were emotionally healthy and self-fulfilled while others existed with "dampened and inhibited powers." After months of research, he wrote in his log: "There seems no intrinsic reason why everyone shouldn't be this way [self-actualizing]. I think of the self-actualizing man not as an ordinary man with something added, but rather as the ordinary man with nothing taken away."[3]

Years later, Maslow's work about "good human beings" evolved into his famous hierarchy of needs, marking a dramatic shift in the field of psychology and igniting a humanistic and positive psychology movement that has altered the way we look at human nature.

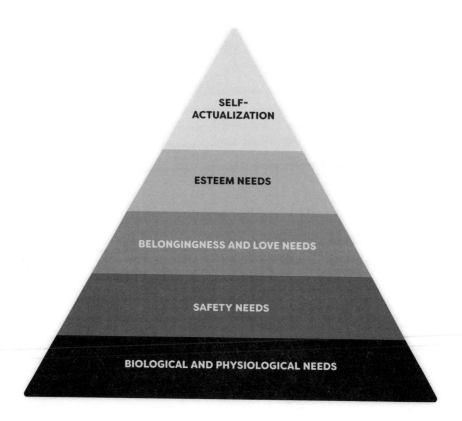

Maslow's hierarchy places human needs in ascending order, with our most basic needs at the bottom, and what he calls our *higher needs* at the top. Maslow recognized that our lower-level needs must be satisfied in order to move up the hierarchy. That means that first our biological and physiological needs must be met; if we don't have air, food, sleep, and shelter, we can't think about anything else. Only after those needs have been met can we put our attention elsewhere.

Safety comes next. If we don't feel safe, emotionally and physically, we're not able to rise any further; a sense of love and belonging cannot be attained if we don't feel safe. And yes, love and belonging are core human needs. Think about it from an anthropological perspective. Back in the caveman days, we needed to feel that we were part of a tribe in order to survive. It's that core desire to fit in that plagues the world's teenagers, not to mention millions of capable adults. Maslow calls these the *lower needs* and often used a vitamin analogy to illustrate his thinking. Pervasive unhappiness, depression, debilitating fears, difficulty with interpersonal relationships—all emotional disturbances—can be attributed to a core needs deficiency. Like calcium and vitamin C, if we don't get them, we cannot be healthy and thrive.[4]

While we oddly think it's okay to deny our needs, science proves otherwise. Only after our basic needs are satisfied can we tackle a higher aim. Achievement, responsibility, reputation, growth, and fulfillment are all accessible once we have overcome this threshold. With no limit to self-actualization, the "fulfilling of yearnings and ambitions, like that of being a good doctor . . . or a good carpenter . . . or, most important, simply the ambition to be a good human being" is the quest of a lifetime.[5]

The lines that govern our lives aren't wrong. They're not bad. They just are. They are our best strategy to meet our basic human needs. We all have lines. Some of them serve us and some of them don't, and it's often difficult to tell which is which because, most of the time, we don't even know they're there. To us, they masquerade as truth—the truth about who we are and the world around us. These lines are the lens through which we see ourselves in life.

As we become teenagers and our hormones kick in at the same time social pressures increase, our lines multiply exponentially (and our creativity continues to plummet).

As we enter college, get a job, get married, have kids, volunteer, and live life, the number of lines continues to increase (and our creativity . . . wait . . . I know I had some somewhere . . .).

If it's true that 98 percent of us are endowed with creative genius until we're five years old and then it's all downhill from there, where does this genius go? Does it evaporate? Are we throwing it about willy-nilly, like a joyful flower girl tossing rose petals at a wedding? Here! Have some genius! I don't need it!

I don't think so. It's my belief that it's still there, trapped. When we live our lives within the walls we've constructed to keep perceived risk out, there is no room for creativity or powerful self-expression. Our most confident, powerful, and authentic self lies restrained behind these barriers to brave, hungering to be set free.

We cannot bravely lead or connect to the want in others without access to our best self.

The problem isn't the lines. We all have lines. Some are real and some are imagined—we may never know the difference. The problem is the *focus of attention* we give the lines that define our lives. Change your focus and you alter the way you see.

And act.

Key Takeaways

➔ Because of our personal histories and life experiences, we unconsciously create barriers to being brave.

➔ We often limit ourselves based on false understandings of our histories and experiences.

➔ Both positive and negative histories and experiences impact our self-perception and our ability to take powerful action. It's not just the "bad stuff" that can limit our mindset.

➔ In attempt to (consciously or unconsciously) meet our basic human needs, we often stop ourselves unnecessarily, without even knowing we're doing it.

➔ If you want to be a brave leader, it's critical to recognize that your histories and experiences do not determine what is possible for you.

7

What Do You See?

I think we are blind.
Blind people who can see, but do not see.

—JOSÉ SARAMAGO

n February of 2007, my husband, Tim, and I packed up our home and moved with our three-year-old son from Seattle, Washington, to Dallas, Texas. I had lived in Seattle for fifteen years. I made dear friends, did some great work, loved the mountains, the water, and the air. It was home. But when Tim landed an exciting new opportunity, allowing this sunshine-deprived girl to start a new adventure, we jumped at the chance.

We bought a lovely home in a lovely neighborhood filled with lovely people. Sunshine was in abundance.

Still, I was miserable. Seattle and Dallas are very different cities with different cultures, and I felt like an outsider. Every experience I encountered, every place I explored, and everything I saw served as proof that I didn't belong. In Dallas, people dress beautifully, all the time. They look good in the grocery store. They look good at the gas stations. They wear makeup and lovely clothes and heels and lots of bling to hockey games. Having moved from a place where it was common to see jeans and fleece in five-star restaurants, I found this disturbing.

In Dallas, people would start talking to me out of the blue—complete strangers! It was the oddest thing. Having moved from a place where we all kept to ourselves and hardly knew our neighbors, it all felt suspicious. Dallas was flat; Seattle had mountains. Dallas was this; Seattle was that, and on and on. I'd compare and contrast and compare and contrast, and all I saw were the differences. The differences reinforced my sense of isolation and the feeling that I didn't belong. The feelings mounted. And while I learned to smile on the outside, inside I felt miserable.

I pouted a lot. I buried myself in carbs and didn't participate. I shut myself up in my life—for two years—and waited for Dallas to pass. It didn't.

And then something triggered me. I don't know if it was something I read or something someone said or really what it was—but I definitely had a triggering incident, as almost overnight things changed. All of a sudden, I *loved* Dallas. I loved the people, I loved my neighborhood, and I loved seeing the sun every day. I'd go out on my walks and look up at the massive live oak trees lining the streets and the bright blue sky, feeling nothing but complete wonder and gratitude. *How can I be so lucky*, I'd think, *to live in such a great place? It's such a good life!*

Here's the thing: Dallas hadn't changed. It was the same, with the same people doing the same things. The same things that bugged me only months before, I now found endearing and lovely. I clearly remember getting off a plane one day at Dallas–Fort Worth after traveling for business, and I looked around at everyone all dressed up waiting for their bags in the airport and I thought, *The people in Dallas take such good care of themselves—why can't everyone live like this?*

True story. Weird, huh?

Nothing in our lives had changed. I was still the same me (although I admittedly dressed better and weighed a little more), but everything was different. I felt different. I experienced the world around me differently. I showed up differently. It was a complete and utter transformation.

The only thing that changed was the way I looked. Before, all I could focus on were the differences, and that's all I saw. And what I saw informed how I felt and what I experienced, and thus how I interacted with the world around me.

I looked for differences and saw differences. Researchers call this confirmation bias. We are wired to look for evidence to support our beliefs. The differences I saw triggered my emotions, so I felt different. It was very real to me. From my feelings came every action that followed. I didn't fully engage, because . . . why would I? I didn't give people a chance or go out of my way or create new experiences because . . . why would I?

I DON'T BELONG IN DALLAS.

I focused on the line I had told myself. I sat back, judged, and played it safe, and I stayed right about everything. It was the truth I lived into. As long as I was focused on that truth, that's all I could see.

So what was true? All of it and none of it.

———

A number of years ago, I was traveling back and forth from Dallas to Chicago, leading communication workshops for twenty-five managers and 175 of their direct reports. For six months, I would do a monthly three-hour session, each month building on the last. We called it the *slow-drip* approach. Our hope was that by giving the attendees tools that they could practice and apply and then meeting regularly to look at what was working and what wasn't, we'd be able to fix some of the bigger issues that plagued the organization, such as morale, culture, trust, and productivity.

There had been a recent leadership change, their stock price was down, and the urgency to improve results hung in the air like a combustible gas. Everyone was on edge, change was rampant, attitudes were tense, and negativity was high. People were not in their happy place.

We divided the group of direct reports into five groups of thirty-five, and one group of twenty-five managers. So for three days straight, I'd go from one session to the next, repeating the same content over and over again. To get a sense of what was going on, the first time I showed up, I thought it would be a good idea to start with the managers. Surely they could tell me what the issues were with the people on their teams. Yep. They told me.

"They're lazy," one manager said.

"They don't care," her colleague chimed in.

"There are problems all over the place, and they hardly seem to notice."

"Why don't they just do their jobs?"

"I don't have time to babysit them."

"I don't know what the problem is . . . Maybe it's the whole millennial thing."

One after another, they shared the horror they faced every day. They were stressed and frustrated and fed up.

"That's terrible," I said empathetically. "It looks like I've got my work cut out for me, don't I?"

So for the next two and a half days, I met with their direct reports. To say I was anxious would be an understatement. These people scared me. For three days straight, two four-hour sessions a day, I walked into a room of strangers, and thirty-five blank stares looked back, the managers' voices echoing in my mind. "They're lazy." "They don't care."

But something, probably instinct, told me there was more to it than that. Why would all these people simply not care? It didn't make sense.

So that first month, I started each session with the direct reports the same way. I'd say, "How many of you, when your boss asks you if you're having any problems, say no, even though you're really having problems?"

I stood up there silently, with my hand raised, holding my breath and looking out at the faces that tried to make sense of what I was asking. They clearly didn't trust me. I waited. And waited. And waited. My heart racing.

And then, finally, one person slowly raised his hand, looking me right in the eye, defiantly. And then another hand went up. And another. Within seconds, after the first guy so boldly showed what was real, every hand in the room was raised.

And it played out the same way in every session with every group of direct reports. All 175 people admitted to telling their boss, "No problems here," when they were indeed having problems.

Imagine the cost of that.

When I asked the groups, "Why?" I got the same answer repeatedly: "I didn't want him [her] to think I was stupid."

We see what we look for. Did the managers want to see problems? Of course not! "No problems here." Great!

And when those problems that weren't there turned into missed deadlines or faulty solutions or poor execution?

"What? How could this happen?"

THEY'RE LAZY.

THEY DON'T CARE.

So why weren't the direct reports honest? Couldn't they see they were only hurting themselves?

This is where the whole being human thing gets tricky. For a moment, let's step into the shoes of these employees:

- The company had been going through massive layoffs over the course of the past year.

- Their department was hit particularly hard, with more than 35 percent of their coworkers losing their jobs.

- I can imagine that as the managers had to let more and more of their people go, it became harder and harder to stay emotionally engaged with those who remained. Keeping a distance made it easier to do what had to be done.

- I can imagine that if I experienced my boss becoming more and more distant, and I watched my friends walk out the door day after day, carrying their belongings in a cardboard box, I'd become distant too. I'd mistrust and maybe hold back, afraid that I was next on the chopping block.

- Layoffs aside, think about how these managers were showing up with their direct reports, given what they believed. How do you show up with someone you think is lazy? How do you listen to them? How do you talk to them? What opportunities do you give them? What if you believe that someone doesn't care? How do you treat them? Do you invest in them? Do you give them what little time you have to spare if they don't care?

If you look at things from the employees' perspective, you might see their lines fading into view.

IT'S NOT SAFE.

HE DOESN'T CARE ABOUT ME.

What we look for is what we see. How we see informs our feelings. Our feelings trigger our behaviors.

The beauty in returning to teach the same groups for the same company over and over again for six months in a row is that I got to know the people behind the lines. What I discovered was extraordinary. Behind the masks of "I don't care" were two hundred human beings—twenty-five managers and 175 of their direct reports—who cared deeply. They cared about doing a good job. They cared about what others thought and needed. They cared about making a difference.

They were just like the rest of us human beings, trapped within the parameters of their own making.

It is impossible to be and bring our best if we are focused on the lines. If you want to be a brave leader, it's critical to challenge how you see.

Key Takeaways

→ We see what we want to see and look to prove ourselves right.

→ Our perception often blinds us to a more effective way of looking at a situation.

→ Our actions are a direct result of our perception.

→ By simply challenging our perception we can dramatically shift our experience and results.

→ How we interpret the behavior of others is greatly influenced by the way we look at a situation. Our reactions, then, are often triggered by misinterpretations and a lack of information. It's important to look at the root cause of behaviors and continue to seek to understand why someone is doing what they are doing, even if it doesn't make sense to you.

→ To be a brave leader, it is critical to challenge the way you look at the situations in your life.

Step Out of the Box

---

*We define only out of despair; we must have
a formula ... to give a facade to the void.*

—EMILE M. CIORAN

When my son, Jeremy, was just learning to walk, he loved boxes. He'd put things in boxes and take them out of boxes—for hours. It pains me to think of all the money we've wasted buying toys and gadgets when he would have been equally happy with a cardboard box. He'd put himself in a box and pop out like a Jeremy-in-the-box, full of delight. We'd jump back in animated surprise, and his peals of laughter could probably be heard a block away. Is there a sweeter sound in the world? At eleven years old, he still loves boxes. Now he pokes holes in them and turns them into robot parts or shields. He gets angry with us when he discovers a great box that has been put in the recycling bin (we have to smuggle them out of the house). I have visions of my grown-up son showing up someday on a cable hoarding show—his house littered with boxes of all sizes. "It all started with my parents," I imagine my unshaven man-son saying. "They gave me my first box when I was two, and I've been hooked ever since."

The joy of boxes is something we never outgrow. While most of us move beyond cardboard, we humans love our boxes. In our attempt to make sense of the world around us, we unconsciously sort and index and catalogue everything in our path. This goes into this box. This goes into that box. This goes into this box. This goes into that box. We like to know where things fit. It makes us feel less confused, more sure of ourselves, and it gives us a sense of control. We all do it, and most of us are completely unconscious of it. It's like breathing.

This is good—this is bad.

This will work—this won't work.

This fits here—this fits there.

But in order to put something in a box, we first have to decide: Where does this go? Our brain then turns back to its files and does a search. What does this look like? Where have I seen something like this before? It blazes through our history and experiences, searching our memories and sorting through our lines to see where something fits. And when it finds something that looks like it will work, *voilà!* Into the box it goes! Speed is valued above accuracy, because of course we're all busy and important, and who has the time to contemplate what belongs where? Close is good enough. Besides, we tell ourselves, we can always put it in a different box later.

In a world that's shifting at the speed of light, what if we're putting everything—stuff, situations, people, possibilities, opportunities, ideas—ourselves—into the wrong box? What if these things don't fit into a box at all?

I run into this all the time with my program, OnStage Leadership. Is it a presentations skills class? Yes. Is it a presence class? Yes. Is it about influence? Yes. Is it about defining purpose or vision or mission? Yes. How about we categorize it as leadership? Yes . . . Yes. Yes. Yes.

It's not just one thing. The conversation is bigger than one thing. It doesn't fit into a box, and it's easy to miss the bigger conversation because we're so eager to figure out where it fits.

And if you think about it, people especially don't fit into a box. There are no clear definitions of what it means to be a mom, a businessperson, a New Yorker, a woman, a millennial, a leader, and so on. Who we are is bigger than just one thing.

And still, we can't help but squeeze ourselves inside. There's something comforting about a box. We like to feel like we fit. We experience belonging, which, if you remember Maslow's hierarchy, is one of our core needs as human beings. Belonging feels good. Not belonging, not so much. We're apt to box ourselves in and box others out, simply to know where we belong. We do it unconsciously, and in doing so, we miss seeing how powerful we are as individuals, the full scope of what our lives can be, and the impact we can have—because we can't help but put ourselves in a box.

I do "this." I am "this." "This" is what's possible for me.

And that is where things get dangerous from a personal-power perspective. Once we "decide" about ourselves—decide about which box we belong in—it becomes nearly impossible to stretch beyond our own limitations.

We need a strategy! A strategy that gives us a way to look past our perceptions altogether and circumvent our knee-jerk talent for seeing, sorting, deciding, and putting ourselves in a confining box in which we don't belong.

For without the box, the world opens up endless possibilities.

Key Takeaways

➜ To make sense of the world around us, we unconsciously sort and index and catalogue everything in our path.

→ This natural human instinct often limits our perception and our ability to take powerful action.

→ People especially don't fit into a box. Who we are is bigger than just one thing.

→ If you want to be a brave leader, *it's critical to challenge how you might be limiting yourself and others due to confined thinking.*

Vulnerable You

Vulnerability is about showing up and being seen.
It's tough to do that when we're terrified about
what people might see or think.

—BRENÉ BROWN

As I sat down to write about vulnerability, I immediately got hungry, so I got up and got a snack. And then I sat back down to write about vulnerability and instantly thought of an email I forgot to send. Then, I got chilly and needed to put on another layer. And while I was up, I figured I might as well get a cup of tea . . . delicious. Then it was time for a bathroom break. When I made it back to my computer, tea in hand, it occurred to me I should check to see if I had any engagement on my Facebook page that needed a response . . . Oh I love that quote! I should . . . Finally, after a solid forty-five minutes of avoiding vulnerability, I sat down to write about it. I wrote. Erased. Wrote. Erased. Snacked. Wrote. Fretted. Wrote. Erased. Called a friend. Called my family. Wrote. Checked email. Wrote. Checked Facebook. Wrote. Had a glass of wine. Whined. Wrote. Erased. Stood in front of the open refrigerator. Wrote. Ate chocolate. Even though I knew what I wanted to say and have taught this information for years, it took me almost a week to write a few paragraphs.

There's an awesome post about the creative process (an inherently vulnerable thing) that's been making the rounds on Facebook that totally captures my experience:

Creative Process

1. This is awesome.

2. This is tricky.

3. This is shit.

4. I am shit.

5. This might be okay.

6. This is awesome.

Having spent three solid days cycling through numbers 2, 3, and 4 on the list, the irony is not lost on me. Even writing about vulnerability feels vulnerable.

If you look up the word *vulnerability*, you can understand why we're not psyched to embrace it. The dictionary defines vulnerability as "capable or susceptible to being emotionally or physically wounded or open to attack or damage." Vulnerability expert Brené Brown, whose gorgeous TED Talk finally made vulnerability okay to talk about for everyone who wasn't already obsessed with it, like me, defines it as "uncertainty, risk, and emotional exposure."[1] However you define it, vulnerability is scary stuff. I believe vulnerability is both our biggest obstacle as human beings and our greatest source of power. It is the gateway to brave leadership. But knowing this doesn't make it any easier.

We are physiologically designed to avoid vulnerability at all costs. As we take in the world around us with our five senses, the frontal cortex of our brain hastens to sort through the incoming information, maps it to our past experiences, our memories, and the meanings we've made (both real and imagined), and kicks out data in the form of body sensations. These are clues. They're telling you that something's up—you've bumped into one of your lines.

The line could be real or imaginary. It could be based on old information or bad information or a lack of information. Your interpretation of the current event could be accurate or not.

The body sensations, however, feel quite real. Your brain instantaneously tells you that, based on your lifetime of data, there is potential for risk. You are vulnerable. Pay attention to the clues.

The first sign could be a fluttering in your stomach, a tingling sensation. Maybe you feel distracted, like you're avoiding something and don't know why. Maybe you feel uneasy or agitated or confused or hungry.

A favorite modern-day coping strategy when we are feeling vulnerable, especially at work, is to simply ignore it. We power through. We figure that if we ignore the sensations, they'll eventually go away. But they don't. The discomfort continues, and it builds and builds—the feelings and sensations trapped behind our walls of denial.

And so we do weird things to make the discomfort stop. Sometimes we try to numb it. We might eat, a lot, or drink, a lot. We might exercise like mad or work endlessly or disappear into gaming or Facebook, Amazon, or eBay, or any number of things we use to take our minds off how we're feeling.

And because we can sense there's a risk, we protect. Sometimes we emotionally put up walls to make sure nothing bad can get in (or let the world know that we're feeling . . . *God forbid* . . . vulnerable). Sometimes we stop engaging, hanging out in the back corners of meeting rooms, hoping not to be noticed. Our techniques for protection are as numerous and varied as we are unique.

As the sensations build, if we can't think our way out of it or numb our way out of it, our cortex kicks it over to the limbic system, involving the amygdala. Here things get really interesting. As our brain's center for emotion management, there's never a dull moment when the amygdala is involved. Serving up a chemical cocktail of serotonin and cortisol and releasing it into our bloodstream, the amygdala can be blamed for all things fight-or-flight. Once the amygdala takes over, your hands might start to sweat. Maybe you feel a shortness of breath. Maybe your thinking gets muddy or crystal clear in an instant. Or you feel tension in your jaws or your shoulders. Maybe you feel nausea. Maybe your face gets flushed. Maybe your heart starts racing. Maybe your hands shake or you feel like you need to pee. Maybe you get fidgety and tap your foot or your pen, or you pace the floor. Or suddenly you chew your pencils or hair or an entire bag of chips you bought for your son (not that I'd know anything about that). Maybe your voice gets loud or it gets really soft. Maybe you stop talking altogether, unknowingly trying to hide. Maybe your knee-jerk response is to fight, and you argue and are combative—to metaphorically kill or be killed. Or maybe your instinct is to flee and walk out the door. Run! You're not safe! Run away!

On impulse, we sense, process, and react. This is our hardwired survival mechanism, and it happens in a flash. Evolutionarily, this served us well, especially during the caveman days. If you stood in the middle of a prairie and stumbled across a saber-toothed tiger in your path, it was helpful to sense danger and be able to react quickly. You didn't have to stop and think, Wait . . . Oh, look at the pretty kitty . . . What should I do now? Should I pet him? Should I continue along my path? Your body sensations signaled an alert. Your heart raced, your breathing stopped, your instincts took over, and you ran—fast. Our bodies are truly extraordinary.

The problem is our brains haven't quite evolved to keep up with the times. What we interpret as a threat is colored by our experiences and childhood interpretations of the world, and this doesn't always serve us well in the workplace (or anywhere in life for that matter). Seth Godin likes to call the amygdala the *lizard brain* because of its Paleolithic tendencies.[2] Our brains haven't been calibrated with the times.

When our quest as human beings was purely to survive and not get eaten, it totally did the trick, but these days we have higher core needs we're trying to satisfy. Now, not only do we not want to get eaten, but we also care about what others think and whether or not we fit in. We want to know that we matter and that we've achieved. As Maslow identified, we've got a whole hierarchy of needs we're trying to satisfy, and when any of our needs feel threatened, we experience body sensations that signal vulnerability. We get uncomfortable.

While there is no saber-toothed tiger threatening your life at work, physiologically the danger can still feel real.

WHAT'S ALL THE FUSS ABOUT?

So what, according to Maslow, might be causing all the fuss with our lizard brains?

How about with this lizard (me)? What was going on with me as I started to write this chapter? It's not like, if I didn't write this chapter, I wouldn't be able to care for my family or they would stop loving me. I'd had my business for many years before I even sat down to write this thing, so I suspect nothing would happen to it. The stakes were not life or death. So what was with all the torture I experienced in trying to write this particular chapter about vulnerability?

Well (without splashing about too indulgently in the mess of my own lines), I highly suspect that my biggest need that was at risk was love and belonging. Writing about vulnerability created a heightened awareness of my own vulnerability. What if this sucks? What if it's rejected? What if I'm rejected?

As my body sensations increased and my avoidance strategies failed, my amygdala joined the party and did its best to stop me in my tracks. And still, I write—but more about that later. Is this something the cavemen (and women) experienced too? I've never met one, but I sincerely doubt it.

Let's take this into the workplace. Remember that company in Chicago, where the managers thought their direct reports were lazy and the direct reports denied all their problems? Well, if you look at Maslow's hierarchy and consider the situation from the employees' perspective, which needs, from their point of view, may have been in jeopardy? Why might they have felt uncertainty, risk, or emotional exposure?

If the company was going through massive layoffs for a solid year, uncertainty would be rampant. The possibility of the employees losing their jobs put the very foundation of their basic human needs—around paying for food and shelter for their families—at risk.

They clearly didn't feel safe to say what was real for them. With such upheaval in the workplace and the emotional distance and judgment coming from their managers, they likely didn't experience much of a sense of belonging.

Imagine how it feels *physiologically* to go into work every day, in the face of such extreme vulnerability.

If you were in this situation, how might it manifest physically? How might you carry yourself? Where would you hold tension? What might your energy be like? How might you express yourself if you felt that vulnerable?

For months, I traveled back and forth to teach this group of managers and their direct reports. I would stand in front of them, look out at the sea of vacant faces month after month, and, based on my interpretation of what I saw, put them in a box. I made decisions about them. I decided they didn't care. I decided they weren't very nice. I decided they weren't "my people." I decided a lot of things about that group, most of which were wrong. Turns out, they cared a great deal; they just weren't willing to show me. They didn't feel safe to be real at work. It took four months for me to see what was going on with them. Four months! I suspect they were working so hard to protect themselves, the only way they could deal with the physiological sensations they felt in that environment was to mask themselves off from the world.

The more disconnected they were, the worse they performed and the easier it was for their bosses to sit in judgment of them. While their natural human instincts told them to protect, doing so only compounded the problem. It reinforced their feeling of alienation from their bosses (belonging), made them feel bad about their performance (self-esteem), and increased the likelihood that they would be the next person on their team to pack up their desk in a cardboard box and be escorted out the door (safety).

Work can be a vulnerable place to be.

VULNERABILITY ON THE STAGE OF LIFE

When feeling vulnerable, we all have our own unique go-to strategies to protect ourselves. Whether you're in a high-stakes conversation with a recruiter, you're in a stressful situation with your boss, or you're speaking in front of a group of a thousand people, when you feel vulnerable, you protect yourself. It manifests physically. It manifests vocally. It manifests in your actions. What do you do to protect yourself when you feel vulnerable? Do you know?

Some of us do it by trying to hide and stay off the radar. Maybe you'll evade eye contact, slouch your shoulders, tilt your head downward, or make your voice small—whispery or breathy. Maybe you stumble over your words, ummming and aaaahhhhhing your way through a conversation or presentation. Maybe you use cynicism or sarcasm to keep people at a distance. Maybe you fold your arms in front of you like a shield. You might clasp your hands or put them in your pocket.

Some of us do it by overcompensating. If we keep moving, they won't catch us! Or maybe you pace or talk fast or try to make everything perfect—scrutinizing every detail, polishing with a vengeance to eliminate any possible risk. Or maybe you use lots of amazing, extraordinary superlatives or talk louder or become more animated. Or perhaps you keep yourself so busy that you don't have a second to spare—to feel how vulnerable you are.

Maybe you overcompensate by being forceful, convinced if you could take charge of the situation that you could control everything around you (and the vulnerability would go away).

And some of us stop participating altogether. We block out the world or stuff our feelings down deep or vanish in plain sight. These days, it's even socially acceptable to disappear in the middle of a conversation. Aren't cell phones the best invention in the world to do just that? It's all the same thing.

It's human beings dealing with the discomfort of feeling vulnerable. No one is impervious. It doesn't matter how old you are, how experienced you are, how smart you are, how talented you are, how rich you are, or how fancy your title. It doesn't matter where you worship or if you worship. It doesn't matter where you live, which chromosome you have, or if you're nice. It doesn't matter if you're purple or blue. If you're a person, vulnerability affects you.

It affects the way we show up at work, the way we lead, and the way we speak in groups. It affects the way we live.

But vulnerability doesn't have to hold you back from being a confident and powerful leader. If you know how it affects you and take the right actions, it can be used to your advantage.

Vulnerability is our biggest barrier to brave and the gateway to our most powerful self.

Key Takeaways

→ All human beings experience vulnerability. Being brave requires navigating vulnerability, not trying to avoid it.

→ Vulnerability triggers chemical reactions in our brain that produce warning signs and body sensations that are often disproportionate or a misrepresentation of the true risk we face.

→ We all have unique strategies (like overcompensating or withdrawing) to protect ourselves when we feel vulnerable that don't always serve us.

→ If you want to be a brave leader you must *understand how vulnerability affects you, physically, emotionally, and mentally; examine your coping strategies; and ensure you navigate vulnerability constructively.*

10

Where Are You . . . Really?

Presence is more than just being there.

—MALCOLM FORBES

O kay," I said, looking around the room at the rebels who still had their laptops open in the training room. "Time to close them up!"

A few of them looked up, their brows furrowed in frustration, and as if I were forcing them off life support, they slowly pulled their fingers away from their keyboards. One guy in the corner, who pretended I wasn't there, typed furiously, completely committed to his breach of the class rules.

"Come on, Brandon," nudged his coworker. "We all have to do it."

Brandon glanced up at me in desperation, looked back at his computer, and slowly closed the lid with a sigh, resigned to his fate.

I felt like a jerk. I knew they were stretched way too thin as it was, and I prayed that a day away from their computers wouldn't be so overwhelming that it would drown out the good we were trying to accomplish at this retreat. In order to make an impact, I needed them to be present, and shutting their computers was only the first small step. The harder part would be shepherding their minds.

———

When I teach executive presence, they seem shocked. "Presence," I say, "begins with being present."

No way. That can't be! Isn't presence about having enough charisma to command a room and get people to do what you want? Nope.

It begins with being present. It even says so in the Merriam-Webster Dictionary:

pres·ence: noun \'pre-zən(t)s\
1. the fact or condition of being present
2. a noteworthy quality of poise and effectiveness
3. something felt or believed to be present

Whether you like it or not, if you're not present, you don't have presence. Being present, in what speaker and Olympian Vince Poscente refers to as our "24/7 CrackBerry world," seems nearly impossible.[1] Our minds constantly tick off mile-long to-do lists while we put out fires, juggle work with family, and do more with less.

I'm not going to claim to be the queen of being present; I, too, am a work in process, but I've had some great role models. If anyone knows how to be fully present, it's my mom. My artist mother can see forty shades of green in a leaf and will ooh and aah at the way the light reflects off a puddle. She's that present.

"Look, Kimberly!" she'd gasp, stopping the car on the way to school. "It's a watercolor sky!" . . . or a watercolor tree or a watercolor mountain or a watercolor bird. All of nature's gifts are celebrated in my mom's expression of childlike wonder and then captured magically on the canvas, as if she's bringing the soul of the world to life.

What would our lives be like if we could bring such presence and appreciation into our daily activities? If, when we listened, we really listened? If, when we spent time with our employees, our friends, and our family, we were that present?

Kids are a great meter for letting you know how present you are. I remember one morning, back when my son Jeremy was about four years old, we were doing our normal routine and he said, "Mommy, come play with me!"

"Not now," I said, typing furiously on my computer. "I've got to send this message."

"In a minute. Let me get dressed."

"Hold on. I need to make your lunch."

After about an hour of him playing quietly by himself in the next room, he disappeared. I finished what I was doing and went to look for him. Coming from the sunroom, I heard giggles. They were cute giggles, which always meant he was up to something.

I turned the corner just in time to see him proudly splattering shaving cream all over our new flat-screen TV, like he was Jackson Pollock. When he saw me, he looked up with a big smile and a twinkle in his eyes and said, "Hi Mommy! Are you ready to play now?"

It's hard to take the time when it feels like there's no time. Yet what is the price that we pay for not taking the time? If a flat-screen TV were all we had to lose, then maybe it would be worth the gamble. But what are we communicating to the people we work with, to our customers, and to the people we love when we don't take the time, in that moment, to be fully present? What might we be missing when we don't truly see and listen?

Think about that company I worked with in Chicago. If those managers were truly present with the human beings they led, do you think they might have realized that there were, indeed, some problems? One hundred seventy-five people! "No problems here!"

There's a cost to not being present.

What I've heard from participants over and over again is that if their leaders aren't present, they start to check out. They stop bringing their ideas. They stop sharing their challenges and their wins. They stop turning to their leaders for support. They stop caring—at least about their leader.

You see, when people sense that we're not invested in them, that they're not important enough, they stop investing in us. They take their want elsewhere, or worse, they stay. As a leader, can you afford that?

THE SURVIVAL BUBBLE

This lack of presence is certainly not intentional; it's often simply a survival mechanism. In the barrage of our daily lives or in the face of stress and overload, sometimes we check out out of necessity. I remember when I first moved to New York, I was like an open vessel, eagerly absorbing all the sights, sounds, and smells. It was so exciting and so exhausting. I would come home from the city and be utterly wiped out. With so many stimuli, people here have to create a protective bubble around themselves to survive or the constant barrage becomes too much to endure.

I don't think this is only a New York City phenomenon; I find it's become this way in our organizations as well. With the advent of the hip, open-concept office space, everyone is around everyone all the time. Yet I'll walk into an office with 150 people all working in the same room, and it's so silent I feel like I'm whispering in church if I speak. What's meant to be energizing in design can become a vacuum if we're not careful.

And in our need to constantly multitask—to send that last email or check in on a deliverable—we disappear into our bubble, shutting out the world around us.

I don't know about you, but I find that the more time I spend in my head, the harder it is to get out of it and be present and inclusive. I stop fully engaging with the people around me because I'm caught in my own web of thoughts.

When I encounter others who are stuck in their heads, I'll do one of two things: Either I'll make assumptions about why they're not present, or

I'll feel like I'm an intruder. I don't want to disturb them and find myself shrinking back from asking questions, engaging in conversation, or being able to connect in any meaningful way.

If we live our lives inside a bubble, might that have an impact on our relationships, on our ability to get things done, or on our company cultures?

On our own sense of satisfaction?

A bubble isn't inherently good or bad. Some of my most creative moments have emerged from my bubble. It's not an all-or-nothing thing. But, as with everything, it all begins with mindfulness. Do you know when you're in your bubble? When it's working for you and when it's not?

We have the power to choose. We forget. Simply because we may be able to survive within a bubble doesn't mean there's a lot of thriving going on.

Recently I listened to a terrific conversation between Jonathan Fields (Good Life Project Radio, one of my favorite podcasts) and MIT professor, technology researcher, and author Sherry Turkle. Sherry talked about the challenge of having "technology that is always on, and it is always on us"[2] and discussed how we no longer notice when we've disconnected from the people we're with and have turned our attention to our devices. We're not aware when we take our eyes off our child or when we have broken the conversation. Solid research indicates that if you're having a meal with someone and you simply put your phone on the table, the depth of the conversation will be lighter—you won't talk about anything of consequence, and you'll feel less connected and emotionally invested.

"The phone is there as a marker," she said, "that this conversation could be interrupted."

The erosion in our ability to be present is severely affecting our relationships, which impacts not only our sense of connection and belonging but also our engagement and our ability to get things done through others. If you want to lead, that is a problem.

———

There's an African Zulu greeting that I love: *Sawubona*. It means "I see you." (I suspect director James Cameron borrowed this saying for his film

Avatar.) It says, I see your personality. I see your humanity. I see your dignity and respect.

Imagine what might be possible if we were to be so present with one another in this way. What kind of connections could we create? What might we accomplish together?

If we want people to experience us as genuine, worthy of trust, reliable, and believable, if we want to earn their want, then we have to find a way to cut through the noise in our lives and be present with the people around us.

Where are you?

Here would be good.

Key Takeaways

→ Presence begins with being present.

→ A lack of presence is rarely intentional; it's often simply an unconscious survival mechanism.

→ As a leader, if you are not present with those you lead, you put their want at risk.

→ When we are concentrating deeply, people often misinterpret our lack of presence. It is vitally important to *choose* how and when we are present with others, rather than operating on autopilot.

→ If we want people to experience us as authentic (genuine, worthy of trust, reliable, and believable), then we must find a way to be present with them.

→ If you want to be a brave leader, you must ask yourself, *How present am I with those I wish to lead and influence? How do I know that they experience me as being present?*

PART III

PUSHING

THROUGH

TO BRAVE

11

A Matter of Focus

All the world's a stage, and all the
men and women merely players . . .
—JAQUES IN ACT II SCENE VII,
AS YOU LIKE IT, WILLIAM SHAKESPEARE

In Moscow, at the turn of the century, a young man who was an actor, director, and theater administrator became curious. As the son of one of the richest families in Russia, he had a keen sense for business that caused him to take notice. Why, he wondered, did some actors consistently attract huge audiences, while others did not? What were they doing differently?

With the heart of an actor, the eye of a detective, and the mind of a businessman, he studied and questioned the Moscow Art Theatre performers he most admired and married his observations with his personal experiences on stage, until slowly certain themes started to emerge. Even before the field of psychology was widely accepted as a discipline, Constantin Stanislavski set out to codify a system to teach the techniques that the most successful actors were using to create truthful, inspired performances. What Stanislavski came to understand still influences the craft of acting today—and in my world (and now yours), leadership.

What Stanislavski discovered was that the most powerful performances—the ones that drew the biggest crowds, the loudest applause, that kept the audience at the edge of their seats with bated breath—were by actors who did something different than all the others. They seemed to be driven by an invisible force, their concentration unwavering. They were able to replicate powerful performances night after night, consistently, unaffected by whoever might be in the audience, the critics' reviews, or the backstage drama of the day. They brought presence.

As he probed more deeply, he found something unexpected. Neither talent nor looks nor experience set the actors apart and gave them the mysterious, almost magnetic quality. They weren't smarter than the others or more outgoing or charismatic. The key, he found, to their extraordinary performance and consistently positive results—the one thing that they seemed to be doing differently from all the others—was simply a matter of focus.

YOU IN THE SPOTLIGHT

Imagine, for a moment, that it is opening night at your local theater and *you* have the starring role in a play that's received a lot of hype. (Congratulations!) Let's say the theater seats maybe . . . two hundred people. That's considered a relatively small house. (Just to calibrate, an Off-Broadway theater seats 100–499 people, and a Broadway theater seats over five hundred.) The audience is filled with patrons who have paid a lot of money to see you perform. Their expectations are high. For them, this is a special occasion. This has probably been on their calendar for months. They probably got all dressed up, paid for a nice dinner out, maybe hired a babysitter—the whole thing. They've invested a lot. Most of the audience members are complete strangers, but you have a handful of friends and family out there who have come to show their support. There's likely a critic or two or three peppered in the audience, with pens poised. You know their reviews will be in the next day's edition of the local paper, and you can hardly wait to read what they have to say. You also have several colleagues sitting out there—actors who auditioned for the production but were not cast, and they're likely *not* hoping for your success. (They probably even auditioned for your role.) The house lights go dark. A hush falls over the sold-out crowd. The music is cued. You walk onto the darkened stage from stage right (which is the actor's right). The stage lights come up and all four hundred eyeballs are on . . . you.

Can you picture yourself? How do you feel? What's happening in your body? Maybe you feel electrified—your senses on full alert. Maybe your heart is pounding out of your chest. Maybe your fingers are tingling. What's happening with your breathing? (Are you breathing?)

As you speak your lines and go through the blocking you've rehearsed over and over again for the last month, what goes through your mind? Maybe you wonder where your friends are sitting? Maybe you hope to impress the critics? Maybe you want to prove to the other actors sitting out there that you deserved to get the role? Or maybe you try to prove something to yourself—to finally know that all those years of studying and starving and auditioning have been worth it. This is the big break you've been waiting for. (Yay, you!) You're feeling excited and scared—totally amped up on adrenaline. What a rush! You vow to make the audience laugh and cry. (It's better than *Cats*.) You vow to show them what a truly amazing actor you are. You care deeply about doing a good job. The stakes are high. You've worked hard for this moment. This, you promise yourself, is only the beginning.

All these thoughts happen simultaneously as you perform. This conversation goes on in your head while you perform your role on stage. Because you—the actor—are a human being, and that's what human beings do.

Except not the actors that Stanislavski studied.[1] The best actors, the ones giving truthful, powerful, and inspired performances, innately did something different. They were able to circumvent their natural human tendencies around wanting to impress others and prove themselves. They were also able to divert their attention away from the emotions naturally triggered by being in the spotlight. The excitement and fear and vulnerability that most others experience when standing in front of an audience was left waiting in the wings and did not influence their performance. Their energy was instead channeled into igniting a live moment in time on the stage. What Stanislavski came to learn was that these amazing actors instinctively understood how to focus their attention. And he figured out how to teach others to do the same.

LIFE EMULATES ART

If you think about it, life at work isn't terribly different from being in the theater's spotlight. While executing your job responsibilities, your brain is hard at work multitasking, much like an actor's. You are constantly trying to impress others, to prove yourself, to say all the right things, and to navigate your own emotions while not letting them show.

What you may not realize is that when you're at work, like an actor, you are also on stage. People are always watching. They are judging. They have high expectations. They have a stake in your performance. Even when you think nobody is paying attention, they are.

I remember listening to one of my unhappy workshop participants talking about her boss's boss, the vice president of the department, Bob, in one of our sessions. "I've been working here for seven years," she said, "and he's never once said hello to me. I see him in the hallway four to five times a day. I see him in the lunchroom. I see him in our department meetings. Nothing. Ever. He never even acknowledges me. I know that he's a busy guy, but you would think that he would care enough to at least make an effort!" Since her boss's boss also happened to be my client, and

I thought he was a pretty good guy, I was surprised. This didn't sound like the Bob I knew. But when all of her colleagues nodded their heads in agreement, I knew there must be some truth to her claim.

The next time I saw Bob, I said, "Do you realize that people feel like you ignore them? They think they're not important to you. I'm pretty sure that's not the message you want to convey."

"But I'm not their boss," he said, confused. "They don't report to me. Why should it matter?"

"You're the leader of the department. Everyone looks up to you. They need to know you see and value them. They need to know you care."

"But how do I do that? I don't even know them!" he protested.

"Get to know them. Start by saying hello in the hallway. Ask about what they did over the weekend when you're standing in line at the cafeteria. If they mention their kids, ask them how old they are," I replied. "You know, have a conversation!"

At the last session of our workshop, when I saw the unhappy participant, she didn't seem so unhappy. She sauntered up to the front of the room and pulled me aside, smiling wryly. "You said something to Bob, didn't you?" (She caught me!)

"Why do you ask?" I replied, playing coy.

"Because yesterday I got caught in a twenty-minute discussion about baseball with Bob during lunch, and that was something that never would have happened before! He's a much nicer guy than I realized. I see him chatting it up with everyone in the hallway now. It's hilarious!"

As a leader, you are always on stage. It's not that Bob was a bad guy or that he didn't care. It's that his focus was on business—all the stresses and demands of his big job. He was completely blind to the fact that the people in his department needed more from him—that they expected more from him. He was on stage.

A few years back, I coached a strategy director who told me about how his CEO would make snarky comments about other people in the office behind their backs. The CEO seemed to think it was funny or that he was somehow bonding with people. "If he's saying things about Sherri, I know he's saying things about me," the director confided, a month before he took his talent and left the company.

You are always on stage, and how you show up has an impact. And if it's negative, beware.

If you get frustrated and walk out of a meeting without saying anything, there is an impact.

If you don't make eye contact when you speak, there is an impact.

If you are overwhelmed and you snap at your colleague, there is an impact.

If you avoid having tough conversations, there is an impact.

If you always have your face in your phone when you're with other people, there is an impact.

If you're so busy that you don't acknowledge the humans around you, there is an impact.

If you say snarky things about people, whether they're there or not, there's an impact.

You may not like it, it may not be fair, but it's what's real. At work, especially in a leadership position, you are in the spotlight. Everything you say and do has an impact.

You may not read your critics' opinions of you in the paper the next day, but like an actor, make no mistake, you are indeed being reviewed.

> ## *What do you want your impact to be?*

And you are being reviewed by everyone—your colleagues, your clients, your boss, your direct reports, and your vendors. (I so hate the term *vendors*. Let's call them *partners*, shall we?)

If you choose not to pay attention to your impact and simply go about business as usual, ignoring the real needs of the people around you, be prepared. Impact ignored has costly consequences: disengagement, high turnover, sagging productivity, and low morale point to a leader who is not paying attention to impact.

If you think you're focused on the business but you ignore the people, you're not focused on the business.

But let's say you're not the ignoring type. Let's say that you really care about what others think and feel about you. Great! How do you find out? Well, they might tell you, but most likely they won't. You're stuck reading their expressions, body language, and remarks, trying desperately to make meaning of it all.

What do people think of me? Am I doing a good job? Do they like me? Am I a success? Am I a failure? You are reading the lines.

Sometimes you decipher the meaning correctly, and a lot of times you don't. Unconsciously, your old lines impact your interpretation of new lines, and truth becomes elusive. You see what you look to see. Not because you're stubborn, but because you're human.

It's a conundrum! We need to be sensitive to how we're perceived, but when we get so focused on what other people think about us, ironically, all we can think about is ourselves. It brings to mind an old joke I've heard dozens of times: What does he think about me? What does she think about me? Well enough about me, what do you think about me?

Don't worry. It's not that you're more egotistical than anyone else; we're all special this way. Caught in our own harsh interrogator's light, we scrutinize our every move—our confidence and power waning with every interaction.

In doing so, we make decisions about ourselves. Where do I fit? What can I do? What is possible for me? We need to know how far we can step out of the lines we have drawn in the sand.

Whether the lines are perceived as positive or negative makes no difference; they serve their purpose. They define your boundaries, your actions, and, largely, you. They influence your performance, how you experience yourself, and how you show up in the world. Effusive in their praise or harsh in their delivery, it is nearly impossible to bring your most authentic and powerful self to the game when you're focused on the lines.

So now what? If you can't focus on running the business because of the potential negative consequences on the people around you, and focusing on what others think about you can lead you down a slippery slope, where do you focus your attention?

On the impact you want to have *outside* yourself.

At least that's what Stanislavski discovered to be true for actors. And as Mary McCarthy said in "The Vita Activa," printed in *The New Yorker* in 1958, "There are no new truths, but only truths that have not been recognized by those who have perceived them without noticing."

And if, at work, we're always on stage, maybe Stanislavski's truth is one worth noticing.

Key Takeaways

➔ At work, we're always on stage, because people are always watching.

➔ The heightened situations in our lives negatively impact our performance when our thinking is self-related (e.g., *What do they think about me? What if I mess up? What's in it for me?*).

➔ People who perform powerfully when the stakes are high are able to take their focus off of themselves.

➔ If you want to be a brave leader, you must focus your attention outside yourself. Ask yourself, *What do I want my impact to be (on my employees, my clients, my students, my patients, my industry, my organization, my culture, my community, etc.)?*

12

Bull's-eye

*The direction of your focus
is the direction your life will move.*
—RALPH MARSTON

N o, no, no!" my director snapped from the back of the rehearsal studio. "It's too general. You're playing generalities. You're not a mime up there. Your character is a real, living human being who is after something. Don't pretend. Do."

Do? I thought. Do . . . What to do? My mind was totally blank.

"What do you want?"

I want you to get off my back, I thought as I peered at him sideways, sitting there all high and mighty. I felt like I wanted to hide.

"Get specific. What does your character want? For real? What's she after?"

What does she want?

———

I remember when I was in college, I used to always wish I had a crystal ball. I wanted to know what my future would bring. I wanted to know what mistakes to avoid. I wanted to find the right path.

For years, I took a backseat in the design of my own life. I was good at certain things, and teachers and adults I respected were quick to say, "You're so good at this, you should . . ." So I did. I did what others said I should do. I didn't really think about it at all. For years, I just let life happen—allowing myself to be guided by the winds of happenstance, rather than choice.

I don't think my story is unusual that way. From what I've seen, many lives unfold within the dotted lines of someone's helpful advice, an opportunity that presents itself, following logical next steps, or by doing what was simply expected—allowing others to set the path on our behalf. The question is this: At what point do we start actively participating in the design of our own lives, rather than as bystanders with a hope and a prayer that it's all going to work out for the best? When do you start going after what you want—for real? What do you want?

It's a big question. If we had to articulate it, most of our *wants* would be generalities. I want to be happy. I want to be successful. I want to get my boss (or director or spouse or mother) off my back. As most of us know all too well, wanting to be happy or successful gets us no closer to truly being happy or successful. It's missing the key ingredient—action. As my acting professor (as much as it drove me nuts) loved to say, "Don't pretend. Do."

Do what?

What Russian actor and director Stanislavski uncovered is that a general want does not provide the kind of focus that will get powerful results. Generalities can't harness attention, which leads to poor performance, both on and off the stage.

Imagine a big dartboard thirty feet in front of you. Now, imagine you are blindfolded. Can you picture yourself? Now, blindfolded, throw a dart at the dartboard. What are the odds that you might hit that bull's-eye? Thirty percent? Fifteen percent? If you're anything like me, it's more like .001 percent. Unless you are a world-champion dart player, I suspect you might have some difficulty.

Now, imagine the same dartboard looms in front of you. It's in the same place, but this time you take the blindfold off. How are your odds now? 40 percent? 60 percent? If you're a killer dart player, you might boast 90 percent. Even I can claim, with my dart-throwing skills as woeful as they are, that my probability of success goes up.

Now that you can see the bull's-eye and know where it is, you can do something about it. You can strategize. Maybe you need to throw the dart a different way or adjust your aim. Maybe you need to get a dart mentor. Whether you're a great dart player or not, because you can *see* the target, you have options for specific action. You're not just throwing the dart in a general direction.

When you stop throwing generalities, the likelihood of hitting your bull's-eye goes up exponentially simply because you can see what you're trying to hit. If you don't hit it, you can do something differently and try again. You can get closer the next time. Your results get better with each throw. That's the power of focus.

THE QUEST FOR SURVIVAL

She looked frazzled and tired. Her eyes were like a portal into her mind, and I could see all the balls she was frantically juggling. She was in a million places at that moment. Not with me at all.

"Are you okay?" I asked. "You seem stressed."

"It shows?" she sighed, defeated.

"A little. What's going on?"

As she unpacked her life in a mind-bending thirty seconds— last-minute client emergencies, travel plans, volunteer commitments, family crisis, and contractor issues—I could see she was flooded. Like so many of us, life's commitments had hit a frenzied pace, and she was overwhelmed.

"I'm crazy busy, and I'm not enjoying any of it," she confessed. "I feel like I just want to run away."

As she talked, I could feel the pressure she was under, and my body responded empathetically—my chest grew tight, my breathing became shallow, and my mind started to swim. I had been there before, more than once, and my muscle memory kicked in—a visceral reminder of what a painful place that can be.

In today's world, with so many demands on our time and energy, it's easy to get swept away in the tide of our tasks. Although there are many pithy quotes out there making the social media rounds (that I admittedly "like"), leading us to believe that we can choose to not be overwhelmed, for most of us human beings, I think that's pretty aspirational. In my experience, the choice tends to follow the feeling, because the feeling overtakes us before we can see it coming.

Our focus gets hijacked. We throw our darts haphazardly at the world and wonder why we feel so drained and overwhelmed. We focus on keeping our job. We focus on staying off the radar. We focus on hitting our deadlines. We focus on getting our kids through school. We focus on getting out the door. We focus on paying our bills. We focus on getting dinner on the table. We focus on just getting through the damn day so we can get up and do it all over again tomorrow. We focus on survival. And all of our actions fall out of that. What do I need to do to survive? We're simply reacting to the world around us to get through the day—to survive.

It's no wonder we feel overwhelmed and lose ourselves in the fray.

Without a clear and specific focus *beyond survival*, we're just throwing darts in the dark, hoping something will stick.

This focus on specific action in order to have an impact outside yourself—that internal drive that stems from the core of who you are—is what Stanislavski would call your *Super Objective*.

Key Takeaways

→ By focusing your attention on the *impact* you want to have *outside* yourself, you harness your attention, which makes it possible to cut through vulnerability, show up authentically, and ensure you bring your most powerful self to the situation.

→ A focus on specific purposeful action to have an impact outside yourself is called your *Super Objective.*

→ Focusing on your Super Objective makes it possible for you to adjust your actions, clean up your reactions, and behave more consistently as your best self.

→ Focusing on action to achieve impact—your Super Objective— aligns who you are on the inside with the actions you take in your life, to ensure people experience you as authentic (genuine, worthy of trust, reliance, and belief). The want of others is simply a by-product of powerful, purposeful action.

→ If you want to be a brave leader, *it is critical to get clear about your Super Objective and take consistent, mindful action to achieve it in every situation you face*—especially when the stakes feel high. (There is a tool at the end of chapter 15 to help you uncover your Super Objective.)

13

Goals Are Not Enough

*Somebody ought to tell him
his ambition is showing.*

—HARRY ESSEX

This is where all the gurus step in and declare that goals are the answer. What do you want? You want to hit your goals! Set your mind on a goal, do everything you can to not get derailed, and success and fulfillment are destined to be yours! We love goals! Our bosses love goals! Our companies love goals! And now, our shareholders not only expect us to hit our goals but exceed our goals every quarter. It's all about the goal!

Don't panic. I'm not saying goals are bad. (Blasphemy!) What I am saying is that, despite the golden promise of success and fulfillment that we expect from hitting our goals, they are not enough to ensure that we're bringing our best, most constructive, real self to the game. On their own, goals are inherently flawed.

WHAT'S THE PROBLEM WITH GOALS?

We love fast. The faster we can get from point A to point B, the better. We have become an immediate gratification society. We want information at our fingertips, instant responses, and ready-made food. We want our triple, no foam, extra-hot, three-pump, skinny vanilla latte in under three minutes or we furrow our brows and check our phones in agitation. We're all busy and important and have no time to wait. While in 1997 it was considered good if your Internet page loaded in under ten seconds,[1] according to *The New York Times*, "These days, even 400 milliseconds— literally the blink of an eye—is too long."[2]

We have become a very impatient people. We want what we want, and we want it *now*. We focus on a goal, and our job is to make it happen, fast. We must increase revenue, decrease costs, get the sale, make our employees perform, focus on the goal. And we must hit it—fast. But fast can lead us down a slippery slope.

Early in my career, I did a brief stint in hospitality sales. I had never done sales before, so it was a whole new world. I was on the group sales team for a large dinner cruise. A fancier version of Gilligan's three-hour tour, we'd fetch people at the pier for a glamorous evening of microwaved buffet delicacies and dancing to your favorite eighties tunes while cruising the harbor and taking in the Seattle skyline. Each member of our team was responsible for a different market. Three of us had the corporate market, someone else the military market, and the star of our team, Kathy, had the association/convention market. For the first three months, I was in awe of her. Everything she touched seemed to turn to gold—fast. Like in many inside-sales organizations, we had our goals on the wall, and every time we'd make a sale, they'd ring the Pavlovian bell in celebration.

Kathy was always getting to ring the bell. When you hit a milestone, we got to play the slot machine for cash. Kathy was always getting to play the slot machine. She was always the first to hit her goals, the darling of our boss and the envy of the team. We all wanted to be like Kathy. I buckled down and made twice the number of calls. I started a fax campaign (don't laugh). I was committed, but still my bell didn't ring.

Within a few of months of my arrival, Kathy was rewarded for her outstanding performance by being given the only outside-sales position ever created in the company. She would breeze in and out of the office like a bubble, shopping bags adorning her wrists, to make a quick personal call before running out to a meeting. Since Kathy was so busy wooing potential clients at hospitality functions and wowing hotel concierges with her obviously brilliant sales presentations, I inherited her market. It was an eye-opening experience.

"You should thank me," she said as she flitted out the door. "I've left you with a nice book of business."

And so it began, my days spent uncovering what was really behind all the bell ringing. Massive discounting, freebies, false promises, and outright lies had apparently made booking business a piece of cake. Kathy hit her goals all right, but the business she booked was anything but profitable, and the clients' expectations anything but realistic. Her outstanding performance was smoke and mirrors. But she hit her goals.

We get what we reward. If we reward speed of sale, it's human nature to find the fastest path to get there. If we reward number of sales, it's human nature for people to find the easiest way to get the most for their efforts. Speed and numbers don't always equal profitability or a positive customer experience, and making these goals the sole focus for reward only opens the door to compromising values in a big way.

Goals are not enough.

Sometimes, blinded by media-fueled images of what it means to be happy and successful, we set our aim on an illusion.

I remember when my husband, Tim, first got the offer that led to our move to Dallas. They offered him a sexy title, a nice salary, and a fancy office on the thirty-first floor with floor-to-ceiling windows overlooking the city. He had always wanted these things. But we moved, and he was miserable. Within months, the title meant nothing, the salary wasn't worth it, and he hated going into the office no matter how fancy it was. But he hit his goals.

Unfortunately, sometimes our goals come at a bigger price than we anticipate. I've met so many amazing goal achievers in my time—road warriors, senior executives, entrepreneurs, creatives, consultants, emerging leaders, and so on—their health, relationships, and satisfaction all crumbling around their feet, and they keep pushing harder.

They're ambitious. They want to hit their goals. But when we focus solely on goals, our ambition to achieve those goals can easily lead us astray from our best selves and our most fulfilling life. Convinced that we're doing what we need to do to hit the target, we become numb to the repercussions of our actions, often until it's too late.

YOUR BRAIN ON GOALS

We are a goal-addicted society, and it's no wonder. Our brains love goals. Achieving goals brings us rewards—which could be money, a promotion, or simply kudos and approval—and rewards bring us pleasure. According to *Harvard Health*, neurotechnologies and research show that "the brain registers all pleasures in the same way, whether they originate with a psychoactive drug, a monetary reward, a sexual encounter, or a satisfying meal. In the brain, pleasure has a distinct signature: the release of the neurotransmitter dopamine in the nucleus accumbens, a cluster of nerve cells lying underneath the cerebral cortex. Dopamine release in the nucleus accumbens is so consistently tied with pleasure that neuroscientists refer to the region as the brain's pleasure center."[3]

When we hit our goals, we get a shot of dopamine and we feel good. Give me more of that!

If you map goal focus to Maslow's hierarchy, you can easily see how we're programmed to keep it up. Goals give us access to every point on the pyramid.

If you consistently hit your work goals, you can assume that you'll be able to feed and shelter your family, keep yourself relatively safe, and that your boss will love and adore you and promote you through the organization. It's no wonder that goals are often referred to as the key to success.

Goal addiction is not only accepted, it's downright celebrated. We laud those who have sacrificed much to attain their goals. These superhumans who don't seem to need sleep can operate on caffeine and knock it out of the park every time. We call it *ambition*, which makes it exciting and enviable, and steeps us in the approval of all the important people who know what an important quality that is to have.

And that's why it can be hard to notice, even for ourselves, when achieving our goals shifts from being a self-actualization thing to a self-destruction thing. Why swim to safety when the world applauds you as you drown?

The problem with feeling good on dopamine is that the more you get, the more it takes for you to feel good. One day a little square of dark chocolate will satisfy you; the next week it takes the whole bar. Ambition knows no bounds. When we're using that shot of dopamine to make up for not feeling good otherwise, no amount is big enough to fill the void.

Whether it's a Hershey bar, Soul Cycle, Vegas, cannabis, wine, or work, if our hierarchical needs have been left depleted over the years or our health and relationships have imploded, more dopamine is not the answer—it's a time bomb waiting to explode.

While ambition is the glorified fuel that helps us achieve our goals, it can also be a red herring. We pretend that it's all in the name of success, but if you dig deeper you'll discover a less popular truth. Many of us don't believe—deep down inside—how good we really are. We think we need to prove ourselves, so we focus on that. We prove to our boss, our colleagues, our classmates, our spouses, our parents, our teachers, and all those people who've shown up in our lives and have (most often without even knowing it) left us doubting our abilities and our worth. We prove to ourselves. We do everything we can to prove that those lines in the sand aren't real.

WHAT IF YOU HAVE NOTHING TO PROVE?

We were a competitive bunch. In a program in which the freshman class of one hundred gets slashed to twenty-five students by sophomore year, it's no wonder that every one of us felt we had something to prove. We wanted to be chosen, to prove that we were good enough, to prove that we had the talent, and to prove that we had what it takes. The irony was that the more we tried to prove, the worse we were.

I remember getting notes from my theater professors saying something that seemed so counterintuitive: "You're pushing. Stop working so hard," they would write. It made no sense to me at the time. How could I prove I was serious about my craft if I didn't show them how hard I was working? If they could just see how much I wanted this, how much I was willing to do, then I could prove to them that I was worthy. That's what drove so many of us—the desire to prove ourselves.

It's not surprising that actors find themselves feeling this way. (After all, there aren't many other professions out there that require mass applause to let you know that you've done a good job.) But this need-to-prove thing is certainly not confined to the acting profession. I can't tell you how many people I've met—business owners, students, young managers, stay-at-home moms, attorneys, doctors, academics, emerging leaders, senior leaders, and so on—whose primary aim is to prove themselves: prove that they're smart, successful, capable, worthy, as good as . . . No, the need to prove isn't an actor thing, it's a human thing.

Some would argue that proving yourself unleashes a tremendous energy. People work really hard when they're trying to prove themselves. They will push themselves and achieve great things, make things happen, and get lots of great stuff when they're trying to prove. What could possibly be wrong with that?

Well, a lot, actually. When we're focused on proving ourselves, our actions can be destructive.

- Think of the guy who's bragging all the time—the name droppers, the one-uppers, and the ones who always have to be the smartest person in the room. That's proving.

- Are you worried about "keeping up with the Joneses"? Do you have to have the newest gadgets, the fanciest labels, drive the best car, and join the right club (even if it means living beyond your means)? That's proving.

- Do you measure people's value by their credentials and have to tout yours in every conversation? That's proving.

- Do you know people who make a nice living but continue working a million hours at the expense of their relationships, to make or achieve more? Hoping that someday having more will equal happy? That's proving.

- Do you know people who have disregarded their own values to look good or get ahead? That's proving.

- Do you hang out with people you don't like or respect because they're important, cool, popular, or successful? That's proving.

- Do you know people who seem to agree with all the powers that be but never take a stand for anything themselves? That's proving.

- Do you do what is expected rather than what you dream, and then resent it? That's proving.

- Do you push yourself, your team, your kids, and so on to be perfect, even though perfect is a fantasy? That's proving.

- Do you take care of everyone around you at the expense of yourself? That's proving.

To some degree, we're all trying to prove ourselves, and we pay a price for it. When we're focused on proving, we never feel satisfied. We can never be enough, achieve enough, or feel appreciated enough. In our attempts to be validated and seen, we alienate. When we're trying to prove that we're special, we find loneliness. We are surrounded by riches but cannot see them. When we don't believe we're enough, there's nothing we can do to prove it.

When we're trying to prove ourselves, we are our own biggest roadblocks to being powerful. How powerful can we be, after all, if we feel like we need to prove something? Because if we need to prove ourselves, then that means that we need someone else to validate our worth. Why put that in someone else's hands? The more we try to prove, the less powerful we feel.

When actors focus their attention on trying to prove, on trying to get the director's validation or the audience's applause, they push. They force emotion to create an effect and, thus, aren't believable. They're not sensitive to the other actors in the scene, so they don't collaborate and risk the integrity of the production to satisfy their own needs—their need to prove.

A great performance is one in which the actor can move beyond their concerns about what others think and have the courage to focus on powerfully igniting a moment in time and truly connecting with their fellow actors on the stage.

Perhaps that's true for all of us. When we're trying to prove, we're not believable. We stop being sensitive to the needs of others and to being collaborative. Focused on a need to prove ourselves, we lose awareness of what we're putting at risk. It's not that we're bad. It's that we don't know how good we are.

What would be possible, if you had nothing to prove?

There's nothing wrong with having ambition and setting powerful, challenging goals and working like crazy to achieve them. These make the foundation of great work and lasting companies. But despite what we've been promised, they are not enough.

When Ambition is your God, the office is your temple, the employee handbook your holy book. The sacred drink, coffee, is imbibed five times a day. When you worship Ambition, there is no Sabbath, no day of rest. Every day, you rise early and kneel before the God Ambition, facing in the direction of your PC. You pray alone, always alone, even though others may be present. Ambition is a vengeful God. He will smite those who fail to worship faithfully, but that is nothing compared to what He has in store for the faithful. They suffer the worst fate of all. For it is only when they are old and tired, entombed in the corner office, that the realization hits like a Biblical thunderclap. The God Ambition is a false God and always has been.

—*THE GEOGRAPHY OF BLISS* BY ERIC WEINER

There is another way to harness your attention so that your ambition isn't a product of having to prove yourself but rather grows out of passion, excitement, and joy.

There is another way you can channel your energy consistently and constructively and still hit your goals out of the park without sacrificing yourself in the process.

There is another way.

Bull's-eye.

Unlike a goal, Stanislavski's concept of the Super Objective is tied to what drives you as an individual at your very core. It is your purposeful center. It is the birthplace for confidence, powerful action, and extraordinary results.

Why are goals not enough? Because we can aim for so much more.

Key Takeaways

→ Goals are not enough. In our zeal to get the biggest reward quickly, we often sacrifice our values, relationships, health, and best selves in the process.

→ Though achieving goals feels good physiologically (it taps the pleasure center in our brains) and psychologically (it allows us to satisfy many of our core needs), it can be extremely difficult to determine when achieving our goals shifts from being self-actualizing to self-destructive.

→ When we're trying to prove ourselves, we are our own biggest roadblocks to being powerful.

→ If you want to be a brave leader, *it's critical to ensure that your goals are anchored in your Super Objective to ensure your achievements don't come at the sacrifice of your relationships, health, values, and best self.*

14

Action from the Inside Out

Who looks outside, dreams;
who looks inside, awakes.

—CARL JUNG

There's quite a lot of talk these days about the importance of knowing your leadership philosophy. What are your core values, your guiding principles, your beliefs? What is your purpose? This is incredibly important stuff. And yet, a philosophy alone, in my humble opinion, falls short. How many people do you know who believe one thing and yet behave contrary to their beliefs?

It's easy to believe in positive reinforcement, until someone's not hitting their numbers. It's admirable to believe in open communication, until you have to say something that's uncomfortable. To *believe* requires nothing of you. You can sit and believe and believe and believe, and that changes nothing. It simply lives in your head; there is no impact.

Unlike a leadership philosophy, or the way many people think of principles, purpose, and values, a Super Objective lives in *action*. It is always *active*. You cannot achieve a Super Objective without *doing* something.

Here's an example. Tom is a conscientious young manager. He works in an industry that has a great deal of diversity and has not only seen people being treated poorly for being different but has experienced it himself. He has done a great deal of self-reflection about his beliefs and values, and he's crafted his leadership philosophy to help guide him toward being the kind of leader he wants to be for his new team. "I believe in respect and dignity for all people," Tom writes. This is a great philosophy, wouldn't you agree? It's one that reflects his values and his experiences. The only problem is that Tom can believe and believe and believe until the end of time, and it won't change anything. His philosophy, though admirable, lives in his head, not in action.

In contrast, a Super Objective forces action. If I were to translate Tom's philosophy into Super Objective language, it might read something like this: I *champion* respect and dignity for all people. Tom can't *champion* from the sidelines. If he's truly a champion for respect and dignity, it's going to require more from him. It's going to take looking for something to respect in people he doesn't like. (He didn't say he champions respect and dignity for people just like him, he said he champions respect and dignity for *all* people.) It's going to take standing up to people who aren't treating others with respect. It's going to take bridging differences and listening and dialogue. To *champion* would require Tom to put himself out there, to fight for what's right, to question, to look deeply, to seek alternatives, to bring people together, to explore, to intervene, to shake things up, to push ahead, to shatter perspectives, to heal, to poke holes, to lighten up, to celebrate, to tolerate, to expand, to forgive, to invite, to act. It requires him to *act*. He cannot champion from the sidelines. To champion requires *action*.

A Super Objective lives in action, which urges responsibility. It forces you to consider the impact you're having on others and to tell yourself the truth: *Is this really what I stand for or is it just talk?* If Tom's bull's-eye is to champion, he will have to take aim again and again to hit his target, as the different situations he faces will demand it.

A Super Objective puts you on an active path to be your most confident, powerful, and authentic self. It doesn't make life easier; it makes you and your results better.

Excavating your leadership philosophy is a critical first step. It is the process that allows you to get clear about your thinking and begin uncovering internal need—the thing that drives you. But powerful leadership requires more than understanding yourself and your own beliefs and values. It requires not just identifying but *committing* to the authentic, constructive actions that fall out of internal need.

> *How honest are you with yourself about yourself? How honestly do you allow yourself to show up with others?*

In the theater world, the thing that gives an actor a sense of presence—that intangible magic that makes you hang on every word and completely believe that a character is real—is the actor's commitment to two things: honesty and action.

Actors (or rather good actors) are relentless truth seekers. They are continually challenged to understand themselves—to tell themselves the truth about their deepest motivations, greatest fears, and driving needs—and about how honestly they're showing up. They own when they're not being real. They own when they've made a bad choice. They don't hide it. They stay curious about themselves, recognizing that understanding is always evolving. They're honest with themselves.

They're also honest in their interactions with others. They reach inside and, with great courage, have the vulnerability to take down their masks and allow themselves to be seen. How honest are you with yourself about yourself? How honestly do you allow yourself to show up with others?

A good actor is always focused on doing what it takes to overcome the obstacles and to achieve what their character wants most—their Super Objective. Because their Super Objective is communicated through active language, it will set them on an active path that requires them to *act*. They cannot achieve a Super Objective by simply believing or thinking—

> *Are your actions truly consistent with your words and beliefs?*

they must *do*. Actors who are too much in their head or those who are not committed 100 percent are boring to watch. They have no presence (and are typically unemployed). Likewise, leaders whose words and beliefs aren't manifesting themselves in consistent and constructive action aren't trusted. The people around them hold back their best effort. They don't put themselves on the line. They won't be honest. They're not loyal. They keep their passion, energy, excitement, ideas, and commitment locked away inside. Are your actions truly consistent with your words and beliefs?

A clear philosophy is a good start, but you've got to get it out of your head and have it show up in your actions or it does you no good. The people you lead need you to bring your brave self to your leadership game. You are here to make an *active* difference.

IN THE EYE OF THE BEHOLDER

We can have the best of intentions and can be keyed into our Super Objective and focused like crazy, but it may not make an ounce of difference. Sometimes, we simply don't hit the bull's-eye. Who gets to decide if you've achieved your Super Objective?

Not you. Well, you can, but it won't make any difference. Whether or not you achieve your Super Objective, like in our definition of authenticity, lies in the eye of the beholder.

The classroom is the absolute best testing ground for me. My Super Objective is *to connect people to the best of who they are*, and all day long I get to work toward doing that. I try hundreds of strategies. Sometimes, I'll draw them in to make it safe. Sometimes, I'll hold up the mirror, so they can see themselves the way I see them. Sometimes, I'll dig to get to a deeper understanding. Sometimes, the actions I take are effective, and sometimes they're not. Sometimes, they have the opposite effect.

In one session, years ago, a gentle young woman sat in the back row, and she was having a tough time identifying what mattered to her, so I started asking questions. As I probed more deeply, instead of unleashing her thinking as I intended (to connect her to the best of who she was), I saw her disappear into herself. Luckily, I was mindful enough to realize that she didn't feel safe. Instead of experiencing my questions as helpful, she felt like she was being interrogated.

A Super Objective is all about impact. It's critical to pay attention to whether or not your actions have the impact you want them to have. If not, it's on you to change course. You need a new strategy to hit your bull's-eye.

I could have blamed her. I could have thought, *Oh well, she's just one of those people who doesn't get it. She won't let me help her. Her bad.* Because that's what we do, right?

But if I stand for connecting people to the best of who they are, do I only stand for that when it's easy and convenient? No! I have to flex and change and do everything I can in spite of the obstacles to achieve what I'm up to in the world.

When you can name your Super Objective, you can do something about it. You can strategize. You can adjust. You can make sure your actions are in alignment with what you stand for, and if they're not, you can clean them up to ensure that your relationships and results are intact. Since your Super Objective stems from what drives you internally—anchored in your values, strengths, and beliefs—it makes it possible for you to take action on your own to do more of what fulfills you. You don't have to wait for someone to give you permission. You don't have to wait for a new job or a new title or a new boss; you hold the key to your own engagement. You're no longer aiming at general happiness or success because every action you take helps you get closer to your own personal bull's-eye.

You want to be a brave leader? It begins with understanding your beliefs, principles, and values and then translating them into the impact you want to have outside yourself—in active language. It begins with knowing your Super Objective. And then it's time to act.

Key Takeaways

→ A leadership philosophy and knowing your values are only starting points to powerful results. You can strongly *believe* something, but that does not change anything—beliefs alone are not actionable.

→ A Super Objective puts you on an active path to better results. You cannot achieve a Super Objective without taking action.

→ Whether you achieve your Super Objective lies in the eye of your beholder. If you want to be a brave leader, it's critical to ask yourself, *Are my actions having the impact I want them to have?*

15

For the Sake of What?

Success demands singleness of purpose.

—VINCE LOMBARDI

t's true, what you've heard," my friend whispered. "It really is as wonderful as all the rumors say it is. Nobody ever leaves. Everyone is always smiling and holding the door for one another and cheering each other on. If I didn't know any better, it would freak me out. It's almost too good to be true!"

He sat there beaming at me from across the restaurant table, one of my favorite people on the planet, telling me about his new job at Southwest Airlines. Having used Southwest as an example in my programs for years, I was both relieved and excited to hear about his personal experience. It's not business folklore! The stories about Southwest Airlines are true! And they're true for a reason.

When I started doing research on authentic leadership almost fifteen years ago, it seemed that everywhere I turned, every article I read, and every leadership book I picked up, I heard about exalted former Southwest Airlines CEO Herb Kelleher. *Fortune* magazine referred to him as "perhaps the best CEO in America."[1] *USA Today* ranked him in the top five of the most influential business leaders of the past twenty-five years.[2] Dozens (if not hundreds) of books applaud his leadership. (Yes, I realize I'm adding to the fray.) I gobbled it all up.

In an early article I read, he was quoted as saying he wanted to *"build a culture of commitment,"* and evidence revealed itself in everything I devoured about the man. Entire books have been inspired by his gift for *"creating customer evangelists,"* and in workshops, as I'd toss out questions to my participants, it was clear that he had accomplished that.[3]

"What did Herb Kelleher *do*—what actions did he take—to build a culture of commitment, or to create customer evangelists?" I'd ask.

"He'd ride on the planes, working as a flight attendant, serving the passengers! Most CEOs don't do that!" one person would say.

"He encouraged employees to be themselves!" another would chime in.

"No layoffs!"

"No baggage fees!"

"Free sodas when you fly!"

"And they give you snacks!"

"He made sure every employee received a special card on their birthday."

"No cancellation or change fees!"

"He empowered the employees to make decisions."

"I heard he was a regular guy. He walked the halls and had his office near all the other employees."

"He'd work side by side with everyone in the airline. There was no job beneath him."

"He created a *fun* environment!" (Imagine that!)

Actions. He took *action* to hit his target: his bull's-eye. He took *action* to achieve what he was up to as a leader for Southwest Airlines: to build a culture of commitment and to create customer evangelists—what Stanislavski would call his Super Objective.

Now, the purpose of a company, many would argue, is to increase revenue and decrease costs in order to maximize shareholder value, right? MBA wisdom would tell you that goals should be set and measured accordingly. As CEO, certainly that should have been Mr. Kelleher's primary focus, yes? Well, let's think about that for a minute.

There are many ways that airlines have historically gone about increasing revenue. When I ask my participants, I hear: "Baggage fees." "Cancellation fees." "Charging more money."

There are also many tactics airlines have used to decrease costs: "Layoffs." "Reduce benefits." "Kill the snacks!"

These are all perfectly good strategies to make airline shareholders happy. Yet when I asked my participants, "If Mr. Kelleher had done these things, what would've happened to his culture of commitment?" ("Ummm . . . down the tubes.") Or what about his customer evangelists? (LOL!)

When you consider the profitability of Southwest Airlines, you might discover he was on to something. In a decade when most major airlines are showing record losses, Southwest Airlines recently celebrated their forty-fourth year of profitability—achieving record profits, with $568 million in profit-sharing. Sounds pretty good from a shareholder's point of view too, doesn't it?[4]

He hit profitability all right. In fact, he knocked it out of the park! But it was simply a by-product. His actions were not anchored in a spreadsheet; they emerged from a more personal need. He did what he did *for the sake of what*? For the sake of building a culture of commitment and creating customer evangelists. It's amazing what can happen when you actively aim for purpose instead of profits. That's the power of Super Objective.

COFFEE, PEOPLE, AND PURPOSE

It's so easy to lose yourself amid the torrent of opinions out there. People aren't shy about telling you what you *should* do or *should* think. It's great to get multiple perspectives to consider and ideas to try, but how do you hold steady to what you know to be true for yourself or for your organization, in the eye of the storm? The truth is, unless you know what you stand for, you can't.

Several years ago, during my morning reading routine, I ran across a *Fast Company* article about Howard Schultz that caught my eye.

In 2008 Starbucks' stock was falling, and fast. CEO Howard Schultz had just returned after an eight-year absence and was under enormous pressure from the shareholders to turn things around. Starbucks' comprehensive health coverage was under fire by one of their biggest investors, and he insisted that the timing was ideal to cut the $250 million program. Other companies were doing it, so why shouldn't they? Surely it was justified.

Schultz responded with clarity. The essence of their brand, he explained, is humanity. Their culture was built around two primary benefits: providing health coverage and giving stock options to anyone who works over twenty hours a week. And Schultz held so firmly to those beliefs that he went so far as to say, "If you believe the financial crisis should change our principles and core purpose, perhaps you should sell your stock. I'm not building a stock. I'm trying to build an enduring company. We are a performance-driven organization, but we have to lead the company through the lens of humanity."[5]

To build an enduring company steeped in humanity. Some might call that a pretty powerful Super Objective. Every time I think about this example, I get goose bumps. Schultz brought such unwavering clarity and courage.

Most of us aren't in the position to make decisions between a $250 million program and our principles, but we do make choices all the time about our actions. We get so focused on hitting our goals and getting fast results. "Do whatever it takes!" becomes our mantra. We're out of a job, so we take the first one that comes down the pike. We sell to whomever will buy. We rarely ask the question, "Is this what I really want? Is it right for me?"

In 2008, Starbucks' stock was at $3.91 per share. At the time I'm writing this, it's at $60.42. That's the power of a Super Objective.

Consider that the great results we've been aiming for are simply *by-products*. The reason Starbucks has done so well is that they've created a company that people believe in and want to be a part of building. Howard Schultz has brought unwavering clarity around what Starbucks stands for as an organization, and they've courageously held on to that pillar of truth in the face of some mighty winds.

What if you were to do the same? What if you were to bring clarity about what you stand for as an individual and let that inform your actions? Because when storms of change toss you about, and you're being pushed this way and that by the hot air of opinion, you've got to hold on tight to something. Do you know what you stand for? I suspect Starbucks shareholders are glad that Howard Schultz does.

I remember sharing these stories in the classroom at one of the world's largest corporations. After the session, a colleague who had been observing followed me out, shaking his head, and said, "Kimberly, why talk to them about Herb Kelleher and Howard Schultz? The people in this class are managers, not CEOs. How can they possibly relate?"

How indeed? Mr. Kelleher and Mr. Schultz surely aren't mere mortals like the rest of us, are they? I smiled, as I had dozens of stories I could share. People are people. We all have something that drives us. Impact is not reserved for someone with a certain title.

When I walked back in the classroom, I told them about Jim, who I had just met that morning (at four thirty a.m. to be exact). Since I was teaching at a company that was large enough to have their own hotel on campus (no kidding), I had no commute! The only problem was that, because they wanted to encourage people to get out and meet others, there was no coffee service in the room. The coffee was strategically placed in the common areas in the lobby. I desperately needed coffee to fuel my preparations for the day. So, at four thirty a.m. (before human beings have any business being awake), I snuck into the lobby in my socks in search of caffeine, praying that I wouldn't run into anyone. Well, we all know how that works. When you don't want to run into anyone, you always run into someone. That's when I met Jim.

Jim was an engineer who worked the night shift. He was just getting off work and caffeinating before his forty-five-minute drive to his day job, where he worked construction. He had been balancing two jobs for the past seven years, was "lucky because (he) didn't require much sleep," and was the father of two little girls—the "light of [his] life." I learned all this as we both poured our coffee. (He takes his black.) As I was doctoring my cup, I reached for the milk, and to my dismay it was empty. (No!) I must have made a pouty face or something, because Jim immediately said, "No milk? I'll go find you some!"

Now this guy had just worked a twelve-hour shift, was getting ready to drive forty-five minutes in the dark to his next job, and was offering to track down milk for my coffee (for glamorous me, in all my no-makeup-morning-hair-sock-wearing glory).

"Oh no!" I protested in disbelief. "You don't need to do that! I'm grateful that you offered, but you've got a lot going on. I'll be fine!"

He smiled the biggest smile I've ever seen at four thirty in the morning and said, "You don't get it. That's what I do." He beamed proudly. "I put things together for people to make their lives better." And with that, he went off in search of milk.

I suspect that's exactly what Jim brings to everything he does. As an engineer, he *puts things together for people to make their lives better*. In construction, he *puts things together for people to make their lives better*. He does this as a father and as a guy in the lobby talking to a disheveled leadership educator at four thirty a.m. Because that's what Jim does. That's what he stands for. It shows up in his actions and in his words. And did he make an impact? Well, it's been two and a half years since my ten-minute coffee conversation with Jim, and I'm obviously still thinking about him, so I'd say yes. That's the power of a Super Objective.

I have been scouting Super Objectives for years and have found them lurking in the most wonderful places. I'll be innocently listening to a TED Talk ("My name is Kimberly Davis and I am a TED-a-holic") when all of the sudden, BAM! Out jumps a Super Objective! Like when I was watching hotelier Chip Conley's talk, "Measuring What Makes Life Worthwhile," and I learned about Vivian.

In his midtwenties, Chip owned a "no-tell motel" (his words, not mine) in the San Francisco Bay area. It was not the kind of place where you'd see respectable customers returning again and again, yet that's what was happening. Chip started investigating—talking to staff and customers—and he heard repeatedly . . . "Vivian."

"It's Vivian."

And from his customer Dave, who had stayed at the hotel more than a hundred times over the past twenty years, "I can always count on Vivian to make me feel at home."

As it turns out, Vivian was a Vietnamese immigrant who worked as a housekeeper. When Chip asked her, "How can you find joy in cleaning toilets for a living?" she told him she didn't clean toilets. She *took care of people who were far away from home.*

So when Vivian greets someone in the hallway, she's not simply being nice, she's taking care of them, because they are far away from home. When she makes the bed, she's taking care of them. When she cleans toilets, she's taking care of them. Because, you see, Vivian knows what it's like to be far away from home. Vivian doesn't simply do a job; she makes an impact. The by-product is her contagious joy, the returning customers, and the increased revenue.

Not long ago, I had the privilege to speak to 1,500 educators in a school district in central California: the superintendent, teachers, principals, administrators, school psychologists, nurses, cafeteria workers, bus drivers, coaches, custodians, and the president of the school board—everyone who worked for the district was there. They filled the gymnasium on a beautiful sunny day in August—the day before school. I challenged them to think about the impact that they wanted to have over the next school year. After my talk, as I sat on the rental car shuttle, heading back to the airport to go home, I received a tweet from a man who had been in the audience. "I'm so excited to start the day tomorrow! Thank you for helping me find my Super Objective!"

"You're so welcome!" I responded. "What is the impact you are going to have?"

"To sow the seeds of self-confidence!" he replied.

I could feel his excitement in less than 140 characters.

"What is your role in the district?" I asked.

"I'm a bus driver!"

Every single one of us can make an impact.

Imagine what is possible if this man focuses his attention on taking consistent action to achieve his Super Objective. If when the children board the bus, he finds a way to sow the seeds of self-confidence for each unique child. If when a fight breaks out on the bus, instead of reacting angrily, he looks for a way to sow the seeds of self-confidence. If when he observes a kid being bullied, he turns to the victim and sows the seeds of self-confidence and then turns to the bully and sows the seeds of self-confidence. If the last thing he does, when the kids step off the bus to head into school and learn, or into whatever family situation they may find themselves in at home, that in his good-bye he sows the seeds of self-confidence. What a difference this man can make!

That is the power of a Super Objective.

Several years ago, I invited some of my past participants to contribute to my blog, in a section I called *The Super Objective Spotlight*. Every piece was a beautiful testimonial to the power of activating a Super Objective, but one post in particular brings me to tears every time I read it:

> I was a little lost in life and was feeling that my job did not fulfill me
> or give me a sense of purpose. But I was looking at it all wrong. [Now
> I] realize that I need to give myself a sense of purpose, and as long as

I am pursuing my Super Objective, it will translate to fulfillment not only in my career but in all facets of my life.

To let you know a little about me, I tend to be a worrier. I stress about what others will think or how they will feel. That fear paralyzes me, and I end up being unable to make tough decisions, especially when they affect other people. When I stopped worrying about myself and how others would feel about me and instead took actions that support my Super Objective, expanding the potential of others, it became easy to make a decision and feel good about it. When I am present in the moment, truly listening and connecting with the people around me, I am able to confidently articulate a clear course of action. My Super Objective has allowed me to get out of the way of myself and move forward. So much of the anxiety and stress I put on myself is removed, and instead I can have a positive impact on those around me—which was always my goal.

Now I am not saying I am perfect in my quest to obtain my Super Objective. I find myself getting pulled into old habits through the course of daily life. If I catch myself doing that, I remind myself of my purpose. I am almost always instantly able to view the situation differently and react in a way that I am much more proud.

That is the power of a Super Objective.

You might agree that her experience is moving, but moved to tears? Surely I'm exaggerating, you might think. But no, I cry every time. It took me years to dig deep and get the clarity I needed to name what drives me—to connect people to the best of who they are. So yes, to learn that this beautiful, caring, *brave* woman has found a way to bring the best of who she is—to shine her light and make the impact she was born to make—moves me to tears. So often we never get a chance to know if our work makes a difference, because it is our commitment to achieve an impact in the face of that not knowing that gives us the power to be brave. But it's still lovely to find out.

Key Takeaways

➜ Powerful results are a by-product of a focus of attention on action to achieve purpose—your Super Objective.

➜ You do not need to be a CEO, a celebrity, or have a big title to work on your purpose. Everyone can make an impact.

➜ We all have something that drives us. The key is to name it *specifically*.

➜ If you want to be a brave leader, *your focus must be bigger than your job responsibilities*.

UNCOVER YOUR SUPER OBJECTIVE

If you want to live a life of impact, feel engaged, and get your best results, then complete this exercise. There are no wrong answers; just be honest with yourself. You deserve to know what drives you, and the people in your life are worthy of the impact that only you can have.

To begin the process of uncovering your Super Objective, it's critical to first, as poet Anne Sexton says, "Put your ear down close to your soul and listen hard." To identify what drives you at your core, you must first know why you care.

Part I—Why Do You Care?

• Why do you personally care about what your organization is up to (vision, mission, or values)? About the work that you do? About the products or services you offer? About the people you serve?

- If you have direct reports or lead a team, why do you *care* about them as their leader?

- What matters most to you?

Part II–What is the Impact You Want to Have?

- If you lead others, what is the impact you want to have on your team or direct reports?

- What is the impact you want to have on your colleagues?

- What is the impact you want to have on your customers or people you serve or the public?

- What is the impact you want to have on your division, organization, culture, or industry?

Put a star next to the group that you find most exciting—where you personally want to have the biggest impact.

Part III–Craft Your Super Objective
A Super Objective

- Inspires action
- Acts as a filter
- Helps maintain focus

A Super Objective Should Be . . .

- *Focused outside yourself*—on who or what you want to impact (your direct reports, your division, your culture, the organization, your community, etc.)

- *Active*—active language inspires action (use active verbs)

- *Clear*—paint the picture

Crafting Your Super Objective

Think about the impact that you personally want to have as a leader outside yourself. Who or what do you care about most? Where do you get your energy? On the individuals who report to you? On your team? The public? The organization? Your community? What do you do to have this impact? Consider what actions most closely hit on what you're personally up to as a leader and who or what you want to impact.

Examples:

- *I want to sow the seeds of confidence for students.*

- *I want to build a culture of commitment.*

- *I want to create customer evangelists.*

Tips:

- Limit yourself to no more than two actions or groups you want to impact. You should be able to take mindful consistent action around your Super Objective in every situation you face.

- Use language that means something to you personally and ignites energy within you. Stay away from jargon. A Super Objective is designed to ignite energy *within you*, not market you to someone else.

- You should know when you're doing it and when you're not.

- Keep it simple. Brief, concise language is more actionable.

CRAFT YOUR SUPER OBJECTIVE:

For additional tools, videos, and support to identify, activate, and keep your Super Objective alive, go to:

www.braveleadershipbook.com.

16

What's Your Intention?

Our intention creates our reality.

—WAYNE DYER

I f your Super Objective is the compass that directs you toward your best self, then Intentions are the road markers that keep you on your true path during all the crazy twists and turns you encounter on your journey. Your Super Objective is your strategic big picture—what you stand for as a leader—and your Intention is *tactical*. It's what you're going to *do* to achieve your Super Objective in the situations you face. Like the language we use for a Super Objective, Intentions are also *active verbs*—forcing deliberate, purposeful action.

Let's say you're the vice president of internal communications and your Super Objective is to *foster a culture of growth and inclusion*. You discover that one of the managers you lead is a bully: He routinely threatens your vendors, yells at his direct reports, and is condescending to his colleagues. What do you do? What actions do you take with this bully manager if you truly want to foster a culture of growth and inclusion? Would you investigate further? Would you bring people together? Would you coach this manager? What would your conversation with this guy look like, if you were truly aiming to foster a culture of growth and inclusion? What are the *constructive actions* you would take to achieve your Super Objective?

Intentions keep us in check. They force us to think before we act. While every situation brings an opportunity to achieve your Super Objective, it can be incredibly difficult to stay mindful of what you stand for and how you'd like to show up in the world in the complex landscape that is our life at work. Sometimes, when we're on autopilot or in survival mode, we do things that are questionable or aren't going to get us where we want to go. Sometimes, we react. Sometimes, we make bad choices. Sometimes, in an attempt to get from point A to point B quickly, we take the fastest route (which isn't always the most constructive). Sometimes, taking well-meaning advice, we go against our own values or what we know to be true. Being human is no picnic. So how do we get ourselves back on track when our actions go awry (which they will)? How do we show up as powerfully as we can when the stakes feel high? How can we be sure that who we are on the inside is represented by how we show up on the outside? How can we be congruent?

THE PRICE OF INCONGRUITY

We've all met them, or have heard of them—leaders who say they stand for one thing but whose actions tell a different story. Such as the CEO who talks a good game during company meetings or to the press, insisting that he wants to "inspire his people to greatness," yet behind closed doors threatens his direct reports that "heads are going to roll" if they don't hit their numbers. I don't know about you, but I don't find that terribly inspiring. Or there's the director who wants to empower her team but micromanages at every turn. And what about the manager who "wants people to feel safe" coming to him but dishes the dirt behind people's backs?

I was talking to a dear friend of mine who used to be a senior leader for one of the world's largest retailers. This company has enjoyed a great reputation for being people focused and caring about their employees. Many books have been written about their culture, and yet I knew that during my friend's tenure at the company she had been miserable. When I asked her about it—why the discrepancy between what I'd read about the organization and her experience—she said, "That's true at the store level. At corporate, it's a different story. Behind the scenes, the same rules don't apply."

When things are incongruous, people know.

I could share countless other stories that I've heard from friends and participants (or participants who have become friends) about values-driven organizations that have bullies at the helm, about bosses who tout the virtues of transparency only to blindside their teams, about departments that invest in emotional intelligence training for their employees but show little or no empathy during layoffs, about people-centered companies that treat their vendors like second-class citizens, and so on.

It's no wonder that cynicism seems to be at an all-time high, loyalty at an all-time low, and that more than 69 percent of American workers are not engaged, and some say 87 percent globally.[1] With so much incongruity, we don't know what to expect, to believe, or to trust.

THE ART OF THINKING BEFORE YOU ACT

Imagine you're a newly promoted director of sales who stands for "inspiring your people to greatness." What Intention (or action) should you take to inspire them to greatness when someone's not hitting their numbers? Do you threaten repercussions? Do you call them out during a team meeting? Do you stalk them to make sure they're doing what they're supposed to be doing and dictate their every move? Would that inspire them to greatness? Probably not. What actions could you take in the face of them not hitting their numbers, if you were truly about inspiring your people to greatness? Perhaps you could bridge their self-confidence by reminding them of past obstacles they've overcome. Or maybe you could share a personal story about a time when you weren't achieving your best and how you overcame that obstacle to succeed. Or is it possible that they don't have the resources they need to be successful? Maybe you need to better frame your questions to get to the core of their problems and inspire them to greatness in the process? It's all about taking mindful constructive action that is in alignment with who you are as a leader.

> *Actions that are in alignment with your Super Objective are Intentions.*

What if you're a manager who stands for *cultivating* the *strengths* of the people on your team and you know that one of your direct reports is not living up to their potential? What actions could you take to cultivate their strengths? How would you talk to them during your one-on-one meetings? What would your feedback sound like if you were really about cultivating strengths?

Knowing what you stand for makes it possible to bring Intention— deliberate and purposeful action.

Just as every situation will be different and bring about different challenges and obstacles, your Intentions will also be different. Your Intentions are the actions you take to achieve your Super Objective on a situation-by-situation basis. Depending on what's going on, you may use many different Intentions in a single situation to help you achieve your Super Objective. If one doesn't work, you'll need to switch tactics. If you missed your bull's-eye, you'll need to find a new strategy or a new Intention so you can get as close to the target as possible.

You should know that it's quite possible you won't achieve your Super

Objective in the situation! But authentic power lies in your commitment to taking constructive action. Your focus on the actions you take to achieve your Super Objective harnesses attention, which is what gives you presence and makes it possible for you to access the want in others. When your actions are consistent and congruent with what you stand for, people know what you're about and *want* to be a part of it. They want to give you their best. They want to listen. They want to follow.

REACTION OR CHOICE

Every situation we face presents the possibility of reaction. None of us is immune. We all react. Looming deadlines, compounding expectations, lack of sleep, overflowing plates, low blood sugar, client demands, snarky Facebook posts, global warming, Congress, the news—the list for what can increase the intensity and frequency of our reactions is endless. As a pretty passionate and outspoken woman, I have been working on my own emotional reactivity for a lifetime. Without a doubt, having clarity about what I stand for has saved me on more than one occasion, making it possible for me to course correct when I find myself veering in the wrong direction, instead of bringing my best.

The truth is that sometimes I get mad or snarky or I feel sorry for myself, and I don't give two hoots about connecting others to the best of anything. But I always pay the price. I feel it. I know it in my bones. I'm not being the person I want to be.

Many years ago, I led a class for about thirty-five people in a typical hotel breakout room in Philadelphia when I first discovered how valuable my newly minted Super Objective would be. I was team teaching, and we had just finished covering one unit and were transitioning to the next. Now, when you start teaching a new unit, it's critical that you have everyone's attention, because you're often taking the learning in a new direction and you don't want to lose anyone. So I stood up front, I captured the group's attention, and I began.

I began, but while most of the group was with me, back in the far left corner of the room, one of the participants continued to talk loudly to her tablemate and totally ignored the lesson. So I did what most facilitators would do in that moment, I continued teaching as I slowly walked over to her corner of the room, hoping she would sense my presence and . . . hush.

Nope. Didn't work.

The rest of the room kept looking over at her, annoyed, so I knew I needed to deal with the issue but didn't want to call her out. So, I kept talking and then gently put my hand on her shoulder, thinking she would realize what she was doing and, well . . . hush.

Nope. She kept yacking. Loudly.

Now, her tablemate looked up at me, embarrassed, but the talking lady was completely unaware. I thought, *Okay . . . what do I do? I don't want to embarrass her. Nothing else seems to be working . . .* Then, I thought, *Humor! That's it! I'll try humor!* I leaned over with a big smile and whispered playfully, "Okay, Chatty Cathy!"

(Can I tell you how much I regret that?)

She turned to me with a massive scowl on her face and said vehemently (and again, very loudly), "EXCUSE ME?"

The room was so silent that you could have heard a pin drop. I felt like I had been slapped. I felt humiliated. I felt confused. I didn't know what had just happened. Was "Chatty Cathy" an offensive thing to say in Philadelphia? Did it mean something I didn't know it meant? I was completely shocked.

Can I tell you that the last thing on earth I wanted to do at that moment was *to connect that lady* to the best of who she was?

Luckily, my cofacilitator jumped right in without me having to say a word, and the class went on. And, like a beaten dog, I put my tail between my legs and sat down, completely flooded by my own emotion.

In the past, I would have ignored that scary talker lady for the rest of the two-day session. I would have pretended she didn't exist. I would have put a protective shield around that corner of the room and overcompensated for my insecurities and bewilderment. And I would have gone home after the program feeling like crap about my work, about that lady, about the whole session, and especially about myself. Because when we can't show up at our best, we feel it. We can't escape ourselves.

That was the first time in my life I had some clarity about who I was. I had named it. I knew that if I was truly about connecting people to the best of who they are, then something had to happen. I had to *do* something. I wasn't capable of connecting anyone in that room to their best if I wasn't bringing mine.

I tell participants all the time that knowing your Super Objective doesn't make life easier. In fact, it makes life harder. Because all those things we normally do when we react or mess up, we now know they won't get us where we want to be. You can't escape the knowing.

I knew I had to take some kind of action to get myself back on track—to be the person I know I am, at my best. I had to take a risk. I had to be vulnerable. I had to go talk to the scary talker lady. Can I tell you how much I did not want to do that?

At the beginning of the next break, I followed her out, pulled her aside, and said, "Ummmm . . ." (Yeah, it wasn't eloquent.) "Look, I'm sorry if I said something that offended you. That was certainly not my intent. Please forgive me."

And with a shocked look on her face she laughed (loudly—go figure). "You didn't offend me!"

It was like a release valve opened inside of me. We talked, and it turned out that she loved the content so much that she couldn't stop talking about it with her friend. It had triggered something for her, and she was excited. I also learned that she's someone who processes things *orally*—she needs to *talk* about it so it can sink in.

Oh my goodness! It was like finding the Holy Grail! I would have never guessed that that's what was going on with this lady. Never!

Now that I knew what she needed, I could find constructive solutions for her to be able to talk about the content without disrupting the process or the rest of the class. Now that I knew she wasn't scary lady, she became awesome lady.

I would never have gone to talk to her before I named my Super Objective, not in a million years. I would have been a total wimp. I would have let my fear, anger, and discomfort be bigger than the possible outcome.

WORKING INTENTIONS WHEN THE STAKES FEEL HIGH

The higher the stakes, the more likely we are to feel vulnerable and fall prey to our body's natural tendency to protect or defend, which doesn't always serve us well. Focusing on the high stakes or on our body's reaction only compounds the problem. When you need to speak at a conference with passion and eloquence, you end up looking like a stiff robot. Or when you need to have a difficult conversation during a one-on-one, you end up sounding cold and uncaring. It doesn't mean that you're a robotic, cold, uncaring person; it means that you are human and you're in survival mode. Working Intentions allows you to choose your actions, putting you back in the driver's seat.

Think back to the situation about my friend the recruiter (whose candidate professed to be curious about others but didn't ask her a single question). The stakes are pretty high in a job interview—wouldn't you say? If the candidate had entered that conversation absolutely clear about who he was and what drove him, how might that have changed things?

Let's imagine for a moment that he was telling the truth and that he was indeed the curious sort. But curious for the sake of what? What impact outside himself might his talent for staying curious achieve? Maybe it's to unlock motivation in others, or maybe it's to create powerful experiences

> *Working Intentions allows you to choose your actions, putting you back in the driver's seat.*

or to facilitate a deeper understanding. A talent for curiosity could be the foundation for an incredibly powerful purpose.

Let's assume for now that his Super Objective is to *facilitate a deeper understanding*. Imagine that's what drives this man at his core. Yes, he's there to land a job. He hopes to impress the recruiter. He wants her to like him and refer him on to her clients. But what if instead of doing his best to impress her and recite his resume, he directed all of his energy into facilitating a deeper understanding? Imagine he's sitting there, with my friend the recruiter, focused completely on achieving his Super Objective in this situation. What actions might he take?

What kind of questions might he have thought to ask? What kind of research might he have done in advance? How might he have responded to her questions if he was solely focused on facilitating a deeper understanding? Maybe he would have thought to share colorful, rich stories that helped bring his relevant experience to life. Maybe he would have learned something about her during the conversation and found common interests or shared relationships, creating a real human-to-human connection. Maybe he could've brought up current events influencing his industry. Maybe he would have asked her powerful questions that challenged her thinking. Maybe he would have been able to relax and enjoy the conversation, rather than treating it like an interrogation. Maybe . . .

And would she have put him up for the job? Who knows? But she would have likely felt engaged and connected during the conversation. Her guard would have let down due to his authenticity. His sincere interest in her would have shifted the power, taking him off the hot seat and allowing for a more human-to-human connection. One brief meeting could have created a foundation of trust that moved beyond a single transaction to become a mutually beneficial relationship. Everything changes when you shift your focus.

Far too many times, when the stakes felt high, I've made situations much worse than they needed to be because I wasn't mindful of focusing my attention outside myself on impact. A few years ago, I was in negotiations for what was probably the biggest engagement of my career at that time. I had done my due diligence and was armed with market rates, comparisons, and information about what the same company had paid others for services like mine. I knew the value of my work. I had put together a detailed proposal, which we went over in person, without objections, when I met with their team. The meeting was fantastic! I loved them, they loved me, and all seemed great with the world. Together, we were going to change the lives of their emerging leaders, and I couldn't wait! I received the green-light call, and we were going to get started as soon as their contracts person sent over the agreement. How exciting!

And then I received the agreement. I had to read it over three or four times to be sure I was reading it right. Surely, they had made a mistake. Surely, they wouldn't have reduced the fee by almost 75 percent and expected me to sign it? I was floored. If they had issues with the fee, why hadn't they mentioned it during our meeting? It made no sense to me. I ran through a torrent of feelings every few seconds—shocked, humiliated, insulted, disappointed, confounded, nervous, bullied, uncertain, foolish, helpless, frustrated, embarrassed, insecure, disillusioned, and defeated. My emotions were completely hijacked. I jumped on the phone with my various advisors.

"You have to stand up for what you're worth!"

"Know your walk-away point."

"Of course they're going to try to bring it down; that's just the game!"

I hate games. I felt nauseated. My stomach was in knots. I scheduled a meeting with their contracts person and was ready to duke it out. I didn't sleep for three nights, fretting.

On the day of the big call, I was a mess. I felt sorry for myself, mad at them, and just plain cranky. I didn't recognize myself. Knowing that I needed to get ready for the biggest financial fight of my career, I wanted to talk to someone I trusted immediately before that call, so I rang a dear friend of mine who had been in sales for years for a large leadership company. She had been through negotiations of this scale before. I had to be tough. I had to defend the value of my work. I couldn't show weakness.

We were in the thick of our conversation, my angst overflowing, when it hit me: This is not who I am. This is not who I want to be. I stand for connecting people to the best of who they are—how could I do that in this meeting?

"Oh my gosh," I said to my friend breathlessly. "What have I been doing? I've got amazing tools and I'm not even using them!"

What action could I take to connect the *contracts* person to the best of who she is?

I took a long, deep breath and exhaled a week of stress. I was relaxed and calm and centered for the first time in a week.

Five minutes later, the contracts person and I were on the phone. I could feel her tension pouring through the receiver. This was nothing new for her; she fought these battles all day long, every day. This was her life. She was a pit bull waiting for the fight. I breathed deeply and reminded myself to connect her to the best of who she is.

"I don't know how you do it," I said humbly, "talking about these contracts all day long. Your job must be so stressful."

I could hear her audible sigh on the other line. And then there was silence. That was perhaps the first time in her career somebody had acknowledged her as a person, rather than treating her like an enemy to be taken down.

"Yes," she said quietly, "it is."

That changed everything. Instead of adversaries, we were simply two people having a discussion about how this could work out for all parties involved.

And it did. I walked away feeling heard and valued and satisfied with our agreement. Did I leave some money on the table? Maybe. Maybe not. Who knows? But I felt good about it. My dignity was intact. I showed up as the person I know myself to be. That is where confidence begins.

The next time you find yourself in a situation where the stakes feel high, ask yourself, "If I were to be true to who I am at my core—my real, best, most powerful self—and focused on taking constructive action to make an impact, what action would I take?" In your answer to yourself lies both power and responsibility.

That's the key to being brave.

Key Takeaways

→ Your Super Objective is your strategic big picture—what you stand for as a leader. The actions you take to achieve your Super Objective are called *Intentions*.

→ Intentions are tactical—they're what you *do* to achieve your Super Objective in every situation you face.

→ Intentions force you to think before you act and keep your actions congruent with who you are at your core to ensure the want of others.

→ Intentions make it possible for you to get yourself back on track when you are emotionally hijacked, so you can bring your best, most authentic, and powerful self—your brave—to the situation at hand.

→ Brave leaders *choose* their actions rather than operating on autopilot or reacting to the world around them.

17

The Magic If

Empathy is about finding echoes
of another person in yourself.

—MOHSIN HAMID

never imagined my theater degree would serve me as it has, giving me tools that I use daily in my personal and business practices. One acting technique that has become the foundation for everything I do is called the *Magic If*.

When creating a character for the stage, you have to consider everything that makes a person who they are and why they do what they do. You consider the given circumstances. You do what is called a *character analysis* and explore the character's history, values, beliefs, and physical characteristics. You look at the relationships between the different characters in the play. Who has the power? Who tells the truth? Who doesn't? Why?

And you do all of this to come to a single basic question: Given everything you know about your character and the world they live in, what would you do if you were in these circumstances?

If, as an actor, you approach this critical question with any judgment at all, your performance is guaranteed to ring false, and all presence goes out the window. Without a doubt, the audience will find you phony and uninteresting. Instead, you simply have to relinquish any preconceived ideas you might have about anything or anyone, look at the given circumstances, put yourself in their shoes, and move forward. What would happen if we practiced this in life?

The opportunity to practice this lesson always seems to come to me while I'm driving. I remember once, when I was on my way to a meeting and running a bit behind so I was, I admit it, going about seven miles an hour over the speed limit. It was six thirty in the morning. The sun was starting to peek above the horizon, and my wiper blades were doing their best to clear the dew off my windshield as I wound my way through the quiet neighborhood. Within a few blocks, I found myself driving behind a small white van that was going at least seven miles an hour *under* the speed limit. I slowed down, muttering, "Come on . . . come on . . ." As I followed about a car's length behind the van, I could see a large neon yellow sticker stuck to the back window warning, "Do not tailgate!" Suddenly, the van stopped abruptly in the middle of the street. A head popped around from the front, and could I see arms futzing with things in the backseat (more grumpy muttering on my part). I took the next left to escape the pokey van and continued in my frenzy to get to my meeting on time. I parked, centered myself, and got out of my car, when I was met by the woman who was driving the van and who was clearly upset. She shouted at me, "You! You need to learn how to drive! You scared me half to death!" I was bewildered, embarrassed, a bit confused, and full of judgment. Time for the Magic If.

Taking in all the given circumstances—the speed of the van, the message on the rear window, her reaction when she saw me—I can imagine that this woman had a bad experience with someone tailgating in the past. I can understand that, because of her probable past experience, she is more fearful and angry than the situation warranted and that her reaction is probably not about me. I've been fearful in the past. I've been angry in the past. I know how that feels. Now, rather than judging her, I can empathize with her. My reaction is diffused, and I can go on with my day. I can learn what I have control over (my reactions, going seven miles an hour over the speed limit, leaving on time to get to my meeting, etc.) and let go of what I don't (her reaction, her driving speed, her need to search for things in the backseat while driving). The Magic If gives us a chance to step back and think before we react.

> *The Magic If gives us a chance to step back and think before we react.*

How could this impact your life? What if you could step into your client's shoes and see from their perspective? Not just to uncover their possible objections, but to understand the stress that they feel and their hopes for themselves. What would you do differently?

What if you could step into your boss's shoes and better understand the pressure she is experiencing and the fears that she has?

What if you could step into the shoes of your direct report? What might he be balancing in his life? How does he feel about himself when you're around?

And outside of our work environment, what if you could step into your child's shoes? Your neighbor's? The guy behind the counter at Starbucks? The woman sleeping on the sidewalk?

The Magic If activates all of our senses and makes it possible to walk in someone else's shoes, not just cerebrally, but viscerally.

A lifetime ago, back when I had my events company in Seattle, it was so useful to be able to crawl into someone else's experience in advance. I would walk through every moment of the event as if I were a guest.

I'd walk in the shoes of the men, women, senior leaders, clients, and the hardworking frontline employees. I would explore with all my senses, asking myself questions. It didn't matter if it was a big client event, an employee picnic, or a huge global company meeting. I only needed to act as if I were the person experiencing it for the first time, and the details I needed to access would unfold.

When I arrive at the event, where will I park? How far will I have to walk? Will I be wearing heels? What will the weather be? When I arrive, am I excited or anxious or feeling obligated or annoyed or hopeful? Why? What might be running in the backdrop of my mind? Is something going on in the organization that might impact how I feel about being there? When I open the door, what do I see? What do I touch? What do I smell? What do I hear? How do I feel? Every detail is carefully crafted by asking myself, if I were a guest, how would I experience this?

Later, when I was hired to design my first training workshop, a customer experience program for my biggest client, I simply unleashed the same skills. I walked in the shoes of their customers to understand the minutiae of their experiences. I walked in the shoes of the employees asking myself, "How might they discover what we need them to discover from minute to minute?" What do they see, hear, taste, touch, and feel? How, from their perspective, based on all I know about the unique individuals involved, might they receive each moment? How would people in marketing feel? What about IT? How about the senior team? What would I do if I were in their shoes?

I had a past OnStage Leadership participant, turned friend, turned colleague email me not long ago: "I'm reading *The Experience Economy* [by Colin Shaw], and it's got me thinking a lot about how you do your thing. Did this book influence your approach to OnStage? Or are the connections there unintentional?"

I wrote back that I had devoured *The Experience Economy* when I had designed the Customer Experience Program and loved it. (I also loved Colin Shaw's other book, *Customer Experience*.)

"What people don't realize is that it's all the same thing," I replied.

"A customer experience and employee experience aren't any different—it's all about empathy, understanding human needs, and the impact you want to have."

If you want your customers to have a positive experience, you must walk in their shoes and understand the experience you are providing through their eyes. You have to go beyond meeting basic needs and avoid cookie-cutter assumptions—that all people are the same—and understand what might, as author and marketing guru Seth Godin so beautifully says, "surprise and delight" them.[1] How do they feel?

If you want engaged, excited, loyal employees, you must care enough to walk in their shoes and experience your organization, the work that they do, their personal challenges, and your leadership through their eyes. Going to work every day is an *experience*. How do you want them to *feel* coming to work? How do you want them to feel about themselves, feel about your organization, feel about the environment, your clients, their opportunities, and about their responsibilities, their colleagues, and your policies?

Remember the elephant vs. the rider? Empathy is all elephant.

If you want to have rich relationships with your friends, your family members, the people in your community, the members of the nonprofit board you're on, your kid's teacher, with anyone really, the key is to stop, remove your own filter of the world, and try to not only see but experience things from another perspective. Without judgment.

The definition of empathy is to understand and share another person's experiences and emotion—the ability to share someone else's feelings. Research shows that the ability to empathize has a direct correlation to higher job performance and increased customer satisfaction in the business world, and faster recovery for patients in healthcare. It bridges cultures and diverse backgrounds, breaks down barriers, and builds trust. A leader who shows empathy makes it possible for people to feel safe to take risks and to challenge themselves to grow and improve. Empathy is critical to any organization that wishes to flourish.

The first level of empathy is our hardwired emotional empathy. Emotional empathy is our automatic and often unconscious response to another's emotions. Our emotions become contagious, what scientists call *emotional contagion*, allowing us to identify with the physical sensations that someone else might be experiencing by tapping into our own muscle memory through our brain's magical mirror neurons. We can look at someone, see what's going on with them, and by unconsciously picking up their vocal, facial, and nonverbal cues, we'll viscerally feel what they are feeling. That's why when a friend pinches their finger in the door, you wince in pain and feel a rush of sensations in your body, as if it were happening to you. It's not that you're simply an amazing friend (although you may be); it's that your brain is an extraordinary machine that is designed to keep you safe and alive. You see that? It hurts! Don't do that! I can't tell you how many times my emotional empathy has left me in puddles at the movie theater. As we're transported into someone else's world, their emotions become contagious, and we feel their loss and pain and fear and relief, our shared human experience uniting us in what UCLA psychiatrist Daniel Siegel calls the *bubble of we*.[2]

Where the Magic If really comes in handy, though, is in accessing the second and third levels of empathy—those that can be cultivated and can make an extraordinary difference in the way you lead.

The second level of empathy has to do with the ability to see through another's eyes, what researchers call *cognitive* or *mind-to-mind empathy*. According to author and renowned psychologist Daniel Goleman, cognitive empathy "does more than give us an understanding of their view—it tells us how best to communicate with that person: what matters most to them, their models of the world, and even what words to use—or avoid—in talking with them."[3]

This is where the Magic If can really make a difference, as it is anchored in perspective. Going back to our definition of authenticity, what do the people you lead need from you to find you *genuine, worthy of trust, reliable, and believable*? If you can't take their perspective, you cannot know. Asking yourself how you would feel if, based on all their given circumstances, you were in their shoes is the fastest way to know if you're on target or not.

Cognitive empathy can be a powerful tool in negotiating and motivating others. Leaders with strong cognitive empathy are good at understanding the needs of their customers, superiors, and direct reports, which directly translates to stronger relationships and better performance. Cognitive empathy makes it possible for healthcare workers to crawl into the skin of their patients to see the world from their point of view, but to also step back so they can make objective decisions. It is a cornerstone for building trust.

My husband is masterful at cognitive empathy as it applies to work. As an innovator and strategy guy, he spends his days inhabiting the minds of his customers' customers. When he's working with a coffee company, he starts roasting his own beans, lurking around coffee shops, and mocking up new fangled brew machines. When he has a spirits client, he can be found taste testing at Scotch bars, interviewing the patrons, and querying the bartenders (all in the name of customer empathy—the sacrifices he makes). When it's mustard, he becomes a stalker in the condiments aisle, and we inevitably end up with ten different brands we taste test over dinner. He does everything he can to get inside the consumer's head to understand what drives their decisions and where there is opportunity to meet an unmet need that they may not even know they have. Imagine if we were to invest that kind of energy in understanding the people we lead.

Drilling down further, the Magic If helps us access the third level, which is empathetic concern. Empathetic concern comes into play whenever we show that we care about another person's thoughts and feelings. It's heart-to-heart connection, or the Magic If in action. Empathetic concern breaks down barriers, facilitates change, creates trust, and makes the effort of our relationships work.

Imagine what would have been different had the managers in Chicago (the ones who thought their direct reports were lazy and didn't care) employed the Magic If to ignite their empathetic concern. Maybe if they had recognized that their employees were absolutely scared out of their minds—certain that they'd lose their jobs, that their boss hated them, and that the company thought they were totally expendable—they would have found a way to let them know they were concerned and made it safe for them to say what was real. They could have avoided the missed deadlines, the mistakes, and loss in productivity—all the problems they didn't want to see—and could have focused on creating a place where people wanted to come and bring their best.

Recently, I stood in line at a rental car company when a red-faced woman stormed in and asked to speak to the manager. She was furious. The manager came out and stood there quietly, nodding as her emotions flooded the room (with all of us in line trying desperately not to appear like we were staring, which of course we were). She talked so fast and breathed so deeply that I was sure she was going to hyperventilate at any second. He just stood there, with a calm, serious expression, hanging on her every word. When she was done with her tirade, I watched him gently touch her arm, his look of concern so honest and evident, and I heard him say, "It sounds like you feel like you've been treated unfairly."

"Yes! Yes, I have. It's not fair that . . ." she went on to explain.

I have no idea what he said to her after that, but a few minutes later, after I had signed my contract and was heading out to the parking lot, I watched her, with tears of relief in her eyes, take his hand and say, "Thank you. Thank you so much for listening to me."

Empathetic concern is a powerful tool to dissipate heightened emotion. When we let people know we have a sense of what they're going through and show that we sincerely care, it allows the emotion to subside and logic to return.

Neuroscientists believe, for most of us, egoism and empathy are innate. (In spite of your conviction that your boss or ex-boyfriend might be a psychopath, thankfully only about 1 percent of the average population is born with psychopathy[4]—not having empathy or remorse.) In other words, I'm born thinking that it's all about me, and I'm born with the ability to care about your feelings, and in situations where there's conflict between the two, assuming my brain is healthy, it should be able to auto-correct and consider us both. But given how malleable our brains are, my ability to empathize is not fixed. The situations I find myself in, from the time I'm an infant through adulthood, will impact how my brain is wired and how empathetically I think and react. Childhood trauma or neglect can have a devastating impact on a person's ability to empathize. Research also shows that decisions made quickly or under duress dramatically reduce empathy. (Have you had to make a quick decision or two at work recently?) And studies have found that when we're in a more comfortable situation, it becomes harder to identify with the feelings of someone who is experiencing pain or distress, making it easier to judge those who are less fortunate.[5] Perhaps most alarming is a recent study that shows empathy levels have been dramatically declining over the past thirty years.[6]

Given how critical empathy is in being able to lead and influence, it's a good thing that research also shows that we can practice and make choices that will reshape the way our brains function and hone our ability to empathize, which is one of the reasons the Magic If is so powerful. It gives us a simple strategy to practice curiosity and empathy before we enter high-stakes conversations. It creates mindfulness around our relationships and ensures that we're bringing our best, most thoughtful self to the situation. It makes it possible for us to choose powerful actions that can have an impact, and thus achieve our Super Objective.

If it's true that we see what we look for, then what if we were to start looking through the eyes of someone else? How might that change the way we see? How might it change the way we participate in meetings or respond to emails? How might it change the products and services we offer, the cultures we create, or the way we show up in the world?

If in order to lead, we must find a way to access others' wants, then the Magic If is one of the most powerful tools you can use. Without being able to stand squarely in someone else's shoes and view the experience from their lens, all we're doing is imposing our own agenda. And I don't know about you, but that's never made me *want* a darn thing.

Key Takeaways

→ The Magic If makes it possible for us to step into another's shoes and look through their lens without judgment. It is empathy in action. It forces you to ask the question: *What would I do in these circumstances?*

→ It is impossible to get people to want to follow you without empathy. It is the key that unlocks what others need from you to experience you as genuine, worthy of trust, reliable, and believable.

→ Empathy isn't an all-or-nothing thing. Empathy can be understood, cultivated, practiced, and improved even in those of us who don't have a natural knack for it.

→ Customer experience and employee experience are the same. They're both about understanding human needs and the impact you want to have.

→ If you want to be a brave leader and need to tap into the want of those you wish to lead and influence, empathy is critical. Thus, the Magic If is one of your most powerful tools in your leadership toolbox.

18

Own Your Power

*Most powerful is he who has
himself in his own power.*

—SENECA

My husband and I sat on the balcony, camcorder poised and ready, waiting for my son's third grade assembly to begin. Jeremy, then eight years old, had been practicing tirelessly for weeks in preparation, and this was the day he was performing "Duel of the Fates" from *Star Wars* on the piano for his entire school. I may be biased, but he rocked it. We sat there, beaming, proud parents that we are, waiting for the assembly to come to an end so we could hug our kid, when all of the sudden, one of the teachers stood center stage and started singing.

"The snow glows white on the mountain tonight, not a footprint to be seen. A kingdom of isolation, and it looks like I'm the queen . . ."

Then several other teachers stood to join her.

"The wind is howling like this swirling storm inside . . ."

And then the rest of the teachers stood up.

". . . couldn't keep it in, heaven knows I tried."

And then the principal started singing. And then, in a blink, the whole school stood—the teachers, kids, and parents in the balcony—with complete joy and abandon, everyone in the entire building belting out . . .

"Let it go! Let it go!

Can't hold it back anymore.

Let it go! Let it go!

Turn away and slam the door.

Here I stand, and here I'll stay.

Let it go! Let it go!

The cold never bothered me anyway!"

It was the best flash mob ever. It was like a scene out of a movie. The energy in the room was absolutely incredible. It was palpable.

My son got so inspired that he immediately went home, downloaded the song on YouTube, and taught himself how to play it on the piano. For weeks, the song "Let It Go" permeated my house. Jeremy played it incessantly, and being the catchy little tune that it is, both my husband and I often found ourselves humming it out of the blue. When I couldn't sleep at night, the song replayed in my head over and over again, uncontrollably. It became my mantra during my morning walk, for three solid miles.

Rather than fight it, one Saturday morning when I was doing the dishes, I decided it would be good to stop singing my own lyrics and learn the real ones. I could foresee embarrassing moments looming ahead when I mindlessly unleashed my own version while working in the backyard. (I knew my son would be mortified.)

If you don't have kids and haven't an excuse to listen to Disney songs without tarnishing your cool grown-up image, let me give you the quick backstory: The song is from Disney's animated hit movie *Frozen* and is sung by the character Elsa (played beautifully by Idina Menzel). Elsa was born with special powers, but an accident that occurred when she was little caused her parents to make her hide them away—and thus herself away. When she finally releases her powers, she frees herself from the bondage of her old life and expresses the freedom she feels in being able to be herself and own her power in the song "Let It Go."

For months after the release of *Frozen,* the song was everywhere. It won the Academy Award in 2013 for best song. Every parent of every kid who loves to sing and perform has probably heard the song more times than they can count.

For more than a year, there was a "Let it Go" frenzy in the world. The Idina Menzel YouTube video has (at the moment I'm typing—I suspect it will be much higher by the time you read this) more than 512 million views. The Demi Lovato version has almost 447 million views.

So one morning as I was doing the dishes, I cranked up the music, and in attempt to learn the real lyrics, I listened intently for the first time. And then I replayed it. And replayed it. And replayed it again.

I ran upstairs to my husband and said breathlessly, "'Let It Go' . . . it's hitting a universal chord with people . . . it's . . . it's tapping into the need that we all have to be ourselves and own our power. This isn't just a Disney thing; this is exactly what I'm seeing all around me in my sessions. People want the same thing at work! They just want to feel free to be themselves, powerfully . . . to be real . . . to let it go!"

But it isn't an easy thing to do—to "let it go" at work. Most of us have spent a lifetime doing our darndest to, like Elsa, "Don't let them in, don't let them see . . ." and "Conceal, don't feel, don't let them know . . ."

It's the reason the song resonates with so many people. We can relate. It's what we hunger for—to be free to be ourselves. Like Elsa, it's where our true power lies.

The word *power* means many different things to people. When I ask my participants what power means to them, I'll hear things like strength, control, authority, title, fame, wealth, position, and leader, to name a few.

What does power mean to you?

My favorite definition of power is "influence over others, the source of which resides in the person, instead of being vested by the position they hold."[1]

True power is your inherent ability, regardless of your title, where you're from, who you know, or what you have, to access the want in others. It's all you.

Traditionally, most of us have thought of power as something outside ourselves to be gained—a title, a position, money, or control—things requiring someone else's participation or permission. But true power comes from within and manifests in our actions and behaviors. It's not something that can be given or anointed. I'm sure you've known plenty of people who have fancy titles who you wouldn't consider to be powerful. Looking outside ourselves for power only limits our ability to see how we're getting in our own way and thus the possibility of being as powerful as we can truly be. To be powerful in the world, we must first be powerful in ourselves.

> *You need to know yourself well enough to identify what you might be doing, consciously and unconsciously, to dissipate your own power.*

This means we must know ourselves, which is easier said than done. How well do you understand and manage your emotions? How do stress, being overwhelmed, anxiety, frustration, fear, anger, uncertainty, and vulnerability manifest in your body and impact your thinking and reactions? Cultivating your most powerful self begins with this kind of self-awareness. You need to know yourself well enough to identify what you might be doing, consciously and unconsciously, to dissipate your own power.

Most of us have no idea what we're doing that's getting in our way of being as powerful as we can be. Unfortunately, the things that derail us most often aren't talked about in your annual review or traditional business books. But I've always been one to break traditions.

JUST BREATHE

As soon as I say the word *breathe* in a corporate environment, people get squirrelly. They get visions of yogis and start to think I've gone all woo-woo on them. Breathing is one of those things we've been doing since birth so we assume we've got it down, and yet most of us—especially under duress—don't.

Duress at work happens a lot. When we find ourselves in a stressful or anxious situation, our breathing becomes more and more shallow. While we normally have our whole chest cavity and abdomen to fill with air, when constricted in response to the surge of stress hormones, we find ourselves running out of breath—often to the point of cutting it off altogether.

Now here's where it gets interesting: Your brain needs oxygen to function. When we're stressed or anxious, we unconsciously cut off the air to our brains and we wonder why we can't think, can't remember, and can't articulate. Do you get sweaty palms and a pounding heart when you're feeling anxious? They're taking their cue from your brain panicking from the lack of oxygen, which causes your amygdala to kick into high gear.

Moreover, when we run out of breath, since our brain is starving for air, instead of thinking about our actions we become subject to emotionally triggered *reactions*, which put our results at risk. We cannot access the want in others when we're in a reactive state. That's when even the most well-meaning leaders turn to fear and threats and start to lean on their title to get results. Lovely outbursts like "Do it because it's your job!" or "If you don't hit your numbers, heads are gonna roll!" rob us of any real influence we can have. People know they may *have* to do what you say, but their *want* is long gone. If power lies in your inherent ability to truly influence, reactivity renders us powerless.

The first thing to do, when you're feeling stressed, is breathe. It may

> *We cannot access the want in others when we're in a reactive state.*

sound simple, but it's the fastest way to access your most powerful and authentic self.

Actors and singers have been studying the art of breathing since acting and singing began, because they know that in order to perform well under stress (and we've already established that the stage is quite a stressful environment) they need to have their instrument working at capacity.

> *The first thing to do, when you're feeling stressed, is breathe.*

You are your instrument. In order for you to express yourself fully and perform your best, you too must ensure that you can work at capacity under stress. Knowing how to maximize your breath is a critical skill for brave leaders.

What actors and singers are trained to do is to breathe from their belly or diaphragm, expanding the amount of air by more than eight to ten times. If the old saying *breath is life* is true, which would you rather have, two cups or a gallon? I read a quote once (probably on a tea bag) that said, "Breath is the voice of the soul." I so love that (even if the source is questionable). We cannot fully express who we are without it.

Next time you find yourself on a stressful call or you're feeling overwhelmed or anxious, simply take a moment to stop and breathe—low, slow, deep breaths. Allow your stress hormones to subside, your mind to participate, and your best self to emerge. Breath is the foundation of power.

BELLY BREATHING

With your feet shoulder-width apart, your knees slightly bent, and your arms resting by your side, begin by taking long, slow breaths, filling your lower belly with air and allowing your chest cavity to open and expand.

Put your hand on your belly, on top of your belly button. Take in a low, deep breath to fill the space beneath your hand. You should be able to feel your hand rise and fall when you breathe. Allow the breath to move up into your chest cavity, expanding your chest. When you exhale, keep your chest cavity open. Don't collapse. (You'll feel your shoulders slightly round if you're collapsing.)

You now have a massive space for lots of oxygen, which will make your brain very happy. Practice this as much as you possibly can so it becomes muscle memory.

MASTERING THE HEIGHTENED REALITY

As a leader, you're always on stage and people are always paying attention. For example, let's say you're the director of operations for a large casual dining chain, and you're visiting one of your restaurants. You've been making the rounds for three days now, and you're exhausted. You've been driving a lot, your eyes are bothering you, and you're having trouble with your contacts. As you walk into the kitchen to take a look at the back of the house, you look up, roll your dry eyes, trying to get your contact back in place, and the kitchen manager sees you and breaks out into a cold sweat. He's trying to figure out what he did wrong, and he's not the only one. The dishwasher frowns in the corner, and the cooks glance at each other in agitation as they fill the plates. You look at the kitchen manager, who is staring at you defensively, wondering, *What's with the attitude?* You're tired, but your senses are now on alert. Something isn't right, and you're determined to figure out what it is.

Not the best setup for a positive exchange, is it?

Because you're always on stage, everything you do, intentional or unintentional, is noticed. The people you lead are making meaning out of everything you do or don't do and say or don't say, and the meaning they're making is not always in your favor. This puts their want at risk.

If you didn't get enough sleep last night and you're quiet in a team meeting, the people reporting to you will worry they did something wrong. If you're slammed with deadlines and didn't have time to thank your employee for working overtime to finish a report, they'll think you didn't like it. If you just got off a stressful client call and you walk by one of your teammates in the hallway and don't smile or say hello, they'll think you're mad.

It's not that people are paranoid or looking for the worst in you, it's that their brains make meaning out of every little thing. That's what human brains do. And if you need to connect to the want in others in order to influence or lead, it's a truth you can't afford to ignore.

As a leader, you live in a heightened reality. You're on, and people are watching. It's not like going to the ball game with your friends or having dinner with your family. (Although, I would argue you're "on" there too; it just may not impact your work results.) Because you live in a heightened reality, your focus needs to be different.

Most of the time, when we try to focus, we bring tension into our bodies. Like when you're trying to think of someone's name and you can't. *Troy . . . no . . . Trevor . . . no . . . it starts with an R, right? R . . . Ray? No, that's not it . . .*

Picture yourself trying to remember. It's a struggle—holding your breath as you wrestle with the different consonants and vowels. You sit, rigid, every muscle tense, sorting through the card catalogue in your brain. You are so . . . focused. But it's to no avail. You give up in defeat, worried about early-onset Alzheimer's, and go get ready for work.

And then it happens. Your hands are full of shampoo as you wash your hair, warm water cascading over your face . . . Trey! That's it, Trey!

Once the tension subsides and you are relaxed, your breathing returns and your brain can participate, giving you the answer you've been trying to reach. Stepping out of the shower and toweling yourself off, you sigh, relieved that you haven't completely lost your mind.

Tension blocks clear thinking.

Here's another example: You're sleeping. It's two a.m. And all of a sudden, you hear a noise in your kitchen. Every muscle in your body tenses.

Your breathing stops, and suddenly you have bionic hearing. Every sound is magnified. You can hear the sound of your cat's claws on the dining room floor. You can hear the wind rustling the leaves against your windowpanes. Your significant other's breathing sounds like a hurricane in your bedroom. "Shhhhh! Did you hear that?" You lie there, alert, with your heart pounding. You are ready to do (gulp) whatever needs to be done. You are focused.

Or imagine your boss has asked you to present the team's strategy to your boss's boss and all of the other executives. You've prepared diligently for this meeting, but you're nervous. You've never presented to the C-suite before. During the meeting, you're asked a question to which you do *not* know the answer. Like a deer in the headlights, you grow tense and your breathing stops. All eyes are on you. You are focused.

Now this tension-filled, often adrenaline-fueled focus isn't a bad thing. (Without it, most of us would have been hit by a bus by now—or a taxi, if you live in New York City.) You don't need to read a book or take a class to learn how to do this; it's your hardwired survival mechanism, courtesy of your amygdala, and it serves you well.

But it is *reactive*. Your actions are sparked by survival rather than choice.

As a leader, it's critical to bring a heightened focus to every situation you face, but not a reactive focus. Reactivity cannibalizes true power. The kind of heightened focus I'm talking about is not a focus that comes from tension, but rather from *paying attention*. It's a focus that comes from being very, very *present*.

I don't have to tell you how difficult that can be these days.

TENSE? WHO ME?

"I want to send someone on my team," he said, "but I should warn you . . . she's pretty . . . hmmm . . . intense."

"Intense? What do you mean, intense?" I responded gingerly.

"Oh, you'll see. I think the work you do could really help her, if you can get through her tough facade. She's really smart and she cares about the business. She's got great instincts. She's just so . . . unapproachable. I'd like to groom her for a leadership role, but she can't lead if nobody feels like they can talk to her!"

When Jen showed up in my session two months later, without even being introduced, I knew who she was. She was intense all right, her fixed jaw hardening her appearance, vanquishing all warmth. She looked mean and she scared me. I hadn't even met her and already I was worried. We had a lot of work to do.

We are all a product of the stimuli that surround us and the environments we inhabit. A horn behind you honks, and your jaws tighten. Your heart beats a little faster. You hold your breath.

You rush out the door, late to a meeting. You're breathless, your mind is swimming, you're frowning in frustration, and your stomach is in knots. (You hate being late.)

You sit, hunched over your computer. Your eyes are straining, your shoulders are tight, and you have low blood sugar from working through lunch.

These are just everyday moments that over time impact how you mentally, emotionally, and physically show up in the world. They aren't necessarily good or bad; they're just moments. Layer in deadlines, conflicts with colleagues, the need to compete, ambition, insecurity, being overwhelmed, frustration, confusion, uncertainty, the quest for life-work balance, the list goes on, and consider how you wear life's complicated landscape.

With all you have going on in your life, how does it affect you? Because even though we've all developed some brilliant coping mechanisms, life shows.

Consider how you wear life's complicated landscape.

We all manifest tension in different ways, but most of us have become experts at avoiding it. We power through, thinking it will magically go away, or minimize the fallout. But unchecked tension only grows.

I will never forget having this discussion in class and watching Jen standing in the back of the room, listening as if she had seen a ghost. "Jen," I said gently, "are you okay?"

"I didn't realize," she whispered, clearly rattled, "I didn't realize how much I've been holding in." Then, in a flash of insight, she looked up and said, "Every day as I walk out of my house to go to work, I clench my jaws thinking about all that has to be done. I drive to work that way, go through the day that way, and drive home that way. I don't think I ever let myself really relax until my head hits the pillow, if then!"

> **Tension unchecked will own you.**

So picture this: In meetings, Jen's jaws were clenched. And as she'd walk down the halls at work, her jaws were clenched. And as she'd sit at her desk, poring through emails, her jaws were clenched.

And seeing Jen, with her jaws locked tight, day after day, what might the people who worked with her have thought? That she's mad? That's she's stressed? Or, like I thought when I met her, that she's mean? *Whatever you do, stay away from Jen! She looks like she's going to blow!*

After I got to know her, I realized who Jen is and who Jen seems to be are two different people. The real Jen is a passionate, caring, dedicated, intelligent, strong woman. But all that was overshadowed by the way she showed up in the world. Tension unchecked will own you.

A month later, Jen's boss called me. "What did you do to Jen?" he asked, laughing.

"What do you mean?" I responded warily.

"Well, she's totally different. Almost happy! People are turning to her for guidance. She's taking the lead on a number of projects, and I hear she started yoga!"

"That's fantastic!" I said, smiling into the phone, "but I can't take credit for the yoga! Jen's amazing, a real asset to your team."

What actors know is that tension blocks authentic expression. You cannot fully connect with others and bring your best, most powerful self to the game if you're carrying tension. Tension blocks your range of emotions, the ability to accurately express yourself, and the possibility of true connection. If personal power is your capacity to trigger the want in others, then you must have access to your full self so others can experience you as genuine, worthy of trust, reliance, and belief. It doesn't matter how brilliant you are or how good your information is—if tension blocks want, you will not be heard.

That's why actors, before they ever take the stage, will do a full-body warm-up to release their tension. Now, I understand that we're all too busy to do a full-body warm-up before we go into an important meeting.

> *The more specific you can be about what happens to you personally, the better.*

Sure, Jeff, I'd love to discuss the financials with you. Just give me an hour so I can do my full-body warm-up. Not gonna happen. But, like with your Super Objective, if you can name it, you can do something about it. Since we all carry our tension in different places, you have to get to know yourself better. Be a detective. Pay attention to how you stand in line at the grocery store and how you sit at your desk. Pay attention to what happens in your body when you're stuck in traffic or when you're on a stressful call. Get curious about yourself when you have to give a presentation or have a tough conversation or when you're running late or when you're cold or when you're mad. Where do you personally carry your tension? Where does it show up in your body, *specifically*?

To simply say "I feel overwhelmed" or "I feel tense" doesn't cut it. What are your body's cues that tell you you're overwhelmed? Where does it show up in your muscles? Where do you *feel* the tension—in your shoulders, your neck, your hands, your jaws? Because we are all uniquely wired, it's different for all of us. The more specific you can be about what happens to you personally, the better.

Once you have some clarity around what happens to you personally in the face of feeling stressed, vulnerable, or overwhelmed, then you can take targeted action. Removing tension doesn't need to take a great deal of time, but it does take mindfulness. Once you're aware of where you carry your tension, then you need to find an efficient way to release it. Free from tension, you can bring your most powerful and authentic self to whatever situation you face.

TENSION-RELEASE EXERCISES

Working from the feet up, slowly tighten each part of your body. Then, from the top of your head, start relaxing each part of your body, one at a time, little by little, until you've reached the bottom of your feet. This exercise forces your muscles to relax by tiring them. It also helps you be more aware of your body when it's experiencing tension in the moment, so you can relax as needed.

As you identify areas where you hold tension, the following are some exercises to help you work targeted areas.

Quick shoulder exercises:

- Hug yourself. Hold for five seconds, breathing deeply, then switch which arm is on top and repeat.

- Clasp your hands behind your back and gently lift your hands upward.

- Roll your shoulders to the front a few times and then to the back a few times.

Neck exercises:

- Gently roll your head from side to side. Feel the weight of your head as it drops.

- Clasp your hands and, with your chin at your chest, gently rest your clasped hands on the back of your head. Hold for a count of ten, breathing in deeply.

- Place your right ear next to your right shoulder. Gently bring your right arm up and wrap your hand over your head, so your right hand rests just below your left ear. Hold for a count of ten, breathing deeply. Switch sides.

Jaw exercises:

- Let your jaw hang loosely and move your lower jaw in small, slow circles, one way and then the other.

- Massage the hinge where your lower and upper jaws meet (slightly in front of your ear lobes), first with your fingers and then with the heel of your hand.

- Blow air through your lips.

- Yawn big.

THE MIND-BODY CONNECTION

Years ago, I was cast in the role of Denise Savage in John Patrick Shanley's heart-wrenching play *Savage in Limbo*. Inhabiting Denise for months of rehearsal and then for the run of the show was a painful privilege, as it forced me to viscerally experience the ache of unconsciously self-imposed powerlessness. The playwright described Denise as "small, wild-haired, strong, belligerent, determined, dissatisfied, and scared. She is in pain, paranoid, and full of hunger. She has hungry ears."

As most actors do, when I first read the play, I started exploring her physicality. How does she stand and sit? How does she move through space? I'd round my shoulders, my head jutting forth like a turtle, my eyes darting around the room, and my breathing shallow. Her hunger and despair engulfed me like a black hole. As I'd speak her words, I wasn't pretending to feel what she felt, I *experienced* it—my body triggering my mind.

There's a reason that actors delve into the physicality of their characters almost as soon as they have a script in hand. They know that in order to give a powerful, authentic performance, they have to trigger real emotion and draw from their own history. Truth cannot be faked or manipulated, as an audience can sense deception. When actors have to play a character who is sick or sad or lonely or tired or scared—or powerless—the first thing they'll do is inhabit that physicality. They'll round their shoulders, their limbs falling heavily at their sides. The weight of their downward gaze causes their head to tilt forward. Their field of vision will shrink. Their breathing will follow suit, growing more and more shallow. Ever so slowly, they will *feel* what their character feels—sick, sad, lonely, tired, scared, or powerless. They *viscerally* experience this truth. It's not pretend.

This is the case off stage as well. How we carry ourselves physically will viscerally inform how we feel, how we experience the world around us, and yes, how others perceive us. So let's say you've been up all night working on your PowerPoint deck for a big presentation you have the next day. Your slides are gorgeous. Your data is rock solid. You know your clients are going to love it.

But you're tired. You got maybe four hours of sleep, if that. You show up to the meeting, and even though you're dressed for success, your fatigue is obvious. Your slouched posture and slow movements are telltale signs that something is up. Your clients notice, but they can't put their finger on it. Maybe she's not feeling well. Or maybe she doesn't care. Who knows what meaning they make of it? They won't say anything to you; they'll just think it. They'll file it away and factor it in as they make decisions about your future relationship.

Yes, your physicality speaks volumes to them, but even more disturbing is what it communicates to you. While your gorgeous PowerPoint deck may say, "You've got this!" your body says, "I can't." "I'm powerless." And you viscerally experience this truth.

How might this impact how you present or the conversation you have with your clients following your presentation? What effect could it have on your ability to ask probing questions or on your confidence in closing the deal? Probably more than you realize.

It wasn't until recently, when social psychologist and Harvard Business School professor Amy Cuddy's TED Talk, "Your Body Language Shapes Who You Are," exploded on the scene that people gave much credence to the link between physicality and mindset, but her research has made it even more compelling.

"Humans and other animals express power through open, expansive postures, and they express powerlessness through closed, contractive postures. But can these postures actually cause power?" Dr. Cuddy suggested. In her research she looked at the difference between what she called *high-power* and *low-power poses* and the effect they have not only on feelings and behavior but also on the body's chemistry. What she discovered was that not only did high-power poses increase participants' feeling of being more powerful, but they also increased their risk tolerance and physiologically elevated their levels of the dominance hormone, testosterone, and decreased their cortisone—better known as the stress hormone. All this, simply from changing the way they "posed."[2]

I experience this on a daily basis. I'll be standing in line at the post office, glued to my phone, slumping into myself, and feeling tired, heavy, and cranky. The moment I catch myself and make an adjustment—roll my shoulders back, lengthen my spine, and lift my head—I magically feel more energized, positive, and ready to face the day. I become a better me in an instant. Dr. Cuddy suggests that making minor adjustments over time can alter the trajectory of our future and general health and well-being, and I know this to be true. I see it in myself, and I see it in my participants. I see it in the manager who shrinks herself in the morning and owns the room in the afternoon. I see it in the out-of-work executive who won't make eye contact early on but later brings everyone to tears as he connects deeply with each of us and shares his powerful story. And I see it in the small business owner who, after years of toil trying to make ends meet, is rejuvenated as she simply changes the way she carries herself.

We are that powerful.

POWERFUL POSTURE EXERCISES

My favorite exercise to ensure powerful, open posture hails from the Alexander Technique. Frederick Matthias Alexander was an Australian actor who had severe personal health problems and his doctors couldn't figure out what was wrong. In the absence of a clear diagnosis, and in hopes of finding a remedy, he was driven to study what causes muscle tension during everyday activities. His method is now considered foundational for actors, dancers, and musicians worldwide.

This exercise, while best done in the privacy of your home or office, is an exceptional way to quickly improve your posture, lengthen your spine, and give you a more powerful stance.

The Rag Doll:

- Stand with your feet shoulder width apart, with a slight bend in your knees. Beginning with the top of your head, roll down, vertebra by vertebra, until you hang by your waist like a rag doll.

- Allow the weight of your head to roll your head forward, so that your chin is tucked into your chest.

- Slowly, roll your shoulders forward.

- Allow the weight of your head and gravity to roll the middle of your spine downward (you will feel as if you're doing a cat stretch).

- Continue to slowly roll the lower part of your spine, tucking your lower abdomen, until you finally touch your toes.

- Your chin should stay tucked the entire time.

- Allow yourself to hang down, your head toward the floor, your chin tucked, gently swaying back and forth to release your tension.

- When you feel completely loose and relaxed, slowly begin to roll up in reverse, vertebra by vertebra, keeping your chin and shoulders tucked until the very end.

- Roll your shoulders back and down.

- At the last moment, untuck your chin, allowing your head to balance at the top of your spine.

- Imagine a golden thread connected to the top of your head and that it's reaching up into the heavens.

- Your spine is lengthened, your posture is open, and you are completely relaxed.

Now, of course, if you're in an open-concept office, you may get a few weird looks if you go into a rag doll by the water cooler, so I'd recommend a modified version. Simply roll your shoulders back and down. Imagine the thread lifting you up from the top of your head, lengthening your spine. And don't forget to breathe, low and slow.

One of the things actors are reminded to do, especially when they do period pieces and have to play royalty (royalty in the nineteenth century did not slouch), is to keep air under your armpits. Now this could possibly be attributed to the fact that those period costumes, since they couldn't be washed, smelled horrible, but you can't help but carry yourself in an open, powerful pose if you have air under your armpits. Try it before your next important meeting! Or, as Amy Cuddy suggests in her TED Talk, you can don your best Wonder Woman pose and call it a day. That works too!

The question is no longer whether or not there is a mind-body connection that leads us to being more powerful in the world; it's whether or not we'll remember to do something about what we know to be true. Like everything else, it all comes down to awareness, mindfulness, and action.

TAKE DOWN THE MASK

Throughout this book, you've heard me talk about "being masked" and "taking down the mask," and when you think about it in terms of authenticity, it makes complete sense. A mask is simply a protective mechanism we use to hide who we are or how we feel. It's a "face we put on" or a "strong persona" we adopt when we're not feeling good enough, strong enough, or brave enough—it's absolutely natural and often encouraged. Most of us actually have no idea we're putting on a mask, but it has a major impact on how people relate to us. How can people know who you are and experience you as genuine, worthy of trust, reliable, and believable if you're masked? Of course, the answer is they can't.

But what if we think about it in terms of *power*? How might a mask impact how powerful you are and how powerfully you experience yourself?

Let's first explore why we mask in the first place. Most often, we mask unconsciously—we don't even know we're doing it because it has simply become our modus operandi—especially at work. Said another way, it's our way of "faking it until we make it" or hiding our insecurities behind a facade of strength and competence. It's our way of projecting the person we think we should be, often hiding what we truly think, feel, and believe. And, because it feels safe and less vulnerable, we can easily become addicted to it. There's nothing wrong with projecting a positive face even when we don't feel 100 percent secure, but when it becomes normal and hides our true selves, it comes at a huge cost.

There is no one-size-fits-all mask. Some of us become void of expression, our eyes staring blankly ahead. Some of us become overly animated, smiling and nodding our heads "Oh yes! Everything is great!" when on the inside we feel the opposite. Some of us get cocky or snarky or badass, wanting to project or establish ourselves as in control. And some of us just turn ourselves down, like our personalities are on volume control, not wanting to be "too much" or stand out or become a target.

Are there times when you mask your true self from coworkers? From family members? From authority figures? What does your mask look like? Do you know?

Here's a quick exercise that's very easy and powerful. Think of how people at work (or school, or whatever setting you may tend to mask—for me it's networking events) would describe you *if you weren't in the room*. What adjectives would they use if they weren't trying to be nice? Be honest with yourself. If you want, you can actually ask a few of them. Once you have your list, look at each one and determine how well it describes who you really are. If there are major differences, you'll know that you are probably in the habit of being masked. You'll also have a really clear idea of what your mask is—and may even find it useful to give it a name.

Reinforced by our histories and experiences, our organizational cultures, social media bullies, and outdated leadership role models, it's easy to assume it's normal or expected to be masked at work. Unconsciously we think we need to be a certain way to get things done, to fit in, to move up—it goes back to our core needs for belonging. It's human.

There's nothing inherently wrong with being masked—it's not good or bad—it's just that, for many of us, we're not *choosing* when we mask; our mask is choosing us. It's not a decision; it's become our normal way of being and one of our biggest obstacles to being a brave leader.

And there's another hidden cost: It's exhausting to not be yourself! Hiding who you truly are and internalizing your feelings day in and day out wreaks havoc on your health, your relationships, your engagement, your productivity, your self-respect, your joy, your perspective, and your ability to commit and be all-in. If you mask for better results, perhaps you better rethink those pros and cons. You are paying a hefty price.

If you want to be brave and authentic at work and develop the leadership traits that encourage people to *want* to follow you, you'll need to understand your mask and consciously decide if, and when, to use one.

It's important to note that being unmasked is not the same as being unfiltered. A filter can be a healthy mechanism to ensure that people experience you as genuine, worthy of trust, reliable, and believable. A filter forces you to pay attention to the needs of others and employ empathy. You can be, and should be, unmasked yet appropriately filtered for the situation. I can't tell you how many rude and hurtful comments I've heard under the guise of "just saying what's real." Remember, if you say it and it can't be heard, you're just talking to yourself. What do people need from you to hear the hard news and feedback you must say? That is your challenge. You're not powerful if your impact is to hurt or repel others—intentional or not. You need them to succeed.

Being unmasked, on the other hand, allows your humanity to shine through and lets people see themselves in your experiences. If personal power resides in our ability to influence others, we need them to be able to connect to us so they want to follow. Some might think a mask is cool or strangely strategic or that they're playing it safe, but in truth, it comes with a higher cost than you may realize.

I remember having this discussion in the classroom, when a senior executive, who had recently lost her job, got frustrated and exclaimed, "I don't understand why we can't be masked. I was masked my whole career and it worked just fine. We were all like that," she said, referring to her fellow senior executives who worked for the same multinational beverage corporation. "We'd be masked with our employees, but then we'd get on the corporate jet and talk about our kids."

I can understand her frustration. If something seemingly works, why change it? But masking is no longer effective in our new work world. It'll get you the "have to" but not the "want to." People won't give their best for a paycheck exchange, but they'll crawl over broken glass for a person they trust and believe in—someone they know cares and is invested in them. A mask hides our most valuable currency.

Humans hunger for connection. They want to be seen, but connection cannot happen from behind a mask. The problem is that, given how unsafe our work environments often feel, most of us run around doing our work masked. We want to connect but don't, because it doesn't feel safe. As leaders, we need to have the courage to take down our masks first, to give the people around us permission to do the same. Only then can true connection occur. Power lives in *connection*. It's vulnerable, taking down the mask. That's why it's reserved for the brave.

EXAMINE YOUR FOCUS

It seems contradictory: We must bring awareness to how we show up in the world and the impact we have and, at the same time, not overly focus on ourselves. When our thinking becomes self-related, it can get us into trouble.

While I'm sure you can probably think of a few folks running about with an inflated opinion of themselves, the vast majority of us are so focused on what we think is wrong or needs to be improved that we have a hard time seeing our own greatness. Oh, by the way, those inflated-ego folks? Most of them are overcompensating.

Remember, we see what we look for. If we look at ourselves and our lives as a fix-it project, that's all we'll see. We'll get up in the morning and look in the mirror and notice that we don't look like the glamorous models in the magazines when we crawl out of bed. We'll make our way to the kitchen and notice it doesn't look like the HGTV Dream Home. We'll walk into the office and look at the messy desk and think, *I've got to fix that.* We'll go from one meeting to the next, picking apart the way we present, the way we've prepared, the way we look, the questions we've asked, the way we react, and the way we feel. We are, after all, committed to our self-improvement. We wonder what it's going to take to do a complete overhaul, with so much to fix.

And this same self-focus can sabotage us when we lead and present. I remember when I first met Erin, a young leader who showed up to one of my sessions, and thought, *Wow! This woman really has her stuff together! She's poised, articulate, warm, clearly committed to doing a good job.* I was so impressed! Yet through the course of the day, I watched Erin disown all of these wonderful attributes. She was convinced she was a terrible speaker, felt like she was a total work in progress, and didn't trust her own instincts when it came to setting strategy. There seemed to be two Erins inhabiting the same person—the "impressive Erin" and the "fix-it Erin." While her focus on growing and being her best was admirable, she could never measure up to her own expectations of perfection. She set herself up for failure, and I knew it was largely due to her focus. How powerful can we be if we view ourselves as a fix-it project? How powerfully can we influence and lead if that's all we see?

It's not that Erin saw something I didn't see. Her experience of herself was real. When she spoke in public, she paid close attention to her heart racing and her hands sweating, and she hated the way she felt. The more she focused on those sensations, the more her anxiety would mount, and the sensations would increase.

As Erin worked toward a strategy, she felt vulnerable, worried that she'd make a mistake and take her team off course. How could she know what the future would bring? The more she focused on her feelings, the more unsure of herself she became.

What we focus on grows. When we focus on the emotions and sensations we feel, they grow. We can't help but make meaning out of our experience (because that's what humans do). If I feel this way, that must mean . . . If I experience this, that must mean . . . And thus, the feelings and sensations get bigger and bigger—a tidal wave of emotion out of control.

The meanings that we make become the truths we tell ourselves. Erin's truth was that speaking in public was painful. In her mind, this meant she was a bad public speaker. So every time she spoke, her truth became her experience. Erin's truth was that setting strategy is risky, so every time she thought about planning for the future, she froze.

It's not that Erin is an especially insecure or nervous woman. She's bright, experienced, capable, and committed. But the feelings and sensations she experienced were real. Speaking in public and planning for tomorrow are vulnerable things to do. Her problem wasn't with feeling vulnerable—feeling vulnerable is normal. What derailed her was her focus of attention. The more she focused on her heart beating out of her chest, the more uncontrollable it became. The more she focused on the possibility of messing up, the more anxious she felt. Her feelings manifested in body sensations that were hard to ignore.

But our sensations don't define us. We all experience feeling anxious when we leap into the unknown. That's normal. We all experience feeling vulnerable when we feel exposed. That's normal. While the trigger situations and our body sensations may differ, we all have them. That's normal.

But what the most powerful people know (perhaps not even consciously) is that the more we focus on those feelings and sensations, the more they build. The more they build, the more likely they are to hijack our success.

To fully own our power, we must take our focus *off* ourselves. That can be scary, because then what? Isn't it more vulnerability inducing to stare into the abyss? Yes it is! That's why it's so critical to focus on purposeful action—your Super Objective.

Focusing on your Super Objective—specific and constructive action to impact someone or something outside yourself—harnesses your attention, frees you of that self-critical voice in your head, and allows for your most powerful self to emerge.

Your feelings and sensations aren't wrong or bad; they're simply feelings. By shifting your focus, you allow them to flow through you like a river, rather than emotionally flooding you like a dam.

I will never forget watching Erin present later that day. She clearly had a shift in focus. She walked off the stage beaming. For not only had we, her audience, experienced her as the powerful, articulate, and poised woman she is, but she experienced herself that way, and it showed—true power, from the inside out.

KNOW YOUR SUPERPOWERS

One of the things I love most about my work is that I get a chance to help people see and appreciate their natural talents. When we're too close to something, sometimes it's hard to see. We don't see the things that make us shine. Great listeners don't know they're great listeners because they're so busy listening intently. People who ask great questions don't realize what a gift that truly is, because that's what they've always done.

So often, when we think of talent, we assume it must be artistic or athletic, but a talent is simply a natural way of thinking, feeling, or behaving. We're all talented; we're often just too close to see them.

When we're little, we instinctively know that we get more mileage out of focusing on what we do well. When my son, Jeremy, was four years old, he always said to me, "Mom, I can run really fast! Mom, watch this! I'm good at mazes!"

One of my favorite memories is when we had been reading this great little book called *Because of You*, by B. G. Hennessy.

"Because of you, there is one more person who can share, care and listen. When people from different countries share, care and listen to each other, it's called peace."

Then, shortly after we read the book, he came home from preschool and told me about having been a good friend to this little boy at school. "Mom, I did peace! I'm good at peace!" (Now that's a talent the world could use, eh?)

But as we grow up, somehow we get the message that in order to fit in we need to be everything to all people—that who we are isn't good enough—and we diminish and dismiss what we do best. We get so hyper-focused on fixing ourselves that, instead of feeling more capable and effective, we feel less. We lose sight of our talents and, in doing so, dissipate how powerful we are.

There are a number of good strengths-assessment tools on the market, some which are free and some that charge a small fee. (Simply Google *natural talents assessment* and you'll find a plethora of options; one of the most popular is Gallup's Strengths Finder 2.0.) Smart organizations build strength-based teams and partnerships, realizing that cookie-cutter job descriptions rarely suit the unique humans they've employed. They understand that a whole lot more can be accomplished—and accomplished with excellence—if people play to their strengths. And they're happier. Imagine that.

To bring our best selves to our work and our lives, we have to unleash our talents. We cannot influence or hope to lead effectively without owning and leveraging what we do best. As Marianne Williamson said (so brilliantly that Nelson Mandela quoted her), "There's nothing enlightened about shrinking so that other people won't feel insecure around you. As we let our own light shine, we unconsciously give other people permission to do the same. As we are liberated from our own fear, our presence automatically liberates others."

I believe that owning and taking responsibility for your talents may be one of the bravest things you can do.

You are talented. Name your strengths. Own them. Leverage them. That's where your superpowers lie! You may be surprised at how good you truly are.

HOW SMART ARE YOU, REALLY?

There are men and women who have forever changed the trajectory of the leadership (and I'd be so bold as to say the human) conversation, and psychologist Daniel Goleman is one of them. As the father of emotional intelligence, his research regarding emotions and the brain has provided the world with one of our most powerful resources to better understand ourselves and connect with others. *The Harvard Business Review* calls his work "a revolutionary, paradigm-shattering idea," and his book *Emotional Intelligence* was on "the *New York Times* bestseller list for a year-and-a-half, with more than 5,000,000 copies in print worldwide in forty languages, and has been a best seller in many countries."[3]

I don't know about you, but I've met an awful lot of people who are highly intelligent but who struggle when it comes to understanding themselves and others. The good news is, unlike IQ (which is essentially your capacity to learn and is relatively fixed from birth), cultivating emotional intelligence, or EQ, is something we can all do.

Emotional intelligence looks at four different measurements. One axis is all about you: How well do you identify your own emotions? And how well do you manage your own emotions? The second axis focuses on you in relation to other people: How well do you identify the emotions that others are experiencing? And how well can you use your awareness of your own emotions and those of others to manage your relationships successfully?

If you think about it, everything it takes to be a brave leader requires effective emotion management. If our goal is to have the people we lead experience us as authentic (genuine, worthy of trust, reliance, and belief) so we can connect to their want, then a high EQ is critical to success. We must bring awareness to how our emotions affect the way we show up with others, and we must be able to navigate them in real time without reacting and having them hijack our best.

Equally important is that if we're focused on having a constructive impact—on achieving our Super Objective—then we have no choice but to pay attention to the emotions others are experiencing and find a way to manage them effectively.

Let's be clear, whether you like someone or not doesn't matter. Whether you agree with how they are feeling makes no difference. They feel what they feel. If you wish to authentically connect to their *want*, you cannot afford to dismiss or judge them. I know. Life is so hard sometimes.

Taking Stephen Covey's famous advice, we must "seek first to understand, then to be understood" and then be intentional with our actions.[4] All the while asking ourselves, *What does he need from me (given how he's feeling) to experience me as genuine, worthy of trust, reliance, and belief? What is the impact I want to have? What can I do to ensure he feels how I hope he will feel and do what I hope he will do? What actions can I take?*

It takes stepping back to identify and manage your own emotions, using the Magic If to step into the shoes of others, and bringing mindfulness to the situations you face, *before* you act.

I have to confess that this is something I work on constantly, with varying degrees of success. While I didn't have the wherewithal to test my EQ when I was younger, I suspect that my scores wouldn't have been much to brag about. This is definitely a teacher teach thyself kind of thing, and I've been diligent about improving my skills, as I know they make a difference.

My story, I suspect, isn't unlike many of yours. I took after my dad, who was the more reactive of my parents. He's a strong personality— passionate, driven, charismatic, stubborn, and used to getting his way. I was always more like him than I liked to admit. (Although now I see how his qualities have made a positive difference for me—our strengths are often our Achilles' heel.) My mom was the opposite. (My brother got her genes.) Warm and kind and completely averse to conflict, her emotions always pushed into the background to still the waters, which, like a boiling kettle with the lid locked tight, would hiss and spurt when things got too hot. Emotion management wasn't something anyone talked about or thought about in my family. We survived our emotions. They owned us. Like an unwieldy, unpredictable paranormal force, they'd inhabit us, wreak havoc, and be off, leaving us wondering what had happened and pointing fingers at who was to blame. You know, family.

I have a wonderful, loving family. I am grateful to be close to my amazing parents. We all just happen to be human beings, and emotions are part of the deal. Human beings are complicated creatures.

Thankfully, emotion management is starting to catch fire, and education around this critical topic has improved. These days, from the time children are infants, parents are introduced to resources that can help them teach their kids how to identify and talk about their own emotions. Grade schools work with children to help them identify emotions in other people, putting empathy into action. This is a world-changing conversation that is going to take time, but hopefully these children, as they move into the workforce, will be better equipped to influence and lead. For the rest of us (and if you're older than twenty, you qualify), we must hold fiercely to our commitment to do the work. Our EQ isn't going to grow itself.

If being powerful is the ability to influence the choices that others make, regardless of title or position, strengthening your EQ is one of the most important things you can do. At least I know that's true for me.

———

In order for us to truly own our power, we have to have all the working parts in synch—our body, our voice, our minds, our emotions. We have to have an awareness of what we're communicating to ourselves and others, and be actively engaged in personal iteration. If personal power lies in the want of others, then we all have access. That makes it both exciting and daunting. How do we grow ourselves to be genuine, worthy of trust, reliable, and believable so that people want to be a part of what we're up to in the world?

Because then the question is no longer "Can you?" but rather, "Are you willing to do what it takes?"

Key Takeaways

→ We are all far more powerful than we realize.

→ If we define *power* as "influence over others, the source of which resides in the person, instead of being vested by the position they hold," then how personally powerful you are has nothing to do with your title but rather is determined by how you physically, mentally, and emotionally process things around you and show up in the world.

→ Getting to your most powerful self begins with self-awareness. What are you doing consciously and unconsciously that dissipates your power? If you can name it, you can do something about it.

→ When we're in a stressful situation, we start to hold our breath and cut off the oxygen to our brains. Our brains need oxygen to function. When you find yourself in a stressful situation, take low, slow breaths, and allow your brain to fully participate in the situation at hand.

→ Tension blocks authentic expression. Identify where (specifically) you carry tension in your body *before* you enter a situation (especially if the stakes are high), so you can first release it.

→ How you physically carry yourself will impact how you feel. Be sure to carry yourself in an open, expansive posture, with your shoulders back, spine lengthened, and head held high.

→ Many of us hide our feelings and our true selves at work by putting on a mask, whether we know it or not. *You cannot connect to the want of others from behind a mask.* To be authentic, powerful, and brave, you must be willing to take down your mask to give others permission to do the same.

→ To fully own our power, we must take our focus off ourselves. When our focus becomes self-related, it triggers body sensations and behaviors that dissipate our power. Instead, shift your focus outward to achieve purpose—your Super Objective.

→ Name, own, and leverage your natural talents and strengths— they are your superpowers.

→ If you want to better activate the Magic If, tap into empathy and connect to the want of others—work on cultivating your EQ.

→ If you want to be a brave leader, it's critical to *own the power you already have—your inherent power.*

19

Connection Is the Game

*Communication is merely an exchange
of information, but connection is
an exchange of our humanity.*

—SEAN STEPHENSON

One of the things I miss most about the theater world is rehearsal, where toil and sweat mix with heart and soul to create magic—alchemy at its finest. I can viscerally remember every first reading. The actors, director, designers, stage managers, and sometimes producers all gathered around a large table to breathe life into the written word. We'd sit there, knowing that, for the next few months, it would consume every waking thought and demand every ounce of attention, energy, and passion we possessed. We no longer belonged to ourselves, as we lay bare at the altar of the stage, bathed in possibility. We knew what could be if we were willing to go all in—to leap into the dark again and again in the face of the unknown. We knew that what lay in wait on the other side was the one true thing for which we all hunger—connection. Connection with the audience. Connection with universal truths. Connection with one another. Connection with ourselves. And we knew we had to work our asses off to make it happen.

Nowhere else have I found this same awareness—that, in order to truly connect, we have to work at it. It's not something that's going to happen by accident. We treat connection like it's a "nice to have" instead of a "have to have," and we wonder why we feel so disconnected and our results are what they are. It's the big secret! We don't connect in order to play the game of life; connection is the game. It's all there is. Everything else is simply a by-product.

> **We don't connect in order to play the game of life; connection is the game. Everything else is simply a by-product.**

Leadership is about connection. *Connect* is a verb. It's active. Either you actively connect to the hearts and minds of the people you lead so they want to follow, or you don't and they don't (follow, that is). Influence is about connection. Either you actively connect in a way that they want to listen and consider your point of view, or you lose the chance to affect change. Presence is irrelevant if you don't connect. If you're presenting and you don't connect with the people in your audience, you might as well be talking to yourself. It's all about connection. If you want to have any kind of impact at all, the stakes are that high. Your results are simply a by-product of your ability to truly connect with the hearts and minds of others.

A while back, I was leading sessions for a small company that had recently been acquired by a large multinational based in France. There were culture issues and communication issues, and because of the vast amount of change they were experiencing, fear and mistrust were rampant. Overnight, this small band of technical leaders that had proudly grown their company from five people to two hundred on their own—a company that had felt more like a family than an organization—joined forces with a behemoth employing more than thirty thousand people worldwide. As you can imagine, their heads were spinning.

I spent several weeks working with their people managers, a new group every two days, but it was the contrast between the first two sessions that stands out in my memory. As common practice, we had a different senior leader kick off each session. The intent was to highlight the importance of the training to ensure buy-in early on. Never before had I experienced such a dramatic example of the impact one leader can have in such a short period of time.

The first senior leader scheduled to introduce the training was the vice president of operations. Human resources had already put the fear of God into the participants to be there on time for the kickoff, so they started trickling in about twenty minutes before we were to begin. As I always do, I walked around, introducing myself and getting to know them.

When our scheduled start time of 8:00 a.m. rolled around and the senior leader hadn't shown up, people turned their heads in anticipation, looking at the door. The human resources partner (my client) didn't want to begin without the official kickoff, so we waited. I continued walking around, asking people questions to learn more about them, as small talk filled the room.

At 8:15, there was no sign of our senior leader. People checked their phones in agitation.

"Maybe we should go see if he's still coming," I asked my client, sensing the tension in the room.

"No. He's coming. I checked with him this morning. He probably just got stuck on a call or something. He'll be here."

So I continued to walk around the room, trying to put people at ease.

At 8:20, there was still no senior leader. The human resources person paced at the side of the room, her anxiety rolling off her in waves. Participants muttered to each other and shook their heads in frustration.

Finally, at 8:25, the senior leader entered the room, phone in hand, reading something on his screen. He walked to the front of the class, stood in the center, commanding the attention of everyone, and proceeded to type something on his phone.

When he finally looked up, his eyes darted around the room, he sighed as if he were very put out, and said, "Look, I know you guys are really busy. This is probably the last thing you want to be doing. But we all have to do it. So pay attention and learn something because we have a lot of work to do these next few months."

And then he left. Just like that.

I watched the group slink back in their chairs, watched the animated faces I had been talking to earlier on my rounds go blank, and watched every single person in the room disengage in a flash.

When I arrived for the next session, to say that I was anxious about the kickoff is an understatement. I knew the senior leader who was kicking off the second session was the chief financial officer and that he had just arrived the night before from London. I anticipated a jet-lagged man who thought that training was a waste of time and money. I braced myself for having to rally the group back to life after he left.

At 7:40 a.m., twenty minutes before we were to start, a small, thin, blond man wearing John Lennon glasses and a yellow tie walked in, looked around questioningly, and said, "Is this where the training is being held?"

"Yes," I responded, as I put the lid back on my flipchart marker and held out my hand in welcome. "But we don't start for another twenty minutes, so if you'd like to grab a cup of coffee first, you have time. I'm Kimberly. I'll be working with you today."

"Hi, Kimberly. I'm Simon. I'm actually here to kick off the session."

(Can I tell you how much I loved Simon?)

For the next twenty minutes, Simon warmly greeted every person who walked in the room. As he shook their hand, he asked about their role in the business, he asked about them personally, and he asked about what they wanted to get out of the training. When it was time for the kickoff, the energy in the room was already buzzing with excitement and anticipation.

At 8:00 a.m. exactly, Simon didn't walk to the front. Instead, he casually perched on one of the empty tables at the side, smiled, and said, "Good morning! I'm so happy to be here with you." And you could see that he meant it. He was a soft-spoken man, so when he started talking, the room was absolutely silent. People leaned in to hear him, riveted. "You know, I took this session about a month ago," he began, "and when I was sitting in your seat, I thought, I don't need this. I'm too busy to sit in a training session all day. I was wrong.

"Before this session, I used to go into meetings with my team having already decided what we were going to do, and I would spend the time delegating the responsibilities to execute my plan. I didn't realize the negative impact. I had tremendous talent on my team, and I had no idea. Now, I go into a meeting asking questions, gathering ideas, and *together* we come up with the plan and decide how to execute. We now have more fun. Our plans are better. Our results are better. And I'm better for it. I encourage you to take what you learn in here seriously and run with it. There's nothing more important you could be doing."

"Oh, and," he said as he got up to leave, "I'll be sure to pop in and see how it's going before I head off to the airport tomorrow!"

He smiled, wished us all a great day, shook several hands and patted several backs on his way out, and all of us were left like race horses in the gate, excited to take off on our adventure together.

After the first senior leader's kickoff, it took me a solid three hours to reengage the group. It was excruciating. I'd ask a question. Let it sit. No response. Over and over again. Crickets. No head nodding. No enthusiasm. Nada, for hours. But it wasn't the group. After spending a solid half day building trust, sharing stories, and sticking it out with them, they slowly came back to life. By the beginning of day two, they were playing full-out. It was a complete transformation. They were *connected*.

As a leader, you carry a tremendous responsibility, because how you show up affects everyone around you. You are always on stage. The first leader likely wasn't a bad guy; he was probably overwhelmed, super busy, and stressed out. He was "volun-told" to do the kickoff, which likely fell way below his list of priorities. Given what was going on in the company at that time, it totally makes sense. But he left a vapor trail of disengagement behind him like I've never seen before, and while it may have been understandable, it was irresponsible.

Think of the ripple effect. He was asked to speak to a captive audience of thirty-five influential people in the business. Each person in that room managed a team of between eight and fifteen people globally. That's an average reach of more than four hundred people across the organization. And what did he communicate during his brief appearance? That it wasn't worth his time (or they were not worth his time). That he had nothing new to learn. That it was low priority (or they were low priority).

Imagine the impact on this company's culture, on morale, on their ability to grow and stay competitive if the message coming from top-down is that learning is not worth your time, you know everything you need to know, and bettering yourself is low priority. Or worse, you're sending the message that the people you lead aren't worth your time and are low priority. The stakes are higher than we realize. Even when it doesn't seem all that important, we are always on stage.

I think everyone in the room that day would agree that Simon, the CFO, did a brilliant job accessing our want. Every single one of us, although different people, experienced him as genuine, worthy of trust, reliance, and belief. So how'd he do it? Was he some mystical special person who knew the secret formula for success? No. He was simply real, he cared, and he connected.

He wasn't magic; he was powerfully human.

When he arrived early to meet and talk to the participants, he showed them that they were important. Words could never communicate that message so clearly.

By sharing his own blind spot, he was able to connect at a much deeper level. He had the courage to remove the mask of perfection and be vulnerable enough to let us see the man behind the title. By doing so, every person in the room could relate. They opened up their minds to what they could learn and how it could make a difference. By risking being real, he gave them permission to be real too. He gave them permission to be human and work on themselves and pass down what they learned to those they led. He spent maybe twenty-eight minutes in the room at most, and that investment will reap rewards for the organization for years to come. That's the power of connection.

PERFECTION VS. CONNECTION

We work so hard to get it right. We agonize over our slides and polish our pitch. Some of us are even lucky enough to have an entire communications team or a group of talented designers who tirelessly craft our message to hit every point and refute every argument, collectively aiming for perfection. Yet . . . I've seen a lot of great PowerPoint slides in my time that I couldn't recall an hour later. I've heard a lot of data that often sounds like it's being delivered by Charlie Brown's teacher. And I've seen pitches so polished that they sound like they came straight from a can—all shiny and new.

Points can be hit and arguments can be refuted, but the truth is, it doesn't matter how close to perfect we may come if we don't truly connect with the human beings in the room.

When I recall the presentations and courageous conversations that have stayed with me for years—the ones that have reached my soul and held on tight, that have changed me, inspired me, bridged my confidence, helped me see possibilities, lit a fire under my behind, and left me wanting to take action—they weren't perfect; they were so much more than perfect. They were human.

Simon's kickoff was a good example. To lead, to have presence, to influence, and to present powerfully, we've got to find a way to move past our need to be perfect and aim for something far more elusive yet critical. We must risk being *seen*. We must risk being so present that everything else fades to the background. We must be vulnerable enough to be real. We must risk connection.

Are we connecting with each other, for real? If not, then why not?

CONNECTION AT WORK

I remember standing in a circle, after a long day, surrounded by the beaming faces of a group that had just gone through OnStage Leadership together. We were talking about what had transpired over the course of the day, and one person said, "Well, we really know each other now, and that's a big change!"

Yes. It's true. They really knew each other. I smiled and said, "You know, we've spent a little over nine hours together, and look at how connected you are to one another! Think about all the people you've worked with for years, but don't know nearly this well. This feeling you have right now isn't something that's only accessible here; it's accessible to you every day."

I find it interesting how people tend to eschew connectedness in the workplace, and yet what a powerful force it can be. We tend to back-burner building the relationships that make our businesses work, when it's these very relationships that help us bring out our best and deliver collective greatness. Think about it: When you feel connected to someone, when you know them and care about them, you don't want to let them down. You'll go the extra mile. You're more apt to be honest with them, more likely to be invested in them, and more committed to ensuring they win. When I work with people I know and care about, I enjoy the task no matter what it is. It doesn't feel like work; it feels like a shared experience. Regardless of your role in the organization, you are a person first (this should not come as a revelation). Your core need for connectedness, whether you like to admit it or not, is even more foundational than your need for achievement.

So what steps can you take to feel more connected to people at work?

> ❝
> *Relationships help us bring our best*
> *and deliver collective greatness.*

Take Initiative

I read a blog post recently by a young finance intern who wanted to get to know people at his new place of work and wanted to feel more connected, and his question was, "How do I get invited out to lunch?" And I wanted to shake him and say, "Don't wait to get invited! Invite! Take the initiative!" If we're all waiting for someone else to go first, nobody is ever going to go. It doesn't have to be a long lunch or a sit-down thing. Make it easy to say yes to, and nine times out of ten, you'll get your yes. "Hey, I'm going to go grab some lunch (or coffee or fresh air, etc.). Would you like to join me?"

Be Curious

The truth is, people love to talk about themselves, but they want to know you're interested before they dive in. Learn to ask great questions and listen to their answers, and your relationships will soar. Steer away from closed-ended questions that will only give you a yes or no or one-word answer, and aim for rich, open-ended questions that will invite them to engage more fully. Be sincerely curious about what people love most about their work, about their passions, about how they got into their field, and why they do what they do, and it will unlock the foundation for a great conversation.

Be Present

Nobody is going to connect to you if you're not able to be fully present with them. Even though you've got a million things going on, be willing to set your phone aside and bring your full attention to the conversation, even if it's for a brief amount of time. If you can't do that, it's not likely that anything meaningful will ever get said, and powerful connections aren't made through small talk.

Listen for Commonalities

As you get to know someone, one of the fastest ways to cement a relationship is to learn what you have in common. Commonalities give us a jumping-off point for richer conversations. What's fascinating is that we often have more in common than we think; we just need to be willing to stay curious long enough. I've had incredible conversations with people from all over the world, who have different backgrounds, beliefs, and experiences, and have found common ground every time. Humans are humans.

Remove the Mask

It's important to take your mask off and let your authentic self shine through. Real connections cannot be made from behind a mask. The thing to remember is that, as human beings, something we all share is our hunger to be seen and appreciated for who we are. That's how we're wired. It is woven into our core need for belonging. But we have to make it safe for one another to truly show up. Have the courage to take your mask off first to give the other person permission to do the same so real connection is possible.

Share Personal Stories

Our personal stories are the investment we make to gain access to the hearts and minds of others—where connection lives. Stories require us to take our mask down, to be vulnerable, and to put some skin in the game. The amount of emotional energy we get back from others is only equal to the amount of energy we're willing to put out; our personal stories are our currency. Now, to be clear, some stories are appropriate to share in a work setting and some stories are not. Maintaining healthy personal boundaries is important. Generally speaking, if it's a story that you'd share with a therapist instead of a close colleague, it's likely not the right story to share. But, that said, most of us play it far too safe at work, not sharing anything meaningful about ourselves that allows others to know who we are and what we're about. It's important to let people in if we want to have powerful connections. Our stories make that possible.

Connect Like Your Life Depends on It

When someone takes the time to have a real conversation with you, don't take it for granted. While I know we're all terribly busy and important, making an investment in our relationships at work will pay dividends for years to come, so it's critical to be all-in. Pay attention to what's going on with the other person during your conversation. What do they need from you to experience you as genuine, worthy of trust, reliance, and belief? Listen for what they're not saying. Be fully present. Get real. Because the stakes are higher than you might imagine.

––––––

We spend a huge chunk of our lives at work, and it's no wonder that so many people feel disengaged when so little attention is focused on making our relationships more meaningful. But it doesn't have to be that way; we can make a different choice. We can choose to connect. We just have to be brave enough to go first.

Key Takeaways

→ *It's all about connection.*

→ *Leadership* is about connection. Either you connect in a way that people want to follow, or you don't.

→ *Influence* is about connection. Either you connect in a way that they want to listen and consider your point of view, or you lose the chance to effect change.

➤ *Presence* is irrelevant if you don't connect. If you're presenting and you don't connect with the people in your audience, you might as well be talking to yourself!

➤ To connect better at work:

> Take initiative
>
> Be curious
>
> Be present
>
> Listen for commonalities
>
> Remove the mask
>
> Share personal stories
>
> Connect like your life depends on it

➤ A brave leader's results are a by-product of their ability to truly connect with the hearts and minds of others.

20

Six Steps to Prepare for Impact

*Here was a place where real things were
going on. Here was a scene of vital action. Here
was a place where anything might happen.
Here was a place where something would
certainly happen. Here I might leave my bones.*

—WINSTON CHURCHILL, *MY EARLY LIFE*

True connection doesn't happen by accident. Like an actor who rehearses diligently to give a powerful performance, we must hone our craft. We must develop ourselves, elevate our thinking, and focus our actions to ensure we are set up for success. We must prepare for impact.

"But Kimberly," you may be thinking, "I don't have time to prepare. I'm barely able to get from one meeting to the next with my deliverables in hand, much less prepare to connect, for God's sake! What fantasy land are you living in?"

I'm sorry. I don't mean to minimize your plight; I know you're crazy busy. But here's what's real: It's not your busyness that's getting in the way of you preparing, it's your mindfulness. Preparing might take five to ten minutes at most. You can do it in the shower. You can do it on your commute into work. You can do it at your desk or in the hallway or in the line at Starbucks. Preparing doesn't take all that much time if you remember to do it. I promise you, if you do it, it will change your results. Dramatically.

So here's my six-step process to prepare for impact:

1. FOCUS YOUR ATTENTION

First, before you enter any situation, simply focus your attention. Bring your mind to the situation at hand and consider all of the people you might encounter. Now it's time for the Magic If. What do you know about the person(s) involved? What might they need from you? What fears, concerns, or worries might they have? What obstacles might they face?

How do you want them to *feel* after your connection? How do you want them to feel about you? How do you want them to feel about the project? How do you want them to feel about the organization (or your school, community, world, etc.)? How do you want them to feel about their possibilities? How do you want them to feel about themselves? Remember in every situation, it's important to balance emotion and logic—the elephant and the rider. By considering how you would like them to feel, you're partnering with their elephant. Things are less likely to go awry and more likely to work in your favor.

> **"**
> *Amazing results*
> *are a by-product of impact.*

The next question to ask yourself is what do you want them to *do* after they have connected with you? What action would you like them to take? Not in terms of giving you the result you want, which is self-oriented, but as a reflection that you had the impact that you wanted. Remember, your amazing results are the by-product of having an impact; they're not your focus.

For example, let's say you're at a sales meeting with a client (and you're the sales guy), and your Super Objective is to celebrate your clients' success. Imagine you've done a brilliant job of setting your Intentions and taking action to hit your bull's-eye. After your meeting, you hope your client feels confident and genuinely valued. The action you might want them to take directly after your meeting might be to invite you to lunch. Or maybe it's that they'll be so excited that they'll want to put the next meeting on their calendar right away. Or maybe, when their boss sticks her head in the door to say hello, your client can't wait to introduce you. Will you get the business or more business or land the sale? The likelihood is much higher if you pay attention to the impact you have than it

> *How do you want them to feel? What do you want them to do? What is the impact you want to have?*

will be if you go in to strictly sell the guy. And you'll get so much more in the process. You'll get an advocate and a friend (which could lead to more business). You'll get to experience yourself showing up as your best, real, most powerful self. You'll feel more engaged. Work will stop feeling like work, because you're doing what you are driven to do. You'll get to bring your most brave self to the meeting. And yes, don't worry, you'll get to hit your goals.

What actions can you take to ensure to the best of your ability that they *feel* what you want them to feel, *do* what you want them to do—to have the impact you want to have?

The actions you're going to take? That's where you focus your attention.

2. PREPARE AUTHENTICALLY

Okay, so this step may take some time. But it's time you likely would have invested anyway, and now it will be more effectively spent, as it has the benefit of the focus preparation you just did in the shower.

Let's go back to our definition of authenticity. Are you *genuine, worthy of trust, reliance, and belief*? Given everything you have considered about the person(s) involved in your situation, what will they need from you in order to find you genuine, worthy of trust, reliable, and believable? How do you need to prepare to ensure they experience you as authentic?

How you prepare when you're going to meet with your boss will be different than how you prepare to meet with a client, your team, or a recruiter. What kind of research will you need to do? What do you need to bring with you to the meeting? What stories might you share? What supporting data might you need to gather? What questions could you ask? How might you dress? How formal is the setting? What language would be appropriate? What are the boundaries for discussion?

What obstacles might you face in this situation when working to achieve your Super Objective? What Intentions might you use to get closer to your bull's-eye? How can you prepare to overcome your obstacles and take the best actions in your situation?

3. BREATHE AND RELEASE TENSION

Do you know how you show up in the face of stress and anxiety? What happens to you physically, emotionally, and mentally? Where do you carry your tension? Breathe deeply. Identify your tension and deal with it *before* entering the situation.

———

See! That's all the preparation you need to do. That wasn't bad, was it? The next two steps take place in real time, during your situation. Beginning with . . .

4. BE PRESENT

Take the mask down and mute your phone. Fully show up and connect like your life depends on it. Shepherd your mind to keep it in the here and now. Listen with a high-stakes awareness. Cocreate with the other person or people in the space. Are they with you? How do you know?

5. PAY ATTENTION TO IMPACT

Authenticity lies in the eye of the beholder. No matter your Intention, if what you're doing is not having the impact on the other individual(s) that you are hoping it will have, it's on you to flex and adjust your actions (not adjust who you are) to ensure that you're taking into account the needs of the others in the situation, *without judgment*. How they experience you, or how they experience what you say, is not right or wrong; it just is. Great results demand that you deal with what is real, not what you think should be.

6. CREATE RITUALS

This last step is an ongoing process to set yourself up for long-term success. One of the best ways to ensure consistently high performance is to ritualize your preparation. Jonathan Fields, in his book *Uncertainty: Turning Fear and Doubt into Fuel for Brilliance*, calls rituals *certainty anchors*—they're "something known and reliable when . . . you may otherwise feel you're spinning off in a million different directions." I love my certainty anchors.

> *Great results demand that you deal with what is real, not what you think should be.*

We only have so much mental energy, so for me, I want to conserve it where I can so I can spend it where I want. In my life, ritual is everything. On days that I teach or speak, I ritualize the time I wake up, what I eat, where I sit, and how I prepare. Almost every activity leading up to a high-stakes situation I ritualize—a call, a meeting, or a presentation.

Ritual is also my powerful daily practice. For example, every day when I go for my walk, I walk at the same time, every morning, taking the same route, on the same side of the street. My friends make fun of me, but it's teasing I'm willing to endure because it works. When I walk, it becomes almost meditative. I don't have to think about where I'm going or how much time it's going to take; I just go. And in doing so, my creative mind is at work—problem solving, ideating, and envisioning. This is fuel for propelling myself forward. Truth be told, if I didn't have my ritual in place, the whole walking thing wouldn't happen. Life gets busy and it's hard to fit it in. And if I wait until the end of a long day, I'm spent. I don't have the willpower to go out there and exercise. Left to my own devices, I'd curl up with a glass of wine and my book club book or mindlessly peruse my Facebook feed, and my three miles of cardio would be out the window.

Gretchen Rubin, the queen of habits, who wrote *Better Than Before: What I Learned about Making and Breaking Habits*, insists that the key to willpower conservation is to turn behaviors into habits. I take it a step further and ritualize my habits. This is what I do and this is how I do it. So when I step outside my ritualized agenda, I've more of myself to give, more creativity to express, and more energy to share. I'm more powerful in myself. Artists and creatives, business gurus, athletes, spiritual leaders, writers, and philosophers have been touting the benefits of ritual for centuries. This is what I do and this is how I do it. Former President Obama and Facebook's CEO Mark Zuckerberg both wear essentially the same thing every day, because they have so many decisions to make that getting dressed is one thing they don't want to think about—smart guys. Rituals help strengthen our focus and concentration, combat the physiological sensations we experience in times of uncertainty, and make it possible for us to bring our best.

If you want to have an impact that gets you powerful results, you can't pull it from out of nowhere. The unfortunate truth is that no matter how talented you are, or how busy and important you might be, you have to prepare. Brave leaders don't wing it.

Key Takeaways

→ Great results don't happen by accident—brave leaders prepare.

→ Here are my six steps for preparing powerfully for any situation you face:

1. Focus your attention.
2. Prepare authentically.
3. Breathe and release tension.
4. Be present.
5. Pay attention to impact.
6. Create rituals.

21

Presenting Bravely

*Let us make a special effort to stop
communicating with each other,
so we can have some conversation.*

—MARK TWAIN

He stood, rigid and frightened, like a wild animal caught in the headlights on the highway. His eyes darted about, avoiding the audience at all cost. He kept wiping his hands on his pants, giving away his sweaty palms. When he started to speak, he robotically read from his notes, as if being forced at gunpoint. Breathe, I silently told him with my eyes. Please breathe. But he never looked at us, so he couldn't see we were on his side.

———

I've had the privilege of seeing thousands of people present, and what is evident is that the issue isn't about them not knowing how to make eye contact or gestures or how to move about the space. The issue lies deeper than that. When told in their performance reviews that they need to improve their presenting skills, human resources swoops in to save the day with a reputable presentation skills class and they're given the prescription for presenting, like the yucky medicine we had to take when we were kids. Take this, and it'll be better. You'll be fixed. Hold your hands like this. Don't do that. Move like this. Don't move like that. They dutifully study and practice and do their best to incorporate the laundry list of shoulds and should nots, and still . . . when they present . . . not so good.

> *Powerful presenting is not about learning more skills; it's about mastering how you show up in the face of vulnerability.*

Here's the thing: It's not because they're simply bad presenters. We like to think that. We like to think, *Well, some of us got it, and some don't.* And yes, some people are more naturally gifted presenters, but it's complete hooey to believe that it's a skill relegated to a talented few. We just need help getting to the root of the problem. It's not about learning more skills; it's about mastering how you show up in the face of vulnerability.

Speaking is an inherently vulnerable task. When standing in front of a group of people, we feel exposed. As Maslow observed in his hierarchy of needs, we are so hardwired in our need for belonging that the mere possibility of rejection feels like a threat. Our amygdala, sensing danger, works overtime, sending all kinds of crazy chemicals through our system in red alert. *Fight or flight! Fight or flight!* it urges us, as our heart rate increases, our breathing grows shallow, and our heads start to swim. *What was I going to say . . . ?*

It is in this setting that we expect ourselves to present powerfully.

When everything inside us screams, "Run! You're gonna die!" you've got to stay up there and somehow find a way to get your point across and deliver your message while being charming, influential, and inspiring people to action. Fat chance.

Knowing what you shouldn't do with your hands doesn't help you at all, because all of a sudden, as you stand up there getting ready for your big client presentation, all you can think of is what to do with your hands. Learning how to scan the room with your eyes so people think you're making eye contact only succeeds in making you more nervous. The sensations mount. Your reputation as a bad speaker has been sealed. But it doesn't have to be that way.

When we're vulnerable and don't feel safe, we unconsciously find ways to hide, protect, or defend ourselves. It's not rational behavior; it's a survival mechanism.

Some of us protect ourselves by making ourselves smaller. We round our shoulders and slouch. Or we lock our elbows in tight and gesture like a *T. rex*, our hands helplessly flopping about, attached to what look like miniature appendages. Some of us prefer to protect, with arms folded or hands clasped in front of our bodies like a force field (or, often with men, a fig leaf). Some of us try to hide. We lower our voice (maybe if they can't hear me they'll go away!) or evade eye contact (maybe if I can't see them, they can't see me!). Some of us hold our notes like a shield, never using them, but clutching them tightly in case we need to fend off an attack. Some of us lock our hands away in pockets, hoping that they'll "stay" as directed. And some of us decide to take the opposite approach. We overcompensate, gesturing wildly and pacing frantically, channeling our adrenaline through our feet.

These are all things we do in attempts to deal with the vulnerability we feel. Our brains, as they consult our historical lines, try to make meaning of the risk they sense and send warning signals throughout our bodies in the form of body sensations that are impossible to ignore.

It's not that you don't know how to present; it's that you don't understand how to override your amygdala to free yourself from your body's hardwired goal of keeping you safe. Logically you may know what to do, but physiologically it feels dangerous.

One of the most important things to understand is that presenting bravely has nothing to do with giving a presentation. Just thinking about giving a presentation is enough to make many of us break out in a cold sweat. It's the way we think about it that causes all the internal hoopla.

> **Presenting bravely has nothing to do with giving a presentation.**

Being able to present powerfully isn't about mastering eye contact or figuring out what to do with your awkward hands; it's about mastering your *thinking*. It's a focus issue. How you think about it will impact how your body's autopilot deals with it. If it shows up on your radar as a scary, risky, threatening ordeal, your amygdala will treat it as such and send corresponding sensations racing through your body to persuade you to rush to safety.

If, however, no threat appears, you are cleared to do what you need to do: connect. So if you're not supposed to think of presenting as presenting, then how on earth do you think about it?

[Spoiler alert! I am about to simplify what has taken millions of people working countless hours to convince you and everyone else that presenting is reserved for the talented and that you either have the "presenting gene" or you don't. And if you haven't been endowed with the gift at birth, you need to take dozens of courses, hire a coach, or spend years in Toastmasters to overcome your destiny as a terrible presenter.]

Here's the big secret that nobody is telling you: presenting is simply a conversation. That's it. It's nothing more complicated than that. You have been having conversations all your life. You're good at them. When you have a conversation, you don't think about what to do with your hands. Your hands take care of themselves. You don't think about eye contact or whether you move too much. You don't think about your notes. Unless you're a teenage boy talking to a cute girl for the first time, you don't think about your sweaty palms or butterflies in your stomach or saying the right thing. You simply have a conversation. You connect.

It's the same thing when you present. Whether you're presenting to a group of seven people or two thousand people, a good presentation is simply a conversation. It's a conversation with one person, then another person, then another. Presentations are real conversations, for which you're completely present, one person at a time.

Now, you might argue that you can't have a real conversation with two thousand people in the span of an hour-long keynote, and you'd be right. But if you have an honest-to-goodness conversation—a real connection for which you're fully present—with the individual human beings in front of you, I guarantee that every person will feel as if you're talking directly to them. What they pick up is true connection, not a speech that's being delivered in a vacuum. They will feel included.

I would love to tell you that I instinctively understood the power of having a conversation from the platform at an early age, but sadly that's not the case. Having come from a theater background, I was used to having my script. I would work my script and choreograph every movement, direct every pause, aiming for perfection. For years, I would speak, and it would be fine, but it was more like a performance. I'd be on stage doing my thing, the audience out there passively watching, and when it was over, I always felt lonely. There was no real connection because I did my thing, alone.

> **_A good presentation is simply a conversation._**

The feedback was positive, but not great. I couldn't figure out why my results weren't better. I was working so hard!

When I started doing corporate training, I was pretty scared. How could I control my presentation when there were these unpredictable participants in the room? I couldn't. They each brought their own histories, experiences, insights, questions, unique personalities, and learning styles. While there may have been a facilitator's guide, there was no real playbook for success. The first few months I taught, I felt like I was going to throw up; I felt that vulnerable. I held on so tight, trying to control the outcome. I didn't trust myself to let go.

Dancer and choreographer Agnes de Mille once said, "Living is a form of not being sure, not knowing what's next or how. The moment you know how, you begin to die a little. The artist never entirely knows. We guess. We may be wrong, but we take leap after leap in the dark."

This so perfectly captures the experience of brave leadership and, especially, presenting bravely. We can't know what's looming in the unknown, yet in order to connect powerfully, we must leap anyway.

And so I did. In the throes of my own discomfort and fear, I took the leap and, to my relief, my participants caught me. Instead of staying on script, I'd allow our conversations to pull us in new and exciting directions. We'd collectively excavate the aha moments, their discoveries and insights leading the way. In the sessions that followed, with each new group of participants, I leapt again and again and again, and each time I'd risk stepping off the cliff of my security and embracing the unknown, they would be there. The more I would relinquish control, the more they would engage. They never let me fall. My stories ignited their stories. My questions sparked their questions. Together, the content grew richer and the conversations deeper. I was no longer teaching a fixed set of ideas, but rather providing a springboard for exploration. Each of us learned from the other, contributing to the overall experience and growth of the collective. It was no longer my *program*; it was our *experience*—cocreation at its best.

The hardest thing for me to understand was that, in order to leap, I first had to find a way to trust—myself, my participants, and the process. It didn't feel smart to trust. How could I trust when I couldn't know what would happen? How could I trust when I had just met the participants for the first time? How could I trust when the possibility for failure was so high? How could I trust when every cell in my body screamed, "It's not safe!"?

Without trust, one cannot leap. Without leaping, one cannot connect. There is no conversation.

Sure, I could memorize the content, anticipate questions, research industries and culture, bring in assessments, and conduct interviews, but I could never be sure what would happen. Maybe I'd hit a hot button and it would send the conversation into a tailspin, or everyone would disengage. Maybe someone would misread my intent or challenge the ideas or mock the process. With so many things outside my realm of control, why on earth would I trust? I know I'm not alone in this.

The biggest obstacle for most presenters is that they don't trust. They don't trust themselves most of all. This lack of trust has nothing to do with experience, ability, or training. I've seen it in seasoned senior executives as often as I do young adults coming right out of college. Trust in the face of vulnerability is hard.

I remember watching one executive, standing on the stage poised and professional. Her impressive background, the Ivy League schools, and a fancy title with a Fortune 500 seemed to go with the expensive pantsuit she wore. Her presentation was articulate and well constructed. She was controlled, with a little too much polish. I

> *The biggest obstacle for most people when they present is that they don't trust themselves.*

felt like she was speaking *at* me instead of *to* me. She seemed removed and aloof. From the moment she stepped on stage, she clutched her notes like a shield. But she didn't look at them, not once.

Who is this beautiful, intelligent, seemingly successful woman? I asked myself as I watched her. I couldn't tell. She had given a full presentation, and yet even when she finished, I felt no more connected to her than I had before she began. She was still as much of a stranger to me. She was masked, protected, and untrusting. But it wasn't me she didn't trust; she didn't trust herself.

Over the years, I've learned to read the signs. We all have our tells—those little things we do that give us away, even when we try our hardest to hide how we feel. When people present, I can spot them right away. The notes are one dead giveaway. There are hundreds of tells. One is evasive eye contact, or looking right through the people in your audience, instead of connecting with the human beings you're trying to reach. Being too controlled or too careful is another—masked to perfection. These are all mechanisms to combat the vulnerability we feel. And, like protective armor worn in battle, they may get us through the presentation, but they're not likely to get us any closer to being heard.

When I gave her feedback later in the day, I called her on it.

"You don't trust yourself," I said gently. "You were clear and articulate, and you knew exactly what you wanted to say, and yet you evaded your audience and held onto your notes for dear life. You didn't need them."

The look on her face, a mixture of bewilderment and relief, told me I had hit on a painful truth that she had hid for years. It was one I recognized because I've struggled with it myself and have seen it in hundreds of others—men, women, emerging leaders, and senior executives. No one is immune.

"Oh my gosh!" she said, "I know!" Then, with a panicked look in her eyes, like she'd just been found out, she pleaded in a hushed voice, "What do I do? I *need* my notes."

"No. You don't need your notes. You are good. You are well prepared. You are better than you know. Trust yourself. Focus on connecting, and let your audience bridge your confidence. They want to be there for you, but they can't if you don't let them in. You have to risk connecting."

Easier said than done.

Now don't get me wrong, I'm not encouraging you or anyone else to walk into a presentation without your notes and pull it straight out of thin air. Preparation is critical. But like an actor who rehearses before they take the stage, we must let go of the script in order to perform powerfully. We must take down our protective gear and risk being vulnerable in an effort to truly connect. If we don't connect, what's the point?

When this senior executive took the stage later in the day to speak, I could see her eyes dancing, alive with a combination of nervous anticipation and excitement. She was there, fully present with us. And her presence was electric. It was as if she simply needed permission to let her real self show up. When she spoke, every person in the audience was mesmerized. She held us in the palm of her hand the entire time. It was breathtaking. At the end, the audience leapt to their feet in explosive applause. As I watched her, I felt hot tears stream down my face, because I knew what a leap of faith she had taken. I knew how hard it was, and I knew that it would change her forever.

While the risk she took will certainly make a difference in the way she leads and presents in the future, and she'll likely reap tremendous benefits professionally, I saw a much bigger reward—a reward that lies in wait for all those who risk true connection. When we find a way to trust ourselves, we don't only learn to leap. We gain the wings to fly.

PREPARING TO TRUST

Telling you to simply trust yourself isn't likely going to override the intense sensations you'll feel when you need to take the stage. It's important to set yourself up for success, and I've found that the way I prepare makes a tremendous difference.

Preparing to trust yourself is the same as preparing for impact. Before you leap, you need to tap into your most powerful self. As I made the transition from being a control freak to letting go, I became conscious about what was making a difference in terms of how I prepared. I'd study like crazy, inhaling everything I could learn about the topics I was teaching. I wanted to be a resource, add value, and enrich our discussions. I ritualized my preparations. On days I was in the classroom, I'd get up at four thirty a.m. and play through the day in my head, visualizing the participants and walking in their shoes. What might they need from me? I'd ensure my transitions were clean and any directions I'd need to provide were clear.

I'd think through the obstacles that I might face and the impact I wanted to have. How did I want them to feel? What did I want them to do? What actions could I take? I'd remove all tension and bring my full attention to the space. Instead of spending my time wordsmithing, polishing, and perfecting, I was invested in taking *purposeful action*. Rather than showing up to teach as a tense and self-conscious mess, I was relaxed and focused on the participants. Like an athlete on game day, I was ready—no notes, no anxiety, just excitement for the journey to unfold.

And it worked. It was fun, and the time flew by! At first, I was kind of surprised. It felt easy. I had never experienced that before. It wasn't heavy and hard, a burden for me to carry, as it was a shared experience for which we each brought our part. It was a conversation.

I would go through this process every time I'd teach. Even though I'd teach multiple sessions every month, each time I would prepare for impact. While I knew the content backward and forward, I didn't let that stop me from preparing to connect. Remember, ritual strengthens concentration and increases performance.

In the past, I had always prepared with the intent to be perfect—to not mess up. Yes, I wanted to do a good job, but I also wanted to prove myself. To impress others so that I'd get the job, opportunity, accolades, respect, or approval, the list goes on, for which I yearned. Now there was nothing wrong with that wanting—it was human—but it didn't serve me. For in doing so, I unwittingly put my focus completely on myself. The impact I hoped to have was self-oriented—a job, opportunities, accolades, respect, and approval for *me*. Yet since I couldn't trust myself to be perfect, I was set up to fail, which made it difficult to allow myself to be vulnerable.

As I uncovered how to prepare for impact, I shifted my focus away from surviving, proving, and impressing and turned my attention to purposeful action. What did I know about the people I would be teaching? How could I walk in their shoes (Magic If)? What was the impact I wanted to have? Did I want to draw them in? Did I want to hold up the mirror so they could see themselves as I saw them? Or did I want to stir them to action? How did I want them to feel? What did I want them to do? I stopped thinking about myself completely, and in doing so, the lines that defined my life and the sensations that accompany vulnerability melted away. I experienced a natural ease and joy that I hadn't felt since I was girl. And even though I wasn't seeking them, jobs, opportunities, and accolades would find me. Slowly, through this new process, I learned to let go and trust myself—first in the classroom, and then on the platform. For the first time in my career since I had left the theater, I focused my attention *outside myself*, and it worked—a powerful insight that Stanislavski had more than a century ago.

As it turns out, they're no different. A theater audience or a large corporate audience sitting in the dark is essentially no different than an intimate group in the classroom. They all want the same thing—to be actively engaged. When I stopped thinking of giving a presentation as giving a PRESENTATION and started seeing it as simply having a conversation, it changed everything for me. I no longer felt like I had eight hundred eyeballs staring at me, because I would be completely focused and present with one person at a time, working to have an impact on that one person and truly connecting with them. What I discovered was that when I was fully present with one specific person in an audience, for real, they would connect and engage, always giving me something back, to which I could respond. No two moments would be the same. I no longer gave a prepared standard presentation, because it was a living, evolving, collaborative moment in time. We were there for each other. I was no longer alone on the stage. I would connect fully with one person, then another person, then another, completely present and simply having a conversation.

Prepare to trust. Focus your attention outside yourself. Leap. Let them be there for you. Connect. They're on your side

I remember, back in college, when I was getting ready to audition for my first show in the theater department. I was a music major at the time and had no idea what I was doing, so I was terrified. I was sure that I would make a fool out of myself, that they'd all laugh at me, and that the humiliation would linger for decades to come. (I was prone to the dramatic.) Huddled in the hallway of the music department, outside the girls' bathroom, I practiced my sixteen bars of "Life Upon the Wicked Stage" (from *Showboat*—I was into the classics at the time), prepping for my audition.

With students streaming in and out of the bathroom next to me, I sang for the graduate teaching assistant who had so generously offered to coach me, and I felt ridiculous. The more I practiced, the more certain I was of my impending failure. "This is stupid," I said, rolling my eyes. "I'll never get cast."

She sighed and, patting the linoleum floor for me to sit next to her, said seriously, "I'm going to let you in on a secret. Most people auditioning don't realize this, but if you do, it will make a huge difference."

"What is it?" I responded eagerly.

"They're on your side," she whispered, smiling.

"What?"

"The directors—they're on your side. They don't want you to be bad. They want you to be great, as that makes their job a lot easier. They're not looking for you to fail; they're hoping for you to be awesome."

I have to admit that at the time I didn't believe her. I thought it was simply a ruse to keep me practicing. But fifteen years later, when I directed my first play and ran my first audition, her words came rushing back. She was right. As the director, I was on their side. When the actors so bravely stood on that stage, singing their hearts out, praying to be cast, I didn't hope for them to fail. I wanted them to be great. In my mind, I cheered them on. *You've got this. You can do it.*

This lesson is one I seem to have to remind myself of over and over again. We see what we look for. When you look for judgment, disapproval, or competition, you are guaranteed to see it. Likewise, if you look for positive intent and support, you will find it. Most of the time, it is sitting right in front of you, silently cheering you on.

Your clients don't want you to be bad when you're pitching them; they want you to be their solution. Your team doesn't want you to embarrass yourself; they want to enjoy your presentation. Your trade show audience doesn't want to be bored; they want to be actively engaged. With rare exception, most people who will ever see you present want you to succeed. They're on your side.

Again and again, I have found this to be true. Whether I was in the classroom or on the stage, when I would prepare in a way that I could trust myself enough to fully let go and focus on impact, my participants would also show up. When I would risk true connection with another person, they wouldn't let me fall. If I was willing to be vulnerable and let them in, they'd be willing to meet me there. But I had to go first. (Please note: vulnerability cannot be faked. You can't pretend to be vulnerable. False vulnerability feels like manipulation, and people know.)

TEACHER, TEACH THYSELF

I would love to tell you that once you've experienced the power of true connection from the platform that you'll carry this knowing with you always and never go back to your old ways, but it doesn't work like that. The higher the stakes, the easier it is to forget. And nobody is impervious.

———

I stepped out of the car and into the oven, wild-eyed and desperate, looking for a place to eat. It was March in Dallas, and the temperature was already in the high nineties. Heat poured off the parking lot in waves. I hadn't eaten since seven a.m. in New York, and it showed. Two airports, 1,600 miles, and nine hours later, I was no longer a nice person. I was *hangry*. My hands shook. I had to find food fast and pull myself together. Spying a small Mediterranean grill at the end of the strip mall, I made a break for it, sweat pouring down my neck. Food! Surely, that will make it all better. Breathe, I reminded myself as I ate and savored the air conditioning. Still, that feeling in my throat lingered—that familiar tightness. Emotion pooled behind my eyes, threatening to escape. *It's not low blood sugar after all*, I thought as I noticed that my hands still trembled. *It's fear.*

The day before my TEDx Talk, I was a mess. Even though I teach how to present powerfully in the face of stress and anxiety, I was convinced I'd publicly blow it, and it would be recorded for the entire world to see. It felt like it was an all-or-nothing thing. I pictured my fall from grace going viral, my business crashing, and my life's work coming to an end. My imagination spiraled out of control, and the sensations mounted.

As I crossed the scorched parking lot to my car, I felt nauseated. *How can this be happening?* I thought. *Crap, crap, crap, crap, CRAP! No!* My heart pounded in my chest as I slipped inside my rental car and cranked the air. I could barely breathe. I checked myself in the mirror and frowned at my melted face. I sat there, horrified by myself. My suit was damp with perspiration and my mind was swimming. *I can hardly remember my name. How am I going to give this talk?* In twenty-two hours I was scheduled to speak on the TEDx stage about being brave, and I felt like a complete imposter.

In the hours that followed, between my anxiety attack in the parking lot and my talk, I prepared. I prepared to trust and leap when I didn't feel like leaping.

I knew, logically, that my shaking hands, tight throat, nausea—all of it—were simply red flags. I knew, logically, that my amygdala was having a party in my brain and the sensations I was feeling were evidence of a chemical reaction. I knew, logically, that I had presented thousands of times before and that I was completely capable and had something valuable to share. All the logic in the world didn't help me.

I also knew that the painful sensations I was experiencing would keep coming unless I could take my attention off the doomsday chatter in my brain and distract my overprotective amygdala.

Teacher, teach thyself. Focus on impact. Focus on impact. Focus on impact became my mantra. And like small bites of bread that nourish the starving, my courage returned one morsel at a time. I found my bravery as I focused on others.

Back at the hotel, I pulled out the photographs I had packed in anticipation of feeling this way and spread them out around my hotel room. I was surrounded. Dozens of pictures of my most inspirational and cherished participants looked back at me from every angle—extraordinary men and women who had overcome great obstacles to find their courage in my classroom.

This is for you, I thought as I began working to make an impact through my TEDx Talk, in my hotel room. I was alone, but not alone.

The next morning, as I walked into the TEDx lobby and looked around at all the people milling about, I thought, *This has never been about me. It's always been about them. This is about the two women outside on the bench who greeted me so warmly, and the young dark-haired girl standing in line chewing her thumbnail, and the tall guy in the brown sports jacket, leaning against the wall in conversation.* As I walked around and got to know some of the wonderful people I would get to connect with from the stage, I relaxed into myself. My focus shifted off of me and on to the people I was meeting, to my friends who had come to support me, to all the people I had met, and the others I wanted to know. I was there for them—all the people out there who, like me, sometimes struggle with being brave.

As the lights dimmed, I stood in the dark, taking deep, low breaths, rolling my neck gently and my shoulders back. *What is the impact I am here to have?* I asked myself. I am here to connect these amazing people to their best selves, one person at a time. That's why I'm here.

————

A conversation is reciprocal. It requires every person involved to actively participate. Your audience wants to be there for you, but you have to let them. If when you present, you're focused on yourself—on how awkward you feel or what your audience might be thinking about you—the audience will disengage, their role in the conversation unclear. Your awkwardness causes them to feel equally awkward. But if you're actively working to make an impact on them by focusing your energy outward to connect with each person as a unique individual, like Newton's law of motion, you will experience an equal and opposite reaction. The energy you put out will be returned. The people with whom you connect will work equally hard. When you leap, they will catch you.

WHAT GETS IN YOUR WAY?

When I coach someone around presenting bravely, I simply look at two things. I pay attention to what's going on for them emotionally, mentally, physically, and vocally and how it's working for them (in terms of connection). And I look at what's going on emotionally, mentally, physically, and vocally that *dissipates* their ability to connect powerfully. That's it. What are you doing that helps you connect, and what are you doing that gets in your way? It's all about connection. I don't believe in rules. I don't think there is a one-size-fits-all solution. I've seen incredible presenters who have broken every rule imaginable, and yet they capture my attention and hold on tight, and I've seen rule-abiding speakers who have bored me to tears. Rules don't work. Are you connecting or not? When presenting, that's all that matters. Don't worry about the rules; worry about connection.

If you want to present powerfully, begin by asking yourself these questions: What's getting in my way of truly connecting? What do I do to protect myself when I feel vulnerable? These are hard questions to answer, not because you may not know (which is possible), but because the answers can be incredibly uncomfortable.

As I've mentioned, my instinct, when I feel vulnerable, is to try to be perfect. I hate that that's the case. I know better, and yet that's what naturally shows up for me. I want every word to be right and every phrase to illuminate. In my desire to engage, inspire, and stir people to action, I stress and fret and practice and polish. I am so hard on myself and so far from experiencing ease and grace and joy. My attempts to be perfect sabotage my process, my confidence, and most of all, my ability to truly connect. There is no perfect. Perfect is an illusion. But when I feel vulnerable, that's what happens for me *mentally*.

And when I'm doing a number on myself mentally, trying to be perfect but completely aware that I'm not, it manifests *physically* as well. I clench my jaws, my shoulders feel like someone has poured cement into them, and my chest tightens. My mind floods with white noise, like the after-hour TVs of my childhood. (Could it be I'm holding my breath?) The more stress hormones I produce, the more my body responds. The more perfection I seek, the harder it is to attain.

My *emotions* flood in response. I feel overwhelmed. I feel crushing self-doubt. I feel fear of certain humiliation and being found out.

The last thing I want is for people to see me in this state, so I plaster my "everything is great" mask on my face, hoping to lock my vulnerability in tight. But the problem is this: If you hide the vulnerability, you lose truth. It's in the vulnerability that you can find the magic.

How does all this manifest when I present? If I haven't caught myself in the throes of a perfection attack, I'll push—push the energy, push the emotion. Amped up on unfocused adrenaline, I can become overly animated and sometimes shrill. When I'm trying to be perfect, I can come across canned. While I'd hunger for connection, I'd feel alone. As the vulnerability would increase, I'd work harder to make it perfect, the feelings would mount, the sensations continue, and my presentation would suffer.

> *If you hide the vulnerability, you lose truth. It's in the vulnerability that you can find the magic.*

What's getting in my way of truly connecting? What do I do to protect myself when I feel vulnerable? All of the above.

It's not pretty, but that's what's real. However uncomfortable it might be for me to deal with this truth, it also sets me free. Remember, like with your bull's-eye, once you have clarity of focus, you can take targeted action.

What do you do to protect yourself when you feel vulnerable? What's getting in your way of truly connecting?

Armed with awareness, you can take action. Without awareness, you leave too much up to chance. I knew that I was my own biggest obstacle when I presented, but for years I couldn't name what I did that got in my way. The core problem wasn't my shrill voice or my overly animated face. The core problem was my focus. I was focused on being perfect. I was focused on protecting myself from failure. I was focused on proving myself. I was focused on impressing. Embarrassing as it is to admit, my entire focus was on me! I was not, sadly, focused on connecting to have an impact on the individuals in my audience.

Once I could name the specific things I did to protect myself when I felt vulnerable—the things that got in the way of connecting—I could use them as guideposts for action.

Anytime I found myself worried about what others would think, I could redirect my focus on specific purposeful action. What impact do I want to have on that lovely woman in the third row? Taking myself off the hot seat allowed my authentic and more powerful self to shine through.

When I experienced loneliness from the stage, I could use it as a cue that I was not letting others in and to lower my mask to let myself be seen, one person at a time. True connection cannot happen from behind a mask. Am I having a real conversation with a person, or am I speaking at them as a group?

As I would feel my heart rate increase and the fluttering in my stomach, I could stop and take a deep, low breath. I could roll my shoulders back, lengthen my spine, and (if I hadn't stepped on stage yet) gently massage my jaws to remove the tension, allowing the sensations to flow through me, rather than hijacking my performance.

As my breathing would steady and my connection to others improve, my voice and gestures would follow suit. With more air, my voice would resonate a little lower. My hands would relax and take care of themselves in honest conversation.

What I have found is that the more I connect, the less I have to work on presenting. When we present bravely, it becomes an authentic extension of who we are—a sharing of ideas and information, rather than a reflection of our skills, knowledge, or worth. We become the conduit to a shared experience.

PURPOSEFUL MOVEMENT

Here's the good news: If you've done your homework, you're actively engaging in what you want moment to moment from your audience, and you're present and connecting to the people in front of you; whether your movements are purposeful no longer becomes an issue because everything you're doing is tied to purpose.

Nevertheless, I should say something about purposeful movement in the realm of speaking. We've all seen it (and, let's face it, have done it)— the speakers who pace or shuffle their feet side to side or gesture awkwardly. Their movements don't seem to have anything to do with what they're saying. In order to be heard, a speaker needs to remove anything that doesn't serve the intent or the message, and that includes movement. I'm not saying you shouldn't move—quite the contrary! What I'm saying is that when you move, do it with purpose.

You want to propel yourself through space to get to the other side of the stage? Great. But do it only if you're trying to connect to a human being (for real) who is sitting over there. Let that person draw you to the other side. You want to gesture wildly in the air? Terrific! But be sure it's connected to an image you're actively remembering. You want to stand perfectly still? That makes sense if you're trying to center your audience's attention and draw them in. That's purposeful. It just doesn't work when you're doing it because you're terrified.

Every movement (or nonmovement) during your speech, in a perfect world, would have a purpose. Why are you doing what you're doing? It's a lofty goal and something that takes years to do well. But it's a goal worth striving for if you truly want to be heard.

KNOW YOUR OBSTACLES

With every audience, you will face both visible and hidden obstacles. In order to have the biggest impact, it's important to identify all the obstacles that might be lurking and work to actively, moment to moment, overcome them. Some obstacles are obvious: the person in the group who looks bored or disinterested, the individual who actively challenges you, the room temperature, time constraints, and so on. But more often, the obstacles are less apparent. What are the elephants in the room? What fears or anxieties might exist? What frustrations or objections might they have? How might your audience feel about being there, or about you as a presenter, or about themselves? What other things might occupy their minds? What emotions might you trigger? Remember, presence is a by-product of harnessed attention to overcome obstacles. Thus, obstacles can increase your presence if you work to actively overcome them to achieve your Super Objective. Avoiding them or pretending they don't exist won't serve you.

UNDERSTAND YOUR AUDIENCE

If the people in your audience are going to experience you as genuine, worthy of trust, reliable, and believable, then it's critical to consider their needs. What senior leaders will need from you in a presentation will be quite different than what your direct reports or clients or colleagues might need. The success of your presentation will be a direct by-product of your ability to understand your audience.

(Please note: These are generalities and not absolutes!)

When Presenting to Your Colleagues, Individual Contributors, or Clients

Use stories and metaphors to bring your information and data to life and create an emotional connection. Be sure to outline the reasons why things are being done. Help them connect to why they matter. Share why you personally care. If you don't truly care, that's a red flag. If you don't care, neither will they. You have to find something, however small, to sincerely care about and support or you cannot authentically deliver your message. Transparency is critical. If they sense you're holding something back, they'll disengage.

When Presenting to Senior Leaders

Senior leaders have limited time, so it's important to come prepared and use concise language. Typically, senior leaders do not want a lot of information and backstory. They expect you to critically think through your challenges ahead of time, identify the best course of action, and provide the business case to support your thinking. Bring them conclusions. Use metaphors to bring your data to life, and keep your stories brief and relevant. While you may not realize it, senior leaders are people too. You still need to work to connect to their want, and you'll have to do it quickly. Begin with a thought-provoking story or metaphor to engage their hearts and curiosity (yes, senior leaders have hearts too) so you earn the right to share your data and information. If you don't pique their interest from the beginning and find a way to command their attention, you'll lose them before you even begin. Think, *Why might they care?* If they want more information, they'll ask for it, so be sure you have the supporting data to back up your statements and ideas. Anticipate their questions and prepare accordingly. Ask yourself what they need in order to trust, and rely on your decisions, your conclusions, and your ability to lead others.

A WORD ABOUT CONTENT DEVELOPMENT

Think about the people who will be sitting in your audience. Picture them in your mind. They are waiting to hear what you have to say. What is it that you want? What are you passionate about? Why should they trust you? Why do they care? Why do you? Taking into account your Super

Objective (the impact you want to have outside yourself), the people in your audience, and all of the obstacles in front of you, ask yourself, *How do I want my audience to feel at the end of this presentation?* and *What do I want them to do?* What is the impact you want to have on them?

Typically, when you build a presentation, you want to start with the end in mind. Crafting a powerful presentation begins with being clear about what you want, in terms of impact. So often we dive in, dumping data and designing slides without stopping to clarify what we're after in terms of impact outside ourselves. Our content typically reflects our own agenda, without considering the needs and feelings of the people with whom we're speaking.

> **Before you begin designing your content, be sure you're clear about the impact you want to have on your audience from their perspective. Get your own agenda out of the way.**

Every good presentation has three components: a clear beginning, middle, and end. A strong beginning is critical to success. Your audience will decide in three seconds whether or not they want to listen to you. If they don't listen, you cannot influence, and they will not follow. It's important to capture their attention right away and to do so in a way that is authentic to who you are. In addition to being clear about the overall impact you want to have, it's important to break it down even further, to work Intentions. In the beginning, do you want to jolt them? Do you want to draw them in? Do you want to capture their interest? Do you want to welcome them? Do you want to invite them into your world? Consider what you want to achieve with the beginning of your presentation. Think about your audience and what obstacles they might be facing. What is the impact you want to have on your audience from the moment you start?

Based on the impact you want to have in the beginning (your Intention), there are many different ways to effectively open a presentation.

Author and speaker Patricia Fripp has an excellent list of opening options on her website: www.fripp.com.

A considerable amount of research indicates that when we start a presentation with data, an audience is wired to refute.[1] Igniting their logic up front initiates our automatic drive to question. Instead, try beginning with a story or a question to invite them in, lower their guard, prime their thinking, and work to create an emotional connection that will pay dividends in the end. Remember, it's important to align the elephant and the rider. Find a way to ignite their want before you load them up with data.

The best leaders use their own personal stories to connect their listeners to what they believe and spark action. Sharing personal stories requires vulnerability, which lowers barriers and helps to establish trust. Being able to tap into your personal stories to connect others to what is most important is a critical skill as a leader. Without it, people may do what you tell them to do, but they will never follow with their hearts and minds. They will always hold out, and you will never get the best that they have to offer. As a leader, you need to be able to put some skin in the game first. Your personal stories are the currency that gives you access to the passion and energy in others.

When crafting your personal stories, you'll want to include—

- **Who:** Who are the major characters in your story?

- **What:** What took place? What were you doing?

- **When:** When did your story take place (year, month, season, holiday, how old were you, etc.)?

- **Where:** Where does your story unfold (city, state, company, inside or outside, etc.)?

- **Why:** Why are you telling this story?

What brings a story to life is interesting specifics. Focus on creating rich characters and vivid settings. Paint a picture to transport us into your world.

The middle is the section where you support the point of your presentation. Like everything else, you'll want to have a specific Intention for the middle of your presentation. Do you want to build your case? Do you want to cultivate trust? Do you want to draw your audience in? Do you want to hold up the mirror so they can see themselves? Do you want to inspire? Whatever it is, it should be in connection to both your main Intention for your presentation and your Super Objective as a leader.

"The most effective communicators use three essential channels to convey important leadership messages: Facts, Emotions, and Symbols," say Boyd Clarke and Ron Crossland in their book *The Leader's Voice*. As you flesh out your presentation, ask yourself what the facts are. How can you make the facts matter to your audience? How can you appeal to the emotions of your audience? What do they care about? How can you use personal stories, paint a picture of your vision, or use metaphors (symbols) to make your presentation memorable?

In the world of musical theater (think big Broadway shows: *Cats*, *The Phantom of the Opera*, etc.), there's something called the *eleven o'clock number*. It's the showstopper, the biggest moment of the night. It comes right before the finale (just before midnight—thus eleven o'clock). Every show, every meeting, every presentation can benefit from having an eleven o'clock number. It's your pinnacle. It might be the point of your story. It might be your call to action. It might be the moment when you give your audience goose bumps and they realize that you get their pain and truly see them. It might be an unveiling. In order to maximize the impact of your presentation, consider building everything to climax at the point right before you end.

At the end, it comes back to what you want in terms of impact. How do you want to leave your audience? What is the main takeaway you want them to remember? What action can you take to have the impact you most want to have? Maybe you want to lift them up or suspend time. Maybe you want to motivate them to act or excite them. Maybe you want to reassure or empower them. What do you want?

In addition to being a conversation, a presentation is an *experience*. What is the experience you want to provide?

Every person in your audience is a unique human being with worries, frustrations, stressors, and fears. Each has their own history. Each one is listening to you for their own personal reasons. When they walk out of the room after you speak, how do you want them to feel? Not just about you and your presentation (which would be self-oriented) but about themselves or the project or the future or the organization? How can you make your ending leave a lasting impact on each person in front of you?

> *If we present and we don't connect, why are we even presenting?*

When we present, the stakes are high, not only for ourselves, but because we have been given an opportunity to connect and make an impact. Opportunities like these are precious. For if we present and we don't connect, why are we even presenting? Why wouldn't we just send them the PowerPoint slides in an email and call it a day?

When we present, ideas are cultivated, feelings are triggered, and insights are sparked. When we present, we give birth to possibility, incite change, bridge fears, and ignite courage, passion, and commitment. When we present, we help people find the humor in the absurd, release tension, and celebrate their wins. When we present, we remind people of why they matter, why they care, and why whatever it is we're talking about is important.

To present is a privilege. When we speak, we must take the stage with that sense of responsibility. Your ending is the last thing they'll hear from you, and it must have an impact. What is the impact you want it to have? Get clear on that first, and then set your strategy for getting there. Come full circle. Call them to action. Ignite their imagination. Make an impact. This is why we speak.

ROAD MAPS AND MEMORIZATION

So you're ready to craft your powerful presentation. You know the impact you want to have and generally what you want to say. You want it to be magnificent, so you sweat over every word, replay every beautiful phrase over and over in your head, and polish to sleek perfection. And in doing so, you've done yourself a huge disservice.

You see, when we're so focused on the words we're going to say and on being perfect, it gets in the way of the main reason we're there, which is to connect. Unless you have to give a formal or high-stakes presentation that is being videotaped or timed to the minute, writing down every word of your speech, unless you have months to prepare and rehearse, will only cause you to be mechanically glued to your script or leave you searching for the words on the back of your eyeballs, instead of connecting with the human beings in front of you. Instead, I encourage you to craft a road map.

Your road map is simply an outline that maps the major points you want to make, stories you want to use, and supporting data that is required. In a more casual presentation, the only elements that you'll want to craft word for word would be your opening, your transitions, and your closing.

ROAD MAP TEMPLATE

The beginning (How can I engage my audience?)

I want them to feel _____ and do _____.

And to do that I'm going to _____ (share a story, ask a question, draw them in by . . .).

How am I going to transition from the beginning to the middle of my presentation?

The middle (How can I support my case?)

I want them to feel _____ and do _____.

And to do that I'm going to _____ (provide examples, offer data to support and illustrate by . . .).

[Note: For longer presentations, your middle may have its own beginning, middle, and end, in which case you'll need to do this for every section.]

How am I going to transition from the middle to the end of my presentation?

The end: How do I want to leave my audience?

I want them to feel _____ and do _____.

Should I call them to action? Come full circle? What is the impact I want to make? What is the one thing I want my audience to walk away and remember?

As long as you know your road map, you won't need your notes. If the stories are yours, you lived them, so you know them. If you have a lot of data, simply use a card or a slide to reference the information, but only use it to grab the facts you need so you can get back to your audience. When you present, your job is to connect. Notes act as a barrier to connection. Use them sparingly.

There may be times when you have to give a memorized formal presentation. If that's the case, the most important thing you can do is give yourself ample time to prepare. Nothing will make the difference like time and preparation—a lot of time. In order to give a memorized speech and still be your real, relaxed, most powerful self, you've got to get through what TED curator Chris Anderson calls *the valley of awkwardness*.[2] Most TED speakers rehearse four to five months before they take the stage, if not longer. I was only given three weeks' notice before I spoke at TEDx, and I felt it. Even with all the speaking I've done in my life, it was not enough time to get it in my bones. Give yourself the time it requires.

———

So many people I work with declare within minutes of meeting me that they hate presenting. I'm lucky. I get to watch them reframe it in their minds and experience themselves, often for the first time in their lives, presenting powerfully. It's exhilarating to behold someone when they find their voice for the first time. I sit in the audience in the dark, covered in goose bumps and misty eyed, as I listen to them speak from their heart. "What was different?" I ask, afterward.

"So much more confidence."

"I actually felt comfortable."

"Real. We were real."

Yes. Real.

You may not care much about being real in your next team meeting, but consider how this kind of confidence and comfort speaking in front of people might help you influence and lead—true power, coming from within.

———

Breathe. Remove tension. Adjust your body to a more powerful position. Take down your mask. Ground yourself. Get clear about impact. Know your road map. Connect. Have a *conversation*. If you stay connected in conversation, you won't have to worry about your voice, gestures, or movements; they'll take care of themselves. If they feel awkward, you're not truly connecting. Use whatever awkwardness and tension you feel as red flags to breathe and adjust your focus. Focus outside yourself to connect, and your amygdala will stay out of your way.

Repeat after me:

"I, [insert your name], will never think of giving a presentation as giving a *presentation* again."

Key Takeaways

→ Your primary job when you present is to *connect* to the hearts and minds of the people in your audience. To simply deliver information is a lost opportunity.

→ Powerful presenting is not about learning more skills; it's about mastering how you show up in the face of vulnerability.

→ Whether you're speaking to two, twenty, two hundred, or two thousand people, presenting is simply a conversation.

→ Every movement in your presentation should have a purpose.

→ With every audience, you will face visible and hidden obstacles. Ask yourself, *What is the impact you want to have on that person?*

→ Take some time to understand the needs of your audience before you present. What do they need from you to experience you as genuine, worthy of trust, reliable, and believable (our definition of authenticity) from their perspective?

→ Every presentation should have a clear beginning, middle, and end. Anchor each section in Intention to shift the rhythm, keep your audience engaged, and give yourself something specific on which to focus to keep your nerves at bay.

→ Rich personal stories with interesting specifics are what will connect you to the want of your audience. When crafting your stories, be sure to include who, what, when, where, and why.

→ Unless your presentation is high stakes, recorded, or timed, don't write out every word. Instead, bullet-point your "roadmap"—your clear beginning, middle, and end, only memorizing your intro, transitions, and conclusion. If you have a high-stakes presentation, give yourself ample time to practice (months) to ensure it is natural and you can focus on connecting to your audience.

→ If you want to be a brave leader, *connect*, don't just present.

PART IV

A BRAVE
NEW
WORLD

22

Own Your Mess

You cannot escape the responsibility
of tomorrow by evading it today.

—ABRAHAM LINCOLN

Guess what? You're human. You say and do stupid things at times—we all do. Mistakes in and of themselves aren't the issue. Yes, we hope that as we grow and learn and evolve that we'll become more mindful, make fewer mistakes, and that when we make them they're not as . . . ugly. But the key to being and bringing your best isn't only about making fewer mistakes, it's also about how you deal with what happens after you blow it.

We don't like to deal with the mess of our mistakes. It makes us not feel good about ourselves. We get embarrassed or self-righteous or just plain weird. When we know we've said or done something that is not a good reflection of who we are, we prefer to pretend it didn't happen.

Memories are funny things. We tend to safely pack away the times we've shape-shifted ourselves into demon-like creatures, spewing toxic slime throughout the workplace or all over the people we love. Once we've justified our actions ("I was angry" or "Well, he shouldn't have . . ." or "If they'd just do what I told them to do, then . . ."), we move on. So should everyone else, right?

> **The key to being and bringing your best isn't only about making fewer mistakes, it's also about how you deal with what happens after you blow it.**

But it doesn't work like that. We don't like to deal with the mess of our mistakes. We want to move on, but people remember.

Many times, the way I've reacted has left me feeling less than proud. I remember once, when my kiddo was about nine, he kept getting up in the middle of the night asking me for things. It was the night before I was leading an OnStage Leadership workshop, so I had my alarm set for four thirty a.m. the next morning. I had dutifully put myself to bed at nine thirty that night so I'd be rested and ready to go, but around eleven p.m., I heard, "Mommy, can I have a glass of water?"

"Sure, honey," I said, dragging myself from my slumber.

Then around one a.m., I heard, "Maaaaahhhhhm! I can't sleep!"

Grrrrrrr. I am now mad at both my husband for traveling and at my son, the sleepless wonder. I walk to his room and sternly say, "Jeremy, I'm sorry you're having trouble sleeping. Have you tried counting sheep?"

"That never works. Will you sing to me?"

I remember so many times when I've laid down beside my child and have sung him to sleep, thinking, *What a miracle this is. I am so lucky to be here doing this.* I have to tell you, I was not thinking those lovely things at that moment.

"Fine," I whispered in frustration, "but only if you promise you'll go to sleep and stay asleep."

Then, at three a.m., I felt a tap, tap, tap on my shoulder.

"Mom, can I sleep with you? I still can't sleep."

I pretend he's not there as he crawls in next to me. And he wiggles around. And kicks off the covers. And elbows me. And finally . . .

"Out! OUT!" I scream. "Mommy has to get up in an hour and a half and I MUST SLEEP!" I usher him into his own room, like some possessed alien, and hiss, "STAY IN BED AND BE QUIET!"

And then, at three fifteen a.m. as I lay in the dark, feeling my heart pounding in my chest, it hit me—the yuck. I became aware that even though I was so tired and had what felt like an immense responsibility on my shoulders, I had totally messed up. I was not acting like the mom I wanted to be. I felt ashamed, sad, and disappointed in myself.

You see, no matter what the circumstances or how justified we are, when we behave in a way that's not congruent with our best self, we know it. We feel it. We cannot escape ourselves. We carry the shame, sadness, and disappointment around with us like weights, not seeing them for what they are—assassins of our self-belief and efficacy. We cannot be and bring our best if we don't deal with the messes that we've made.

> *No matter the circumstances, when we behave in a way that's not our best, we know it. We cannot escape ourselves.*

I tiptoed back into Jeremy's room, and he bolted up in his bed, alert, like a deer in the wild. "Mom? Is that you?" he whispered in the dark.

"Yes, honey," I whispered gently. "I . . . I'm so sorry I yelled at you. It was wrong of me to yell like that. Will you forgive me?"

"Of course, Mommy. I'm sorry too. I didn't mean to keep you up."

"I know," I said, crawling in beside him. Within minutes, he was sleeping soundly.

When my alarm went off at four thirty a.m., in spite of the early hour, I was glad. I was glad that I had taken the time to make things right. How could I teach what I teach and do what I do and be who I want to be if I hadn't? The answer is I couldn't.

Parenting is a great school for learning how to clean up your messes—and so is work. How often do you find yourself snapping at someone when you're frustrated or stressed or behind on a deadline? Or hear yourself calling someone out in a meeting (let the public floggings begin!)? Or making blanket threats ("If you don't hit your numbers, heads are gonna roll!")? Or saying snarky comments in lieu of dealing with the root problem? What messes have you made in your world? Maybe it's time to clean them up.

> **What messes have you made in your world? Maybe it's time to clean them up.**

People are amazing creatures. They have an enormous capacity for forgiveness when someone has the courage to own their mess. But if that same person leaves the mess for someone else to clean up, their memory is long. They may not tell you what you've done that fractured their trust and belief in you, but they have filed it away as evidence of who you really are. They'll carry wariness into the relationship like a shield. They'll hold back and play it safe, or get the heck out of Dodge. If you care about results, you need a different outcome.

You're human. You're going to make a mess from time to time. Get real about what's yours to own. Clean it up. People know. You know.

KNOW YOUR TRIGGERS

Don't you hate it when things don't go your way? Something happens, you're triggered, and then your sunny outlook on life gets obliterated in mere seconds. What a mess! I'm reminded of a recent pharmacy misfortune. I needed a basic prescription refilled, one I've had refilled dozens of times, and nothing seemed to go right. One place didn't have it—it would take days to order. I trekked to another place—they didn't have it in (their supplier was back ordered). "I can't say when we'll get it in," the sheepish guy at the counter said, shrugging his shoulders. The third place I went told me they needed two weeks' notice (two weeks?). What should've, in my mind, taken fifteen minutes to do cost me the better part of a day. I was highly agitated. My inner toddler was throwing a big-time temper tantrum. Didn't these people know I had a lot to do? My perfectly scheduled schedule was totally ruined. What a horrible day! How unfair! Poor me!

Rather sad, don't you think? I let a normal situation have such a negative impact on my day. The funny thing was, on my way to the first pharmacy, I was in a totally different mindset. I felt a sense of gratitude as I gazed up at the blue sky and the warm sun, happy that I had fit my exercise in and content that I was so productive that day. Life was good!

And then . . . BAM! Gratitude, happiness, and contentment were obliterated by frustration, intense agitation, and self-centeredness. It was all about *me*. *My* schedule! They were disappointing *me*!

Now, when I stepped back for a minute and let my rational brain look at this situation, I could see that it wasn't a huge crisis. No one died. There were other pharmacies in the area. I had transportation to get there. It was not a medical emergency. It really wasn't that big of a deal. But my insides didn't know that. I felt mad and wanted to lash out.

The reason this blip in my life merits discussion is that we've all been there before. One of the joys of being human is that certain things cause us to become emotionally hijacked. Something happens that triggers us and the feelings ignited are much bigger than the situation merits, typically causing a strong reaction that we regret.

I have memories of the nasty looks and snippy comments I've made when my lizard brain has taken over, which don't make me feel terribly proud. But my pharmacy situation proves that, even for me (cue: "Hallelujah Chorus"), change is possible!

In the past, those poor pharmacists would have certainly known that

I was mad, and I would have made sure that they knew they were the reason why my day had been ruined. (Can you hear the drama in that?)

But I'm a victim of my amygdala no more! (Well, at least I'm working on it.) Thankfully, in that situation, I managed to keep my inner turmoil in check and was able to treat the poor pharmacists with the kindness and respect they deserved—no nasty looks and no snippy comments. I didn't stuff the feelings. I knew they were there, but I was aware that they were disproportionate. Instead of reacting, I got curious.

I've long believed that our feelings are guideposts. They lead us to understand ourselves better. The problem is that we often misread the signs. We interpret things on a surface level and react, instead of digging deeper for what is at the core. Instead of making meaning of our feelings when we have them, what if we were to question where they point us?

Why was my inner reaction to the pharmacy thing so huge? I got curious. What was really going on for me? It wasn't that the pharmacists didn't care. They did. They were just doing their job. They weren't trying to make it hard for me. In fact, they were doing everything they could to be helpful.

As I looked at the situation more closely, I realized that what was going on had nothing to do with the pharmacists and everything to do with my inability to control the situation. My inability to control the situation was the trigger.

If I connect the dots in my life and map out the times I've overreacted to situations, a great number of them are related to feeling out of control. Having a clear understanding of this trigger changes everything.

One of the things that is so optimistic about the work that's been done around emotional intelligence is that it shows us that we don't have to be victims of our emotions. We can get curious, we can understand, and we can be better. As we uncover our triggers, the feelings may still come up, but our reactions can be contained. We can stop the mess before it happens.

Think about how this plays out day after day in the workplace. Our frustrations with client demands get redirected onto the people we lead. Our feeling of being overwhelmed blinds us to extraordinary work that's being done. Our stress boils over in the way we respond to people on our team. We get triggered time and time again, without paying attention to the mess we leave in our wake. Getting real demands that we take responsibility for ourselves.

Find a way to stay curious about how you're feeling, and let that lead you to understanding, instead of reaction. Your team will thank you. Your family will thank you. And your local pharmacist might just thank you too.

A LITTLE THING CALLED THANK YOU

You know how there are moments in your life that stand out in your mind no matter how much time has passed? I will never forget how I felt in a meeting I had with a senior leader fifteen years ago. I felt like a commodity.

I was running my events company in Seattle, and after months of intense preparation and giving it everything I had, I knocked out a killer company meeting for my client, and the entire organization was talking about it. What had historically been a boring information download had been transformed. People streamed out of the meeting buzzing with excitement. They were inspired by what the company was about, energized by what they were doing, and proud to be a part of such a cool organization. We had overachieved on our goals, and it was an amazing experience.

After the meeting, we went back to the office and I met with the vice president of communications—my work had fallen under her charge. We sat down, and she immediately started talking about what needed to be done in preparation for the next meeting, four months away.

I stared at her, astonished by how swiftly we were moving on, without pausing to acknowledge what we had accomplished. My brain wasn't ready to make that shift.

"So how did you feel the meeting went today?" I asked.

"Good. Now about . . ."

I honestly didn't hear what she said next, amid the white noise in my mind, and it must have shown by the look on my face.

"Kimberly, what's the matter?" she asked impatiently.

"Well, it just feels like something's missing."

"Missing? What's missing?"

"I feel like the meeting was really great. It may be a strange thing to say," I said sheepishly, "but I guess I just expected to hear that you were happy or . . ."

"Kimberly, if you're looking to hear thank you, your thank you is your paycheck. Maybe next time we'll just say thank you instead of paying you."

I felt like I had been slapped in the face. I knew right then that that arrangement wasn't going to work for me. The next day I let them know that I would complete everything I was currently doing, would help them in the transition to find another company to work with, but I would no longer be available to take on additional projects.

> **Heart and soul cannot be commoditized.**

Two hours later, the vice president of communications followed me out to the parking lot with a big bouquet of flowers and an apology note.

Here's what I know to be true: Nobody gives their best for a paycheck exchange. I didn't need flowers or fanfare; I just needed to know that, if I was willing to invest my whole self into something, it mattered.

We like to pretend that business is just business and niceties like saying thank you don't matter. But what differentiates great companies that attract and keep extraordinary talent willing to give it their all—to put their heart and soul into what they do—is that they recognize the human investment being made. Heart and soul cannot be commoditized.

When I was living in Seattle, and my husband and I had blended our two households, which included my two old cats and his two old cats. (We ran the geriatric cat house for a brief period of time. Don't judge us.) We had all these cats, but we both liked to travel, which turned out to be a frustrating inconvenience. While cats are fairly independent creatures, they still need to be fed and their litter boxes cleaned. Thank goodness for dear friends. My friend Elizabeth, who claimed that we were closer than relatives, had four dogs who she happened to walk every day past our house! How perfect could that be? So, Elizabeth, being the good friend she was, agreed to take care of our cats for us while we were away.

And then, three months later, we went away again. Of course, I thought, Elizabeth would be more than happy to help out! We're closer than relatives, right? No.

When I told Elizabeth about the upcoming trip and asked if she could help, she exploded on the phone.

"It's not MY job to watch *your* cats! If you don't want to take care of your **#%! cats, you shouldn't have them!" she screamed, clearly not happy about the whole cat-sitting thing. She then said a few more colorful things that I've since blocked out and hung up.

I called and apologized. I sent apology letters. When we went on our trip (I found a different cat sitter), I bought her a gift and delivered it to her door to apologize. My apologies weren't enough.

We were closer than relatives, and I blew it. My friend Elizabeth had gone out of her way to help us and I had totally taken her for granted. (Can you imagine trying to corral four big dogs outside while running inside to feed four old cats?) That time she helped us? I forgot to say thank you.

Part of owning your mess is to see where you haven't acknowledged the hard work that people are investing all around you to make your life and your organization better. Pay attention to the amazing things going on—the days people come in early or leave late to finish big projects, the extra care and attention people bring to their work, the obstacles they have to overcome to help you—don't let it go unnoticed. Tell them: I see you. I see what you're doing and how it's making a difference. Say thank you to your direct reports, your boss, your contractors, your colleagues, your clients, your vendors, your family, your kid's teacher, and your friends. It matters.

Because if you don't, the people who care the most about giving their best will find someplace else to invest themselves. Or maybe they'll stick around and it will stop being to your benefit.

People need to know that they're seen and that they matter. That is the greatest gift we can give each other, and it's one that will pay dividends for years to come.

If as a leader you need their want to succeed, then this is one mess you can't afford not to clean up.

Key Takeaways

➔ We all make occasional mistakes and have reactions we're not proud of.

➔ The people you lead and need to influence have a tremendous capacity for forgiveness if you're willing to *own your behavior*. While you may move on, if you haven't made it right with others, they won't forget and it will cost you their want. Apologies without excuses and justifications are critical.

➔ You cannot escape yourself. No matter the circumstances, when you behave in a way that's not congruent with your values, purpose, and best self, you know it. Misalignments become assassins for your self-belief and efficacy.

➔ We all have emotional triggers rooted in our personal experiences that lead us to react poorly. Stay curious and observe your feelings to better understand your triggers and stop your reaction before it costs you the want of others.

➔ Nobody gives their best for a paycheck exchange. If you want to be a brave leader, it is critical to recognize and appreciate the effort and work that is being done to make your business succeed. Otherwise, you risk the passion, commitment, loyalty, creativity, trust, enthusiasm, and energy—the want of the very people you need most.

23

Cultivating Brave

You get nothing at birth
except things to transcend.

—MILTON GLASER

Maya Angelou once said, "Do the best you can until you know better. Then when you know better, do better." For me, every day is a commitment to do better. Sometimes I succeed, and sometimes I don't. But here's my commitment to myself: Give up trying to be perfect to be authentic, and give up trying to prove to connect. In exchange, one conversation, one meeting, one presentation—one situation at a time—I get the chance, however small it might be, to make an impact.

I want to share with you some of the things that I do to cultivate brave for myself. This is by no means an exhaustive list. You will certainly find other strategies that make a difference for you (and I hope you'll share them), but here are some of the things that work for me:

COMMIT TO MASTERY

My dad's commitment to mastery is something I'm incredibly grateful to have inherited. For as long as I can remember, he has gotten up at four thirty a.m. to read. He reads journal articles, the newspaper, and studies with an intensity that few can match. While he retired from practicing medicine quite a few years ago, he still keeps himself current on the latest research and attends association meetings and conferences. He has reignited his passion for the guitar and Spanish, practicing both for hours each day, and is on his way to becoming a master gardener. My dad has modeled growth and development my entire life. His hunger for knowledge—for mastery—has been contagious.

I have always admired professional actors' commitment to mastery. They work and hone themselves and their craft, always tweaking, improving, and iterating, never satisfied. There is no good enough; there is only a hunger to be better. Mastery is elusive and always out of reach.

For years, before my son was born, I would have my morning Zen time. (There's not been much Zen since he showed up on the scene.) I'd journal and meditate and devour personal development and business books, highlighting every page so heavily that my husband teased me that I should just dye the pages yellow and be done with it. Recently, in my attempt to KonMari my office, I went through all my beloved books and stumbled upon Joan Evelyn Ames's beautiful book, *Mastery: Interviews with Thirty Remarkable People*. I thumbed through my notes and highlights and dog-eared pages of this book that I grew to love more than fifteen years ago, inspired all over again by the incredible people she had interviewed. They were masters from every discipline—artists, business magnets, sports legends, media moguls, educators, scientists, and spiritual leaders. I was astonished to realize, years later, how much of my life's work was a reflection of those interviews. The influences that make us who we are are often relics of our past.

The masters spoke of an eagerness to learn, flexibility, and commitment to quality; of discipline, abandon, and focus; of an urge to investigate, of being with the struggle, and admiring the work of others; of humility and patience, and having a childlike quality; of hard work, time invested, and tenacity. They spoke of caring, vulnerability, and courage.

- Architect James Ingo Freed talked about "playing the edge," not doing the safe thing.

- Opera singer Margaret Harshaw believed that "freedom is the highest form of discipline."

- Environmental artist Mary Miss mentioned a "desire and willingness to keep walking."

- Athlete and coach Bill Dellinger insisted that it's important that you allow yourself to succeed—that "success breeds success."

- International orchestra conductor Gisele Ben-Dor talked of the importance of being genuine. "It has to be you a hundred percent, for better or worse."

As it turns out, masters do not think of themselves as masters. They are simply people working diligently to be their best selves and are committed to making an impact. Some might call them brave.

Dan Pink's research identifies pursuing mastery as one of the top three things we need to feel motivated—autonomy, mastery, and purpose. As much as we think we'd like a life of leisure in which we could kick back and do nothing, it turns out that wouldn't be terribly motivating; working on improving ourselves is key to satisfaction and engagement. As Pink says, "The joy is in the pursuit more than the realization."[1]

The wonderful thing is that working toward mastery is totally within our realm of control. We can continue to grow and better ourselves without permission.

A commitment to mastery is critical to cultivate brave. You will never hit your bull's-eye every time. In order to achieve what you stand for as a leader, in all the crazy situations you find yourself, you will need an arsenal of Intentions. To be your best self, you'll have to take one mindful action after another, working diligently to get closer to your target every time, course correcting along the way and cleaning up your messes. A focus on achieving your Super Objective, your purpose in action, forces mastery. It requires you to get better and better. And in doing so, you ironically drive yourself.

Mastery is an endless horizon; it's like trying to reach infinity: you know you can go on and on forever.

—LEGENDARY WINEGROWER RICHARD PONZI,
IN *MASTERY* BY JOAN EVELYN AMES.

SET HEALTHY BOUNDARIES

The saying goes that your strengths are also your Achilles' heel. The things that we do well also tend to get us into the biggest trouble. One person's ability to take control of a tough situation can make a positive impact or disempower everyone around them. Another person's talent for solving problems can also make them a terrible listener. For me, my curiosity about people, my desire to step into their shoes and look at the world from their perspective, to see what's underneath all the surface stuff and connect the dots, coupled with my sincere passion for helping others, has (quite obviously) led me to do the work I do today. It's why I loved the the-ater. These gifts serve me in my life. But they've also caused me problems when I've neglected to put the brakes on. If I don't carefully monitor how much of the world's "stuff" I take in, my brave gets lost in the cacophony of other people's pain. All the problems, frustrations, and general nasti-ness leave me feeling sad, tired, frustrated, and depleted. I lose my ability to have a positive impact.

There are so many negative influences out in the world—negative, snarky posts and negative, snarky people. We are inundated with tragic, fear-inducing, depressing images and stories in the media. I'm not suggesting you live a sheltered life under a wet rock or only surround yourself with happy-happy-rainbow-sunshine people, but I am suggesting that you bring some mindfulness to what you let in to your world. Negativity breeds negativity. We cannot be and bring our most confident, powerful, and authentic selves if we're focused on the negative. Set boundaries around what you watch, with whom you share your time, and what influences you allow. Fiercely protect your mindset.

That said, if you're anything like me, this won't be an easy feat. Setting boundaries can sometimes feel like you're being mean or selfish, or by disconnecting from the media hoopla that you're being naive or foolish, but it is one of the healthiest things you can do. There's a real question to be explored around self-preservation. How much negativity can we be exposed to and still be our best selves? As recently as the early nineties, scientists discovered something called *mirror neurons* in our brains. Mirror neurons explain why, when you're with someone and they stub their toe, you react in pain as if it were happening to you. Our brains mirror another's experience. Mirror neurons are at the heart of empathy and explain why the Magic If is such a powerful tool. Asking yourself, "What if I were in this person's circumstances?" forces you into a visceral understanding of another's situation as the mirror neurons in your brain replay it physiologically for you to experience. As neuroscientist Vittorio Gallese says, "At the root, as humans we identify the person we're facing as someone like ourselves."

Map this to Dr. Amy Cuddy's work around power poses and you can see how, if your mind mirrors what it sees, spending a great deal of time with people who are not in their happy place can have a dramatic impact on your own feelings and behaviors, even to the point of altering your brain chemistry.

I used to take long walks with a friend who loved to dissect and condemn every move her boss would make. We had known one another for the better part of two decades and she was notorious for always having the worst boss in the world, so eventually I stopped believing that the boss was the problem. For three solid miles, she'd demonize the boss of the month, completely ruthless in her rant. I found myself feeling empathetically torn. I cared about her and knew she was venting, but I could feel myself getting more and more tense with every step. While she may have been my friend, it was her boss's shoes I couldn't help but occupy, and it was a painful place to be.

I would offer different perspectives and challenge her to consider another way of looking at things. I would encourage her to talk with him and explore solutions. "Kimberly, I don't want you to coach me," she'd say, frustrated. "I just want you to listen." As much as I loved her, it didn't feel good to be her sounding board. Every time we'd meet, it would be the same thing. In her presence I was tense, and in her wake I was exhausted. My best self was nowhere to be seen. Then I'd feel bad for feeling bad. For days afterward, my mind would replay her monologue, seeking the perfect thing I could've said that would've empowered her and made a difference in the way she looked at things. But there was no perfect thing I could have said. And even if there was, she had no desire to hear it. She was committed to having the worst boss in the world. That's what was real. I allowed myself to become emotionally entangled in her ick and it cost me. We cannot be our best self if we're covered in ick.

And it's not only other people's ick we need to worry about; our own negative self-talk can take us down. I wouldn't tell my worst enemy some of the things I've muttered to myself. Of course, now that I'm getting more mindful, it can be a bit embarrassing. I'll catch myself saying something mean and cynical and then my healthier alter ego will stop, reframe it, and use it as a learning opportunity. I talk to myself all the time. It's a good thing I have a home office or people might think I'm nuts.

I've come to learn that pain is part of the human condition. To cultivate brave, we cannot avoid or eliminate the negative, painful experiences, but we can shift the way we interact with them. Set healthy boundaries for yourself; you cannot have the impact you need to have if you don't.

SURROUND YOURSELF WITH BRAVE

Brave doesn't happen in a vacuum. I've discovered if I want to be my most confident, powerful, and authentic self, I need to surround myself with others who are committed to doing the same. They bridge my confidence, remind me of my aim, celebrate my wins, challenge me, cheer me on, help refocus my attention, teach me, provide a constructive sounding board, call me on my crap, give me a good kick in the pants, and inspire the heck out of me. I am absolutely certain that, were it not for the brave people in my life, I would not be doing what I am today.

So how do you find all of these brave folks? Well, the first part of the process is to work on your own brave (which, trust me, is a life-long journey). "We attract people with our common level of emotional health," relationship expert Dr. Margaret Paul says, and I have found this to be so true.[2] If you spend your days engaged in self-defeating, unhealthy activities, don't expect the superstars to find you all that interesting. But if you actively work on growing your brave, it's like a magnet to others who are working toward being their most confident, powerful, and authentic self.

Of course, that's a long-term strategy. To foster healthy relationships more quickly, it's important to remember that we see what we look for. If you actively look to find purposeful people who are working to have a constructive impact, who take responsibility for their actions and reactions, and who are committed to learning and growing themselves, then that's what you'll see. If you're focused on engaging with the negative, snarky people, then those are the people who will engage with you. *You're that powerful.* The first thing to do is to prime your thinking. They may not be on your team, in your neighborhood, or around your dinner table, but if you actively look for brave people, trust me, you'll find them everywhere.

If you don't already have people like this in your life and you're at the beginning stages of cultivating your own brave, social media is an excellent way to meet a lot of people who share your commitment to personal and professional growth. Identify inspirational influencers to follow. Read posts that will expand your thinking and elevate your attitude. Connect with as many brave people as you can.

I've found Twitter chats an especially wonderful tool for this. In the span of an hour, you can connect with people all over the country (or even all over the world, depending on the chat) who are interested in similar topics. There's a chat for everyone, and they take place all throughout the day. There are chats about education, leadership, influence, writing, politics, and parenting. You name it, there's a chat. Again, be careful about choosing the best chat for your goals. Some chats will naturally attract the brave, and some will attract the trolls. You want to protect your mindset as you leap into the fray. Simply do a quick Internet search for Twitter chats in your area of interest (for example, type *education twitter chats*) and you will find links to all the chats available, the times that they are offered, and often a brief description of what they discuss. When it's time for the chat to begin, you simply log in to Twitter (you'll need to set up an account), do a search for the chat by putting the hashtag in front of the chat name (for example, one of my favorite education chats is #G2Great), hit enter, and the conversation will unfold. If you end up participating in chats frequently, you'll find tools like TweetDeck make it infinitely easier to keep up with the conversation, as often over two hundred people will respond simultaneously. In the course of a one-hour commitment, you can increase your brave community exponentially.

> *Being acquainted isn't enough to make someone want to support you and your work; it takes a relationship to gain access to their want.*

But, of course, social media friendships can never be a surrogate for rich, meaningful, personal relationships, and rich, meaningful, personal relationships take time. There are no shortcuts; there is just investment. The problem is, with our crazy schedules and busy lives, it's hard to make the time. We think that relationships are a "nice to have" instead of a "have to have," so we back-burner them, assuming they'll be there when we're ready. But relationships don't work that way. We can't simply hit the pause button and come back to them later. I can't tell you how many people I know who have found themselves unexpectedly unemployed, starting a new business, or needing help, and they've no one in their corner. They've isolated themselves in their job, only making small talk to get the work done, and while they may have a lot of connections on LinkedIn, they don't have *relationships*. Being acquainted isn't enough to make someone want to support you and your work; it takes a relationship to gain access to their want.

Relationships begin with true connection. Instead of thinking about them in terms of what you can get, consider looking at them with the mindset of what you can give. Make genuine friendships rather than contacts. Be curious about people, listen as if the stakes are high, and stay fully present. Create for yourself a brave community. Not only will they be there, should the going get tough, but they will inspire you to be better and give you a chance to have an impact that matters. Partners in purpose make the journey much more rewarding.

CREATE YOUR OWN PROCESS

There are some great tools in this book that have helped a lot of people. But you are not just anyone, you are you! What works for you may be different than what works for me. There are so many incredible resources out there to help you grow and be effective. (I've included many of my favorites at the back of this book.) I encourage you to learn and absorb as much as you can from a wide variety of teachers, leaders, writers, philosophers, psychologists, artists, scientists, and other insightful people who share your day. Observe and test what works best for you. Put all that you learn into your personal sieve and, from that, cull the essence of your own process. So many people will rush to tell you that they have all the answers, but it's not true. Nobody has all the answers. This is your life on the line. These are your results. Trust your instincts. Even Stanislavski, as influential as he was, said, "Create your own method. Don't depend slavishly on mine. Make up something that will work for you! But keep breaking traditions, I beg you."

TAKE BABY STEPS

One of my biggest challenges is that I've always been a "boil the ocean" kind of girl. I tend to think big picture, and sometimes the enormity of what I'm trying to accomplish feels so big and overwhelming that it leaves me frozen in my tracks. Such was the case when I decided to write this book. Simply thinking about sitting down to write a book made me want to vomit. It felt so daunting and unachievable that it took me a good three years to get myself started. But then I channeled Bob.

One of my favorite movies of all time is *What About Bob?* Bob (Bill Murray) is a troubled man filled with crippling phobias and fears who seeks the help of psychiatrist Dr. Leo Marvin (played by Richard Dreyfuss) who professes that the path to power is found in baby steps.

"Baby steps to the elevator . . ." I hear Bob say in my head, adding the right amount of levity to my stressful situation.

I'm lucky. Getting to the elevator for me is a piece of cake. (It's all relative, isn't it?) The reminder is what I need to get me moving through what scares me.

So before I started to write this book, I sat down to write my first blog, then another, then another. Baby steps. Pretty soon, I had hundreds of blogs, and in the process had developed discipline, found my voice, increased my confidence, grown my audience, grown myself, and with every small step, found the courage to write.

Boil the ocean with baby steps.

NURTURE AND GROW YOUR WHOLE SELF

I would love to tell you that when I sit down to write, or get ready to speak or teach, that I'm able to push myself into high gear and crank out great work, because I am a disciplined machine. But alas, that's not true. I'm not a machine, I'm a person, and I suspect you might be the same. What I've learned is that compartmentalizing my work self from my whole self is a recipe for disaster. If I don't get exercise, especially in the winter, I get blue, my creativity and productivity plummet, and my work suffers. If I eat bad food, I feel heavy and lethargic, and my work suffers. If I don't get enough sleep, I can't concentrate, I'm cranky, and my work suffers. If I don't take a break once in a while, my output stinks, my back hurts, and my work suffers. My best, most powerful self is left drowning in a busyness delusion. We are people, not machines, and we need to treat ourselves as such. If you're not taking care of your whole self, trust me, there's not a lot of brave going on.

MAKE A POSITIVE IMPACT

By far the most selfish thing I do to cultivate brave is by doing something (anything) to make a positive impact. It is an energy and satisfaction infusion that cannot be matched. It is self-perpetuating, making me want to be a better me. It reminds me of my Prius; the more I drive it, the more it charges the battery. It forces me to get out of my head, to look beyond my own nose, and to connect to other people. It is the key to cultivating brave.

Key Takeaways

→ Commit to mastery: There is no end point to being a brave leader. To be your best self, you'll have to take one mindful action after another, working diligently to get closer to your target every time.

→ Set healthy boundaries: Set boundaries around what you watch, with whom you share your time, and what influences you allow. Fiercely protect your mindset.

→ Surround yourself with brave: Brave doesn't happen in a vacuum. If you want to be your most confident, powerful, and authentic self, surround yourself with others who are committed to doing the same.

→ Create your own process: *There is no single answer or system to be brave*, as every person is unique. Learn and absorb as much as you can from a wide variety of teachers, leaders, writers, philosophers, psychologists, artists, scientists, and other insightful people who share your day. Observe and test what works best for you.

→ Take baby steps: Huge accomplishments are simply a series of small steps. Focus on the single next step in front of you.

→ Nurture and grow your whole self: Compartmentalizing your work self from your whole self is a recipe for disaster. Exercise, eat healthy, sleep, take breaks—you are a person, not a machine. Machines are not brave.

→ Make a positive impact: Do something (anything) to make a positive impact. It will force you to get out of your head, to look beyond your own nose, and to connect to other people. It is the key to cultivating brave.

24

A Brave Legacy

What vision do you aspire to? . . . If you really look in the mirror, what kind of person do you want to be? Obviously, this doesn't happen by accident. You have to work for it, train for it . . . Anything is tough if you want to be good . . . It's like asking, what do you want to grow into? What does self-actualization mean to you?

—ABRAHAM MASLOW, BRANDEIS UNIVERSITY, 1965

t was November 2004. I was eight months pregnant. I felt like a whale, and a friend had invited me to attend a community event held at a local church. After being squeezed into a pew, trapped on either side by well-meaning people who blocked my escape to pee, a lovely dark-haired woman stood up, took the microphone, and started talking about her experience with the 3-Day Breast Cancer Walk. She talked about making a difference. She talked about training hard. She talked about the extraordinary community of walkers. As she talked I disappeared into my thoughts, my hands resting on my swollen belly. *I want to be the kind of woman who makes a difference*, I thought. *That's how I want my son to remember me.* It was the first time legacy had shown up on my radar.

Before that day, I had never walked more than a couple of miles (because, you know, I'm not athletic). Before that day, I had never participated in a fund-raiser, except selling oranges for my high school choir in the dead of winter. They all froze in our garage. Before that day, it had never entered my mind to do something so time-consuming and hard for no pay. (Of course that was before I became a mother. Thanks to my son, I'm now quite accustomed to spending a lot of time working hard for no pay.)

Within the hour, I had waddled over to the information table and signed up. It would be three months before I could train and six months before the event. I had no idea who would walk with me. I knew I'd still be nursing. But it felt like something I had to do. For the first time in my life, I was compelled to be a part of something bigger than myself and make an impact.

That afternoon changed my life forever. From that point forward, I was hooked, not by long-distance walks (although I am a big fan), but by purpose. Never before had I experienced, with such clarity, that what I wanted to do wasn't about me at all—it was bigger than me. Never before did I work so hard for something that didn't ensure some kind of personal reward. Dan Pink, in his book *Drive: The Surprising Truth about What Motivates Us*, said, "We're designed to be active and engaged. And we know that the richest experiences in our lives aren't when we're clamoring for validation from others, but when we're listening to our own voice—doing something that matters, doing it well, and doing it in the service of a cause larger than ourselves."

I was "driving" myself, perhaps for the first time, and I felt so very . . . alive. One step at a time, I was becoming the woman I wanted to be.

In 2009, former banker, singer, songwriter, and palliative care worker Bronnie Ware wrote a blog that took the world by storm. She didn't anticipate such a response, she was only guided to write what she knew, but after spending years serving people during their last three to twelve weeks of life, in a role where "there is no room for trivia. You go straight to the core of things," what Bronnie knew was regret. When she posted her blog, "Regrets of the Dying," it took off almost instantly. Within a few months, more than a million readers had engaged with the piece, and by the year's end that number had tripled. She's since written a book, *The Top Five Regrets of the Dying*, which has been printed in twenty-seven languages. Bronnie's words clearly hit a universal chord. The most common regret of all: "I wish I'd had the courage to live a life true to myself, not the life others expected of me."

So many of us have historically looked at life as an either-or; we can either be true to ourselves (which is often seen as selfish, short-sighted, or naive) or we can be successful (which is often viewed as giving up our own needs to attain the world's approval or riches), but never the two shall meet.

What I've come to believe is that it's possible to forge a legacy that allows us to be both. For it is being true to who we are that allows us to tap into our best, and all the riches in the world feel meaningless if they're not anchored in something greater than ourselves.

I've had the privilege to work with a lot of senior executives who have found themselves in transition—amazing men and women who have been in the workforce over twenty years and for a multitude of reasons have found themselves, often for the first time in their careers, thinking about what's next.

Most had accomplished a great deal. Most had impressive "stuff" that they purchased with their impressive salaries. Most had title-related power at their jobs. People on the outside looking in would say these executives were successful. Yet interestingly, many of them did not think of themselves that way. They didn't feel successful.

Many of them were road warriors, with an impressive collection of airline miles. Many had struggled with relationships. Many had missed dance recitals, birthdays, prom nights, Boy Scout outings, helping out with homework, parent-teacher conferences, and so on. Many of them, twenty, thirty, or forty years later, found themselves asking *why*? What was it all for? They had climbed the ladders, done what they were supposed to do, achieved impressive heights, had a nice home, sent their kids to good schools, and built a life that exuded success, so why didn't they *feel* successful?

There's nothing wrong with working long hours; to do great things often takes great sacrifice. There's nothing wrong with being ambitious, moving up, making a nice living, or having nice things. But I've found that when our definition of success is anchored in all the externals of life—the title, the salary, the stuff, or even those less obvious ones that I struggle with, approval and recognition—we ultimately lose. We can never earn enough, have enough, or be enough to feel successful. If who we are is anchored in externals, it's like building a foundation on quicksand.

What a conundrum! We all want all the stuff, the recognition, and to have the world's seal of approval, yet we don't want our identity to be dependent on those things—we want to feel we have value, with or without the society's gold star, because we do.

So what's the alternative? In a world that throbs with images of what it means to be successful, how do we chart a different path?

As we've discussed, the key to authenticity, connection, and bravery is focus. When we focus our attention on the externals, we often lose ourselves in the fray. We get mired in battling our own lines and trapped in a never-ending loop of reactions. While we may get results, they're often at a cost to ourselves, to the people around us, and to our organizations. What is achieved then is often a fraction of what is possible.

Instead, if we focus our attention on the impact we want to have *outside ourselves*—on purpose, our Super Objective—we put ourselves on an active path that is inherently connected to what matters to us the most. When focusing on impact, we always pay attention to how our actions affect others and our organizations and adjust our tactics along the way.

When focusing on impact, you can make powerful choices on your own about how you approach any given situation. You don't need permission from your boss. You don't need a new job title. You have complete autonomy. Focusing on impact forces you to get better and better, to improve and grow, to seek mastery. Because we're paying attention to impact, our results are exponentially better.

Autonomy, mastery, purpose—to circle back to Dan Pink's research one final time, your Super Objective makes it possible to drive yourself.

If we want to feel successful, we need to stay true to ourselves and take consistent, constructive action toward that end. The externals that we seek are but a by-product. The good news is you don't need a new job to do that. You don't need a new title. You simply need to ask yourself, "I do what I do for the sake of what?" "What is the impact I want to have outside myself?" What impact do you want to have on your direct reports, colleagues, clients, organization, industry, students, patients, or community? What impact do you want to have on your family? Ask the question and then act.

Almost nine years ago, I was facilitating a leadership program for a big pharmaceutical company in the northeast. The director of training for the pharmaceutical company sat in my room, and at some point I had used an example from my colorful theater days. Being the resourceful guy he is, after leaving my session, the training director sought me out on the Internet, learned more about my background, and walked into my classroom the next morning and changed my life. He changed my life by seeing possibility in me. That possibility sparked the beginning of OnStage Leadership.

Since that day, I have had the opportunity to work with thousands of people to excavate their brave. That possibility is creating a community of leaders who make a difference in their organizations, in their relationships, and in their lives. That possibility became my life's work. I am forever grateful for his ability to see what is possible and take action to make such a profound impact on my life. While he is an extraordinary human being, what he did is something that every leader has the power to do.

As leaders, we are far more influential than we often realize. Our words and actions have the power to change people's lives—to bridge their confidence, to illuminate their natural talents, to create opportunity, and to spark growth. Look around you. You're surrounded by people who need the difference that only you can make. What kind of leader do you want to be? What is the impact you want to have? That is your key to a brave legacy.

I don't know about you, but there are times I don't feel brave, and the idea of making an impact seems so out of reach. Sometimes I have to dig pretty deep to find that brave part of myself, but she's there.

When I was eight years old, going into the fourth grade, my family moved into my parents' dream home. Perched on the top of a large hill, overlooking the valley, with Montana's Mission Mountains as the back-drop, my dad, whose Texas roots had instilled a dream of owning a ranch, was convinced we had purchased paradise. Thus, grazing in the field in front of our new house was a herd of French Limousin cattle that I got to feed every night after school. My parents had purchased the land. My mother, the artist, had a hand in the home's design. Every day for a year we would trek out to the site to see the progress. When we moved in, you would think that most of the work would have been done, but for this eight-year-old, it was just the beginning . . . We had to put in the *yard*.

I was convinced it was going to be the biggest yard on the face of the planet. Why my mother felt we needed so much yard is something I'll never understand. But before there was yard, there was just dirt, and rocks—lots and lots and lots of rocks. Rocks that needed to go before grass could be seeded. And for what seemed like a lifetime to a kid, my brother and I were put on rock removal duty. Weeks went by as we two indentured children spent our summer culling every rock from the premises.

Finally, with all the rocks removed, the topsoil was put in—the terrain having been perfectly prepared—and the grass seed was sown. I remember that night like it was yesterday. It was one of those long, warm summer evenings. We had worked hard all day, our muscles sore but our spirits high, as we watched the sprinkler rotating back and forth while the sun was setting, infusing life into the baby grass seeds waiting to grow. We went to bed happy. No more rocks!

It was about two a.m. when I awoke with a start. At first I thought it was a dream.

"Mooooooooo! Mooooooo!"

I sat up in bed.

"Mooooooo!"

And then I saw them. From my daylight basement bedroom, I saw hundreds of Limousin legs walking past my window.

The cows had gotten out. And they were in *our yard!*

"Nooooooooooo!" I screamed, waking my brother down the hall and running upstairs to my parents' bedroom.

My dad, the physician, who happened to be on call that night, missed all the excitement. But for the next two hours, my mom, my younger brother, and I tromped through the muddy remains of our yard in our jammies trying to get the cows back into the field. And they all went in, except one, the bull.

Now if you've never seen a bull in real life, you may not fully appreciate the enormity of our challenge. The average Limousin bull will weigh 2,600 pounds—more than a Mini Cooper. They're big boys. But you see, I was mad. They woke me up. They destroyed our yard. I didn't care how big he was; he was going in that pasture if it was the last thing I did. Of course that's exactly what my mother was worried about.

My mother was screaming, "Kimberly! You get over here this instant!" in the background, and my younger brother, looking like a street urchin, was covered in mud from head to toe, pleading with me to stand back where it was safe. But no. Instead, I stood two yards from that bull and gave him a piece of my mind.

Now you've got to picture it. I was eight, but I was small for my age. (The mean boys at school called me "Shrimp.") And there I was in my white nightgown and muddy boots, holding a rusty metal bucket of pellets in my hand, staring down this bull with such ferocity. That bull, if he knew what was good for him, was quaking in his hooves.

Well, maybe not so much. But I was fearless. I shouldn't have been; I should have been petrified.

I exchanged words with the bull (something that probably sounded like, "You stupid bull! What do you think you're doing?"), shook the bucket of pellets, sashayed past him with a don't-mess-with-me look in my eyes, walked through the gate to the pasture, and like a little puppy he followed behind me, without so much as a snort.

I think about that eight-year-old girl I once was. I think about her pluck and about her ability to jump in and do what needed to be done—even in the dark and the mud and the mess. I think about her fierce bravery.

> *We all have histories that have made us who we are and experiences that have made us stronger. And sometimes we forget how strong and resourceful we can be.*

There are so many times my grown-up self doesn't feel so brave. Like when I resist doing what needs to be done or if the outcome is in the dark and looks like it's going to be messy. When I feel like I've lost my pluck. Those are the days when I look deep inside and remember her. I remember that those qualities are part of me. Even if I've forgotten and I'm feeling uncertain, inside I'm still that fierce little girl who showed that bull what's what!

And that's true for all of us. It doesn't matter what your title is or how successful you are; we all have times when we don't feel so brave. It's during those times—when all seems lost or hard or just plain messy—that we can look deep inside and find that strength when we need it most. We all have histories that have made us who we are and experiences that have made us stronger. And sometimes we forget how strong and resourceful we can be. But it's there, our bravery. Sometimes it simply needs to be corralled.

One of my favorite authors and teachers of all time, Anne Lamott, says that "becoming a writer is about becoming conscious."[1] I think this is true of leadership as well. To become a brave leader is about becoming conscious—conscious of your own needs and desires, of all the quirky and obnoxious things you do that aren't working for you, of your body and breath and voice and mind, of the impact you have on the people in your life and the world you inhabit, and of how, at once, you are both vulnerable and so powerful.

It's a scary thing, I know. It scares me every day. What a responsibility! I don't promise you that it's going to be easy, but I'll promise you that it will be worth it.

In the theater, they call it *drama* for a reason. Every character is fighting for something. They want something so desperately that they're driven to make it happen. You are cast in the role of a lifetime. You get to play you. So I ask you, what are you fighting for?

> *You are cast in the role of a lifetime. You get to play you. What are you fighting for?*

What is the impact you are here to have on your team, on your organization, on your friends and family, on your community, on this world? Focus on that. That is where you find your brave.

If you dare to be your most confident, powerful, and authentic self—to fight that fight every day—anything is possible. And that kind of commitment makes you a special person. A leader in a world that so desperately needs people to step up and make a difference.

Some might even call you . . .

Brave.

Key Takeaways

→ Only in being true to who we are at our core can we tap into our best; and all the riches in the world feel meaningless if they're not anchored in something greater than ourselves. It is having an *impact* that is the key to a brave legacy.

→ If you want to be a brave leader, it is critical to become *conscious*. Conscious of your own needs and desires. Conscious of all the quirky and obnoxious things you do that aren't working for you. Conscious of your body and breath and voice and mind. Conscious of the impact you have on the people in your life and the world you inhabit. Conscious of how you are both vulnerable and so very powerful.

→ What now, brave leader? What is the impact you will have on your world? *Conscious* impact. Brave.

THE **BRAVE LEADERSHIP** MANIFESTO

WE BELIEVE that our best lies in being more
of who we really are, not less.

We believe that everyone has the ability
to make a positive impact.

We believe that we are all far more powerful than
we know and that true "power" comes from within,
not from title or position.

We believe that being anchored in purpose
gives us the presence we need to influence and
helps us bring the courage to take risks.

We believe that mindful, constructive action
is a worthy pursuit.

We believe that compassion and empathy matter
—that embracing our humanity is crucial.

We believe that there is power in vulnerability.

We believe that we can always be better—that
there is always something to learn and ways to grow.

We believe that real connection—as a leader,
a presenter, a colleague, as a human being—is key to success.

And **we believe** that extraordinary results
are simply a by-product of us showing up as authentically and
powerfully as we can.

This is our definition of **"BRAVE LEADERSHIP."**

For me, it's something worth fighting for.
Want to join the fight?

Be a Work in Progress

RECOMMENDED RESOURCES

We are all apprentices in a craft
where no one ever becomes a master.

—ERNEST HEMINGWAY

My work has been influenced by countless others. I stand on the shoulders of some great researchers, academics, business experts, artists, psychologists, scientists, and writers who have not only informed and inspired what I do, but have set the stage for having these bold conversations in a work context. I owe a great debt of gratitude to the work contributed by Dan Pink, Bill George, Brené Brown, Dan and Chip Heath, Anne Lamott, Natalie Goldberg, Elizabeth Gilbert, Constantin Stanislavski, Uta Hagen, Kristin Linklater, Carol Dweck, Simon Sinek, Julia Cameron, Marcus Buckingham, Seth Godin, Shawn Achor, Oprah Winfrey, Martin Seligman, William Bridges, Tom Rath, Patrick Lencioni, James Kouzes, Barry Posner, Jonathan Fields, Daniel Goleman, Nathaniel Branden, Amy Cuddy, Gretchen Rubin, and countless others. Their courageous work has helped me be more brave. Here are but a few of the resources I find myself turning to again and again:

- *Authentic Leadership: Rediscovering the Secrets to Creating Lasting Value* by **Bill George** This is one of the first and most important books in what has essentially formed the "authentic leadership movement." It has strong case studies and data to support how critical it is that leaders show up authentically in the workplace.

- *Better Than Before* by **Gretchen Rubin** This book examines our habits and helps us understand what gets in our way of setting ourselves up for success. I find myself thinking about her work constantly! It has helped me stop the comparison game and find constructive strategies that work for me to deliver on my promises to myself and others.

- *Big Magic: Creative Living beyond Fear* by **Elizabeth Gilbert** While the focus of this book is creativity, it delves into how to show up powerfully in the face of fear—regardless of the task at hand. If you want to move through your personal obstacles to greater success, I highly recommend this book.

- *Bird by Bird* by **Anne Lamott** Reading this book is what started me on my writing journey, and its tear-stained and dog-eared pages are proof that it has made a difference in my work. If you want to learn how to mine your heart to communicate with others, whether through writing or speaking, then this is one of the most powerful resources I can recommend.

- *Drive: The Surprising Truth about What Motivates Us* by **Daniel H. Pink** This terrific book (which is quoted throughout *Brave Leadership*) helps you see how vital "purpose-driven" thinking is to our personal and business success and better understand what motivates the people we lead. Highly recommended!

- *Emotional Intelligence 2.0* by **Travis Bradberry, Jean Greaves, and Patrick M. Lencioni** This is a fantastic resource with an easy assessment to help you identify your EQ and provides strong strategies for strengthening the areas that impede your success in work and life.

- *Encouraging the Heart: A Leader's Guide to Rewarding and Recognizing Others* by **James M. Kouzes and Barry Z. Posner** This book is recommended for anyone looking to lead in a way that others will WANT to follow. It echoes *Brave Leadership* in that at the heart of leadership is caring.

- *Fierce Conversations* by **Susan Scott** This book provides simple but powerful tools that will support you in conversation, especially when the stakes are high.

- *First, Break All the Rules: What the World's Greatest Managers Do Differently* by **Marcus Buckingham and Curt Coffman** This is an outstanding book. If you manage others and want to learn how to maximize your team's strengths, then you'll love this book.

- *Getting Naked: A Business Fable about Shedding the Three Fears That Sabotage Client Loyalty* by **Patrick Lencioni** This book does a terrific job of building out the business case for one of the most important *Brave Leadership* points of view: that there is power in vulnerability.

- *It's Always Personal: Navigating Emotion in the New Workplace* by **Anne Kreamer** I love this author's courage, as she's taking on a subject that few are willing to confront but one that is at the core of professional and personal effectiveness.

- *Mindset: The New Psychology of Success* by **Carol Dweck** This is an outstanding book that allows you, in simple language, to understand how the way you think can dramatically change your outcome.

- *Presence: Bringing Your Boldest Self to Your Biggest Challenges* by **Amy Cuddy** Leveraging years of research, this book expands the important conversation of mind-body connection that Ms. Cuddy first brought forth to the TED stage, and provides rich stories and practical tools to show up more powerfully.

- *Start with Why* **by Simon Sinek** So many companies and leaders begin with what and how they do what they do, but the real power lies in your why. This is a fantastic book that will help you understand why your Super Objective is one of the most powerful leadership tools you can use.

- *Strengths Finder 2.0* **by Tom Rath** This is a fantastic resource to better understand your strengths and how to maximize what you do well.

- *Switch: How to Change Things When Change Is Hard* **by Chip and Dan Heath** This book talks about change in a real and accessible way and provides practical tools to lead through change and constructively navigate your relationships.

- *The Artist's Way* **by Julia Cameron** This beautiful book helps everyone reclaim their inner artist. I highly recommend it.

- *The Gifts of Imperfection: Let Go of Who You Think You're Supposed to Be and Embrace Who You Are* **by Brené Brown** This is a brilliant book grounded in significant research that explores the price we pay for not living our true selves and strategies to get there.

- *The OZ Principle: Getting Results through Individual and Organizational Accountability* **by Roger Conners, Tom Smith, and Craig Hickman** When it comes to books that help you understand your role in driving constructive and effective action, this is one of the best. This will get you back on track when you find your results fleeting and yourself feeling less than powerful.

- *Transitions: Making Sense of Life's Changes* **by William Bridges** This is a fantastic book that provides real strategies for dealing with both professional and personal change in our lives.

- *Uncertainty: Turning Fear and Doubt into Fuel for Brilliance* **by Jonathan Fields** This book has some great strategies that can make a difference in dealing with the vast amount of change and uncertainty we all face in today's business environment.

Favorite Videos:

1. Dan Pink's: RSA Animate (on YouTube) "Drive: The Surprising Truth about What Motivates Us."

2. Amy Cuddy's TED Talk: "Your Body Language Shapes Who You Are."

3. Brené Brown's TED Talk: "The Power of Vulnerability."

4. Chip Conley's TED Talk: "Measuring What Makes Life Worthwhile."

5. Benjamin Zander's TED Talk: "On Music and Passion." (This talk has little to do with leadership but it is a gorgeous example of authenticity when presenting.)

Acknowledgments

I've seen and met angels wearing the disguise of
ordinary people living ordinary lives.

—TRACY CHAPMAN

When I think of all the people who've made *Brave Leadership* possible, I am full of gratitude. No one crosses the finish line alone.

The crossroads of my life are marked by the extraordinary professionals who have seen something in me, given me an opportunity to show what I could do and the chance to grow. Their names are like mile markers in my memory: Fred Lockyear, Michele Glisson, Jennifer Hurshell, Sherri Quesnel, Mike Cook, Cecil Johnson, and Gary Rifkin. My life's work is a result of their ability to see possibility in me.

When I launched OnStage Leadership back in 2008, my early supporters fueled my business and allowed these tools to make a difference in the lives of the hundreds of men and women who have showed up in my classroom. Their trust in me, belief in this process, and advocacy has kept this work alive. Thank you, Greg Pattakos, Paul Allen, Mary Andereck, Kim Sosolik, Frank Lloyd, Charity Wallace, Mario Cabrera, Elisa Johnson,

Mark Nagel, Ralph Elwell, Joy Evans Ayres, Carolyn Jordan, Rani Craft, Raul Trevino, and Shari Barth.

To my dear friend, Alise Cortez, who has been there for me more times than I can count. Your immeasurable support has kept me afloat both personally and professionally.

To my walking buddies, Haley Hines and Cindy Knight, thank you for helping me gain clarity, keeping me inspired, and reminding me why I need to stay the course, every step of the way.

To my husband, Tim Sutton, who encouraged this wild and crazy vision I've been chasing and loved me through the ups and downs. You opened my eyes to a world I would have never known without you. Who knew that my purpose wasn't in the theater but rather waiting in the wings?

To my incredible OnStage Leadership stage managers, especially Cathy O'Neal, who has been my partner in crime from the beginning.

To my parents, Jack and Marsha, who have not only given me permission, but have celebrated my "brave" from the day I was born. There are no words to express how grateful I am for you. I will never forget sitting around my kitchen table in Dallas, when you so courageously let me walk you through this strange new program I had developed called OnStage Leadership. You have always been my greatest champions—my first participants, my first blog readers, my first book editors. You have always made me feel safe to try new things, to put myself out there and live out loud. That is the incredible gift you've given me that I hope to pass on to others.

To my brother, Todd, who is the most loving, positive, and resilient person I know. Your belief in me has given me the strength to keep pushing forward when I wanted to quit.

To my dear friend and mentor, Donna Fenn, thank you for taking this fledgling under your wing and infusing her with the support and guidance that made this thing possible.

To Leah Spiro, thank you for taking the time to read *Brave Leadership* in its early stages. Your validation provided the fuel to keep moving forward.

To my first editor, Alice Anderson, thank you for taking me out of my writing vacuum and giving me the thoughtful feedback I needed to make this better.

Thank you to the entire team at Greenleaf Book Group, especially Daniel Pederson, Lindsey Clark, Kimberly Lance, Pam Nordberg, Kristine Peyre-Ferry, and Chelsea Richards. Your talents made this book something I'm proud to share, and your professionalism made this process a joy.

To the brave men and women who have showed up in my classroom with open minds and big hearts—your willingness to ask the hard questions, share your stories, and bring the courage to take down your mask and play full-out has not only made this content better, but you've made me better.

And to my son, Jeremy, thank you for reminding me every day why the work I do is important. It's important so I can be the best mom I can be to you. It's important so I can participate in creating a world that celebrates authenticity, constructive action, and making a positive impact. It's important so, like my parents did for me, I can hope not only to unleash, but celebrate your brave.

Notes

INTRODUCTION

1. Mihaly Csikszentmihalyi, "Flow, the Secret to Happiness," TED Talk, 18:55, February 2004, https://www.ted.com/talks/mihaly_csikszentmihalyi_on_flow.

CHAPTER 2

1. Bureau of Labor Statistics, National Longitudinal Surveys, United States Department of Labor, https: //www.g.s.gov/nls/nlsfaqs.htm#anch41.

2. Alison Doyle, "How Often Do People Change Jobs?" *The Balance*, last modified July 28, 2016, https://www.thebalance.com/how-often-do-people-change -jobs-2060467.

CHAPTER 5

1. Heather Davis, "What Comes After the Knowledge Era?" *21st Century Leadership Literacies* (blog), January 28, 2009, https://leadershipliteracies .wordpress.com/2009/01/28/after-knowledge-era/.

CHAPTER 6

1. Arizona Technical Council "TEDxTucson George Land the Failure of Success," YouTube video, http://www.youtube.com/watch?v=ZfKMq-rYtnc.

2. Carol S. Dweck, *Mindset: The New Psychology of Success* (New York: Ballantine Books, 2006).

3. Edward Hoffman, *The Right to Be Human: A Biography of Abraham Maslow* (New York: McGraw-Hill, 1999), 170, 173–4.

4. Ibid, 208.

5. Ibid, 208.

CHAPTER 9

1. Brené Brown, *Daring Greatly: How the Courage to Be Vulnerable Transforms the Way We Live, Parent, and Lead* (New York: Avery, 2015); Kate Torgovnick May, "5 Insights from Brené Brown's new book, *Daring Greatly*, Out Today," *TEDBlog*, September 11, 2012 (1:30 p.m.), http://blog.ted.com/5-insights-from-brene -browns-new-book-daring-greatly-out-today/.

2. Seth Godin, "Quieting the Lizard Brain," *Seth's Blog*, January 28, 2010, http:// sethgodin.typepad.com/seths_blog/2010/01/quieting-the-lizard-brain.html.

CHAPTER 10

1. Vince Poscente, *Age of Speed: Learning to Thrive in a More-Faster-Now World* (New York: Ballantine Books, 2008).

2. Sherry Turkle, "Owned by Your Phone: It's Complicated," Good Life Project, podcast audio, http://www.goodlifeproject.com/sherry-turkle/.

CHAPTER 11

1. Constantin Stanislavski, *My Life in Art* (London: Penguin, 1967), 423, 431.

CHAPTER 13

1. "How long should a page take to load?" User Experience, http://ux.stackexchange .com/questions/5529/how-long-should-a-page-take-to-load.

2. Steve Lohr, "For Impatient Web Users, an Eye Blink Is Just Too Long to Wait," *The New York Times*, February 29, 2012, http://www.nytimes.com/2012/03/01/ technology/impatient-web-users-flee-slow-loading-sites.html

3. "Understanding Addiction: How Addiction Hijacks the Brain," Helpguide.org, https://www.helpguide.org/harvard/how-addiction-hijacks-the-brain.htm.

CHAPTER 15

1. Kenneth Labich, "Is Herb Kelleher America's Best CEO?" *Fortune*, May 2, 1994, http://archive.fortune.com/magazines/fortune/fortune_archive/1994/05/02/ 79246/index.htm.

2. "Most Noteworthy in Business," *USA Today*, July 30, 2007, http://usatoday30 .usatoday.com/educate/college/casestudies/20070821biz_leaders.pdf.

3. Herb Kelleher, "A Culture of Commitment," *Leader to Leader*, 1997, no. 4 (1997): doi: 10.1002/ltl.40619970408; Jackie Huba and Ben McConnell, *Creating Customer Evangelists: How Loyal Customers Become a Volunteer Salesforce* (Lewis Lane Press, 2012).

4. "Southwest Airlines Reports Fourth Quarter and Record Annual Profit; 44th Consecutive Year of Profitability," Southwest Airlines, January 26, 2017, http:// www.prnewswire.com/news-releases/southwest-airlines-reports-fourth-quarter -and-record-annual-profit-44th-consecutive-year-of-profitability-300397175.html.

5. Jillian Goodman, J. J. McCorvey, Margaret Rhodes, and Linda Tischler, "From Facebook to Pixar: 10 Conversations That Changed Our World," *Fast Company*, January 15, 2013, https://www.fastcompany.com/3004348/facebook-pixar-10-conversations-changed-our-world.

CHAPTER 16

1. Amy Adkins, "Majority of US Employees Not Engaged Despite Gains in 2014," *Gallup*, January 28, 2015, http://www.gallup.com/poll/181289/"majority-employees-not-engaged-despite-gains-2014.aspx; Steve Crabtree, "Worldwide, 13% of Employees Are Engaged at Work," *Gallup*, October 8, 2013, http://www.gallup.com/poll/165269/worldwide-employees-engaged-work.aspx.

CHAPTER 17

1. Seth Godin, "Beyond Showing Up," *Seth's Blog*, January 28, 2013, http://sethgodin.typepad.com/seths_blog/2013/01/beyond-showing-up.html.

2. Daniel Goleman, "Empathy 101," *Daniel Goleman* (blog), October 13, 2013, http://www.danielgoleman.info/empathy-101/.

3. Ibid.

4. Christopher Bergland, "The Neuroscience of Empathy: Neuroscientists Identify Specific Brain Areas Linked to Compassion," *Psychology Today*, October 10, 2013, https://www.psychologytoday.com/blog/the-athletes-way/201310/the-neuroscience-empathy.

5. Ibid.

6. Jamil Zaki, "What, Me Care? Young Are Less Empathetic," *Scientific American*, January 1, 2011, https://www.scientificamerican.com/article/what-me-care/?page=1.

CHAPTER 18

1. http://www.businessdictionary.com/definition/personal-power.html.

2. Dana R. Carney, Amy J. C. Cuddy, and Andy J. Yap, "Power Posing: Brief Nonverbal Displays Affect Neuroendocrine Levels and Risk Tolerance," *Psychological Science* 21, no. 10 (2010) doi: 10.1177/056797610383437.

3. Daniel Goleman, "About Daniel Goleman," http://www.danielgoleman.info/biography/.

4. Stephen R. Covey, *The Seven Habits of Highly Effective People: Powerful Lessons in Personal Change* (New York: Simon and Schuster, 2004).

CHAPTER 21

1. Jerome Bruner, *Making Stories: Law, Literature, Life* (New York: Farrar, Straus, and Giroux, 2002); Kate Harrison, "A Good Presentation Is about Data and Story," *Forbes*, January 20, 2015. http://www.forbes.com/sites/kateharrison/2015/01/20/a-good-presentation-is-about-data-and-story/#616a7a62b835.

2. Chris Anderson, "How to Give a Killer Presentation," *Harvard Business Review*, June 2013, https://hbr.org/2013/06/how-to-give-a-killer-presentation.

CHAPTER 23

1. Daniel H. Pink, *Drive: The Surprising Truth about What Motivates Us* (New York: Riverhead Books, 2009): 125.

2. Ibid.

CHAPTER 24

1. Anne Lamott, *Bird by Bird: Some Instructions on Writing and Life* (New York: First Anchor Books, 1995): 225.

Index

About the Author

 Former actress turned authentic leadership expert and TEDx speaker Kimberly Davis shares her inspirational message of personal power, responsibility, and impact with organizations across the country and teaches leadership programs worldwide, most notably her program "OnStage Leadership," which runs in New York City and Dallas, Texas. Additionally, Kimberly teaches Authentic Influence and Executive Presence for Southern Methodist University's (SMU) Cox School of Business's Executive Education Program, and partners with SMU in teaching for the Bush Institute's Women's Initiative Fellowship program (empowering female leaders from the Middle East) and for the National Hispanic Corporate Council. Kimberly lives in Austin, Texas, with her husband Tim, son Jeremy, and their feisty cat, Sulley Magee. You can learn more about Kimberly and the programs she offers at www.braveleadershipbook.com.

This journey has always been about reaching your own other shore no matter what it is, and that dream continues.

—DIANA NYAD